# IN FURIOUS SKIES

*To the memory of my uncle Reg Harwood who assisted in sowing the seeds of my fascination for Second World War aircraft so many years ago. Also, to my parents Trevor and Jean Heath, for all the books, technical explanations, the building of Airfix kits and the weekend trips to the air shows now many years ago. If it wasn't for you, this book would never have been written.*

# IN FURIOUS SKIES

## Flying with Hitler's Luftwaffe in the Second World War

**Tim Heath**

PEN & SWORD HISTORY

AN IMPRINT OF PEN & SWORD BOOKS LTD.
YORKSHIRE – PHILADELPHIA

First published in Great Britain in 2022 by
PEN AND SWORD HISTORY
An imprint of
Pen & Sword Books Ltd
Yorkshire – Philadelphia



ISBN 978 1 52678 523 7



A CIP catalogue record for this book is available from the British Library.



Typeset in Times New Roman 11.5/14 by
SJmagic DESIGN SERVICES, India.
Printed and bound in the UK by CPI Group (UK) Ltd.

Pen & Sword Books Limited incorporates the imprints of Atlas, Archaeology, Aviation, Discovery, Family History, Fiction, History, Maritime, Military, Military Classics, Politics, Select, Transport, True Crime, Air World, Frontline Publishing, Leo Cooper, Remember When, Seaforth Publishing, The Praetorian Press, Wharncliffe Local History, Wharncliffe Transport, Wharncliffe True Crime and White Owl.

*For a complete list of Pen & Sword titles please contact*
PEN & SWORD BOOKS LIMITED
47 Church Street, Barnsley, South Yorkshire, S70 2AS, England
E-mail: enquiries@pen-and-sword.co.uk
Website: www.pen-and-sword.co.uk

Or
PEN AND SWORD BOOKS
1950 Lawrence Rd, Havertown, PA 19083, USA
E-mail: Uspen-and-sword@casematepublishers.com
Website: www.penandswordbooks.com

# Contents

# Foreword

*by Bob Collis*

Most books dealing with the subject of the wartime Luftwaffe tend to fall into distinct categories. Some detail at length the campaigns fought, while others refer to the flaring personalities within the Nazi hierarchy. Many focus on the machines and their crews.

*In Furious Skies: Flying with Hitler's Luftwaffe in the Second World War*, written by Tim Heath, has managed to weave together from his extensive files the tangled strands of history covering all of the different aspects of the wartime Luftwaffe's chequered history in a concise, apolitical and thoroughly readable manner.

By far the most compelling part of Tim's narrative are the accounts from the people themselves. From the excited, naïve exuberance of the Hitler Youth in gliders, through the cocky, self-assured and all-conquering young men of the Blitzkrieg, to the steely-eyed, cynical group of dwindling but highly experienced men who finally mutinied against their leaders as the tide of war changed. Their accounts I have found both sad and uplifting.

If there is a lesson to be learned from the history of the wartime Luftwaffe, it is to be found within the covers of this book.

Bob Collis
Author, historian and archivist
18 August 2021

# Author's Note

My interest in the Luftwaffe began around the age of eight. At the time it was a typical boyhood fascination as the Second World War was still considered recent history, so much so it was rarely if ever mentioned or debated in any of the history lessons throughout the entirety of my school life. I vividly recall my mother's uncle, Reg Harwood, whom we used to visit almost every Saturday night back in the late 1970s. Reg was a widower living in a quaint former farmworker's cottage on the outskirts of the village of Harvington near Evesham. His living room was typically cosy, and I recall being amazed by the rows of highly polished antique brassware that adorned the fireplace and mantelpiece. He had worked as a foreman at the nearby Bomford's farm at Church Lench and recalled many stories from the years of the Second World War. One was how he often used to see Wellington bombers of the Royal Air Force towing targets and the crews of other bombers firing their machine guns at them as part of their training regimen; the discharged brass cartridge cases often came clattering down onto the corrugated roofing of his outbuildings. He then opened one of two old wooden biscuit barrels he kept on his sideboard and presented me with four of the spent cartridge cases that he had collected from his former address. If that wasn't enough to light the fires of enthusiasm further, he also had in his kitchen, on top of an antique wooden box either side of a chiming clock, a pair of 20mm cannon shell cases which Reg explained had been fired by a British aircraft and these had been given to him by a friend many years earlier. These two 20mm cases looked huge to me back then. Reg eventually gave them to me and today they are two of my most sentimental items due to the memories attached to them from my childhood and of a man who nurtured my interest, albeit it inadvertently, in military aircraft.

My fascination with German aircraft of the Second World War period lasted a great many years, and eventually I would meet many people connected either with the German air force or those involved in archaeology and the recovery of German aircraft crash sites in the UK. I began writing to Luftwaffe veterans, attempting wherever possible to document their experiences. At the time I had no idea at just how valuable the material I had gathered would be, as I was researching purely out of personal interest. Along the way I met many fascinating individuals, many of whom were old hands in researching Luftwaffe aircrews killed on operations over the UK. I learned a lot from them and as most steadily curtailed their research activities due to old age, and the expense of airmail letters to the various institutions in Germany, I continued. For a few years I teamed up with an ex-prison officer named Eddie Clarke from Chelmsford in Essex and together we would go through wadges of paperwork regarding German airmen lost over the UK. Eddie had been working closely with the German War Graves Commission based at Kassel in Germany, by making all research material available to the commission and any German families who might still be searching for information on their relatives. Together we acted in an unofficial capacity as a liaison between the UK and Germany where our research work was concerned. It was also around 1997 that I began to submit my research findings to the UK-based militaria magazine, *The Armourer*. My first real exclusive for the magazine was a two-part article on the loss of German fighter pilot Gefreiter Richard Riedel in November 1940. His family had kindly supplied me with a set of the very first photographs of him that would ever be published. It was also from this article and some of the letters I received following its publication from some notable names in the aviation history field, that I learned that this was also a cutthroat business where there are those who are prepared to take your hard work and publish it in their books, claiming all the credit and giving you none.

So, to me this book is more than just a book on the Luftwaffe; it is my chance to present what material I have collected over the years since I first began researching this fascinating subject. It is by no means an exhaustive study, as to produce a comprehensive text on this subject would require many volumes, not just one. So, I have attempted to cover as much as possible with the material at hand and write a book that I dedicate not only to Reg but also my parents, Trevor and Jean Heath, who encouraged my love of aviation by taking me and my sister Tracey as a family to many of the big air shows over the years. So, this book is for Reg and my wonderful parents; whilst sadly, Reg passed away many years ago, I am pretty sure my mum and dad will enjoy reading this book. I must also offer special thanks to aviation historian Bob Collis who agreed to read the manuscript and write a foreword, providing he was happy to have an association with it. Throughout, Bob has highlighted and corrected me on any errors in my original draft, thus limiting the chances of falling victim to the 'Anoraks', as Bob puts it in his own unequivocal manner. Bob is one of those 'old school' aviation historians, a colourful yet amusing character, who is never afraid to speak his mind. His wealth of experience and knowledge in the field of aviation and archaeological research are without peer. Thank you, Bob; it has been an honour to have had your assistance with this book.

# Preface

From the early successes of the Condor Legion operating in support of General Franco's Spanish Nationalist Air Force during 1936–9, and the Blitzkrieg (Lightning War) campaigns against Poland, the Low Countries and France of 1939/40, this unique work explores through the eyes of the Luftwaffe fighter pilots and bomber crews themselves, the rise and fall of the what was once the most formidable air force of the twentieth century.

When Adolf Hitler proudly revealed the existence of his Luftwaffe to the world in March 1935, it was soon to become the largest, most modern air arm the world had yet seen. Equipped with some of the most technically innovative monoplane fighter and bomber aircraft, manned by well-trained crews, it soon became evident that the Luftwaffe possessed a high degree of superiority over its future enemies in the West and East.

Following the German Blitzkrieg on Poland of 1 September 1939, the British and French declared war against Nazi Germany. A few months later, France and the Low Countries soon found themselves falling victim to the Blitzkrieg, where the Heer (army) and the Luftwaffe worked together as a cohesive unit to rapidly overwhelm their seemingly unprepared enemy.

As the British Expeditionary Force (BEF) sent to aid the French began their evacuation from the beaches of the little French town of Dunkirk, it was painfully evident that Britain would be the next to face the might of Adolf Hitler's Wehrmacht (armed forces). Hitler knew that Britain would be facing the might of the Luftwaffe alone, and, owing to its previous success, he was confident of a quick and decisive victory over the British Royal Air Force (RAF) which would then pave the way for the proposed seaborne invasion along the English south coast.

On paper it looked an almost certain victory for the Luftwaffe who for the first time in its offensive capacity would be operating alone against the enemy without the support of Heer tanks and artillery. Yet what factors led to the disastrous air campaign over southern England, which effectively signalled the cancellation of the proposed Operation *Sea Lion* (the codename for the invasion of England)? Why was such a mighty aerial force unable to compel the British people into suing for peace through a protracted bombing campaign, a campaign which would prove costly both in the lives of the Luftwaffe aircrews and British civilians, as well as infrastructure.

Failing to subdue Britain, Hitler maintained the pressure with bombing attacks on British cities whilst turning his attention to the East and the Soviet Union. Showing a total disregard for the inherent difficulties of fighting a war on two fronts, Operation *Barbarossa*, the invasion of Russia, was launched on 22 June 1941, an action which would further tactically and strategically stretch the Luftwaffe and its resources.

Despite enjoying early success in the Russian campaign, the Luftwaffe would soon find itself facing an ever-more competent enemy. With much of Russia's aircraft and war production plants moved beyond the range of the Luftwaffe's fleet of medium bombers, the Red Air Force was not slow in reequipping its forces with completely new fighters and bombers that would soon prove a threat to Luftwaffe air supremacy over the Eastern Front.

*In Furious Skies* explores a selection of memoirs of former Luftwaffe fighter and bomber airmen, from their entry into service up until the last days of the war. What was it like to fly a Messerschmitt Bf 109D for the Condor Legion in Spain, to fly a Ju 87 Stuka on a bombing mission in support of ground forces in Poland, to fly a fighter sweep during the invasion of France and squeeze into the tight confines of a Messerschmitt Bf 109E-4 for a combat mission over the South of England in 1940? What was it like to be a crewmember in a Dornier, Heinkel or Junkers Ju 88 on a night mission over London during the Blitz, to witness the often fiery deaths of comrades, to face the ever-increasing odds of survival as Germany's fortunes began to falter? What was it like to be a young German fighter pilot with very little training entering the deadliest arena of the air war in the defence of the Reich, the *Reichsverteidigung*, where a Luftwaffe desperately short of both manpower and fuel faced odds of sometimes ten to one in the skies over Germany's devastated cities?

This account aims to paint a fascinating if sometimes harrowing picture of excitement, romance and fear intertwined with the brutality, futility and wastefulness that is war, where one's own mortality becomes all too apparent. It is the culmination of many interviews, conducted with some of the leading German fighter 'aces' of the war, including Günther Rall and Heinz Knoke. The aircraft, tactics and various weapons combinations are also discussed in detail. The book features memoirs of other lesser-known warriors of the air, men who failed to amass the high kill rates of pilots like Hartmann, Rall, Galland and Knoke but whose anecdotes would otherwise be lost in the mists of time. This is their story, told in their own words, for the first time.

# Chapter 1

# The Clandestine Air Force

Germany after November 1918 found itself a defeated nation with its political and social structures in ruin with much of German society subsisting barely above starvation level. The First World War had been a disaster for Germany, yet the rapidity with which the conflict came to its conclusion was in part to blame for the inept attitude of the Allies when it came to the question of deciding Germany's future, and the reparations Germany should pay for its conduct of 1914/18. It can be said that the Treaty of Versailles was drafted before the blood of those slain in the trenches had even had time to dry. In this context the treaty was drafted in an air of vindictiveness and aversion to anything German, and, quite apart from the inevitable effect it would have upon German society, it was primarily designed to dismember Germany's economic and military powers, thus ensuring Germany would pose no such military threat in the future. With hindsight one can clearly see that the Treaty of Versailles would become the catalyst for serious social and political instability in Germany that would have far-reaching consequences for not only Europe but the rest of the world. Versailles would aid the acceleration of nationalism and fascism as a viable political force in Germany. When Adolf Hitler came to prominence as head of the seemingly unconquerable Nazi Party in Germany in 1933, vengeance was very much a characteristic of the Nazi mindset.

Within the mandate of the Treaty of Versailles were clauses which effectively ended military aviation in Germany, and which precluded any future attempts at resurrecting the German Flying Corps. Under the scrutiny of the Allied Control Commission, Germany was obliged, in 1920, to hand over all aeronautical equipment to the Allies and associated powers. By the end of the war, the German Flying Corps had in its possession approximately 20,000 military aircraft. Of this figure 2,400 were fighter, bomber and reconnaissance aircraft with frontline squadrons. Adhering to the terms of the clauses on military aircraft and associated materials, Germany surrendered 15,000 aircraft and some 27,000 aircraft engines to the Allied authorities. These measures against Germany were considered more than satisfactory, yet there was an unforeseen oversight, an Achilles' heel in the clauses regarding German aviation matters: an exclusion of any long-term clause prohibiting the manufacture and mass production of civil aircraft. Civil aviation at the time, in 1919, was still very much in its infancy. The Allied powers failed to recognize that civil aircraft could easily be converted to a military role and provide a training platform for a military air force. By 1922 there were some size limitations placed upon Germany's civil aircraft, yet the Paris Air Agreement of 1926 scrapped even these restrictions as being wholly unnecessary. This was just the loophole that Germany needed to resurrect an air arm that would become the largest, most modern and terrifying the world had yet seen.

With virtually no restrictions on civil aviation, the opportunity was seized upon and Germany expanded rapidly, including the expansion of airlines, flying clubs and aviation training centres. It was in this guise of a supposedly peaceful enterprise that the foundations of the future German air force were laid.

It is the common belief that Adolf Hitler and Hermann Göring were the founders of what would become the Luftwaffe, the German air force, yet this is not entirely the case. In 1920, General Hans von Seeckt, who was Chief of the Army Command at the Defence Ministry at the time, was convinced that military aviation would be resurrected in Germany at some stage. He concluded that the new Luftwaffe should be developed as an integral component of the German war machine working in cooperation with the army on the ground. This was of course the theory which would prove devastatingly effective during the Spanish Civil War and the early campaigns in Europe of 1939/40.

With Von Seeckt pushing the buttons, he covertly appointed a small group of officers in his ministry to deal exclusively with aviation matters. His foresight becomes perfectly clear when one considers the names of some of these officers, most notably Hellmuth Felmy, Hugo Sperrle, Walther Wever, Albert Kesselring and Hans-Jurgen Stumpff, all of whom became high-ranking officers in the new Luftwaffe. A secret agreement was convened with the new Bolshevik government in Russia for the establishment of a covert training programme at Lipetsk, under the command of Hugo Sperrle. This air training academy was known as the Lipetsk Fighter Pilot School, or Kampffliegerschule Lipezk. It was also referred to as the WIWUPAL – Wissenschaftliche Versuchs und Personalausbildungsstation (Scientific Experimental and Personal Training Station) – and it was in operation from 1926 to 1933. This was merely a name designed to deceive outsiders as to its true purpose. Much work had to be carried out at the Lipetsk air base prior to activities commencing there. In June 1925, the base was ready to commence flying training operations, yet the training of German pilots only began in the spring of 1926. The school trained 120 Luftwaffe pilots, 300 ground crew, and 450 administrative and training staff during its seven-year period of existence. Those who passed through the doors of this secret academy would go on to train others upon formation of the Luftwaffe in 1935. Ironically, many Soviet pilots would benefit from the facilities at Lipetsk, learning new bombing and targeting techniques alongside the German pilots; it was for a short period of time a valuable cooperation of military assets that were mutually beneficial. In addition to this, a secret training school was set up for the training of German tank crews and gas warfare, also in Russia. This operation lasted from 1928 to 1931.

The covert training combined with the small yet flourishing civil aviation industry in Germany enabled German aircraft designers to gain the lead in both design and technological innovation in aircraft. At the same time a steady pool of pilots was stimulated by the Deutschen Luftsport Verbandes (German Air Sport Movement), in effect a National Socialist Air Corps (NSFK). The Hitler Youth proved a vital recruiting ground for the future Luftwaffe, as Gerhard Funck recalled:

> We were encouraged to enrol into the gliding clubs for glider flying lessons in these rather flimsy-looking things without any engines. Many of us were apprehensive at first as it all looked a bit dangerous. But the Hitler Youth leadership were very clever by attaching immense prestige to anyone who jumped into one of these things and flew in one. At first you had to be schooled in the basic rudiments of flight and control. Then you flew a short height from the ground while tethered to a vehicle. When they felt you were competent enough, they would let you fly a glider untethered and freely. Learning everything took time; we didn't just have

> a few classroom lessons then off we went; no, it was quite intense. The more flying we did the more we wanted to fly faster and higher; it was all very clever – this was how they wanted you to feel, to want to become a pilot, you see. If you made the sufficient grade, then you had the opportunity to go on to a proper flying school and learn to fly a powered aeroplane.

In this sense the Hitler Youth not only operated as a means of indoctrinating Germany's youth into the National Socialist ideal, it also ensured that a steady stream of superbly fit and healthy young men would be available to be called upon to join Germany's armed forces.

It is no coincidence that many of the civil aircraft designs being produced in Germany at the time could easily be converted to military use. A good example of this 'wolf in sheep's clothing' approach was the Heinkel He 111 designed by Siegfried and Walter Gunter and constructed by Heinkel Flugzeugwerke. Although initially designed as a civil airliner, it was clear that this, along with other notable twin-engine designs leaving the factory drawing boards masquerading as airliners or postal service aircraft, had every capability of being converted to military use.

The only possible oversight in all of this rapid civil aircraft expansion (with the exception of the Focke-Wulf Fw 200 Condor) was the lack of four-engine designs. This was something which would return to haunt the Luftwaffe in later years and the reasons will be examined in due course.

So, we can clearly see that most of the Luftwaffe bomber aircraft which would become a familiar sight in the skies above Europe upon the outbreak of war in 1939 were brought about by a clever deception. However, the focus was not just on aircraft which would serve as either light or medium bombers but fighters too. With the single-seat fighter aircraft designs the same principle was applied as to that of the twin-engine civil aircraft.

There were many brilliant aircraft designers and engineers who by the very nature of their energetic, innovative and competitive spirit would soon become household names in Germany and beyond. Perhaps the most famous of these names was Professor Willy Messerschmitt, designer of the renowned and instantly recognizable Messerschmitt Bf 109.

The Bf 109 was the result of the collaborative work between Willy Messerschmitt and Robert Lusser of the Bayerische Flugzeugwerke (BFW). The Messerschmitt–Lusser design partnership had already created the successful Bf 108 'Taifun' (Typhoon) as a sports touring aircraft. It was this basic design that would lay the foundations for the later Bf 109 fighter aircraft, which would become Germany's premier monoplane fighter aircraft, replacing the then obsolete Arado Ar 68 and Heinkel He 51 series aircraft which were by that time reminiscent of decades-old technology. Ironically, like the later Focke-Wulf Fw 190 series of German fighter aircraft, the Bf 109 would be subject to continuous development and see service throughout the entirety of the war and in almost every theatre. It was the subject of a Reichs Luftfahrt Ministerium (RLM) requirement for a single-seat fighter in the document LA. 1432/33. Design work on the new German fighter, designated Project Number P.1034, began in March of 1934, some three weeks after the contract to produce the aircraft had been awarded. A basic mock-up (detailed full-size model) of the aircraft was produced and completed by May, followed by a more detailed version which was ready by January 1935. The RLM designated the design as the type Bf 109. The prototype (Versuchsflugzeug 1, or V1) Bf 109 was given the civilian registration of D-IABI and was completed by May 1935. The only issue facing Messerschmitt at this time was that the new German engines designated for this aircraft were not ready. The RLM acquired four Rolls-Royce Kestrel V1 engines by way of a trade with Rolls-Royce whereby the RLM offered a Heinkel He 70 'Blitz' which Rolls-Royce could use as an engine test bed. It would seem an unlikely cooperation in view of the later circumstances where both companies would be pitched against one another in a technological battle for supremacy of the skies. In the event, Rolls-Royce gave Messerschmitt two of their RR Kestrel motors and the Bf 109 V1 had its engine mounting apparatus modified to take the V12 engine upright. The Bf 109 V1 made its first flight on 29 May 1935 from an airfield in the southernmost Augsberg region of Haunstetten. The test pilot for this maiden flight was Hans- Dietrich 'Bubi' Knoetsch, who recalled after his first flight in the Bf 109:

> The Bf 109 is small, has an enclosed cockpit, retractable undercarriage and the most powerful engine we have to date. The cockpit is a little tight but should not hinder the

resource management of a pilot; it is adequate. The general handling characteristics of the aircraft are excellent and even at this early stage it is an excellent aircraft.

In 1935, the first Jumo engines were finally available and the second prototype Bf 109, the V2, was completed in October utilizing the 600hp Jumo 210A engine. The third prototype Bf 109, the V3, was the first to be fitted with armament, yet this aircraft did not undergo flight testing until May 1936 due to the delays in acquiring another Jumo 210 engine.

Following the new fighter's acceptance trials, a design competition went ahead where the Bf 109 V2 was pitched against the Arado Ar 80, Focke-Wulf Fw 159 V3 and Heinkel He 112 V4.

Many Luftwaffe fighter pilots of the 1930s had grown irrevocably accustomed to the open cockpits, low-wing loading, light g-forces, easy handling and relatively low speeds of the biplane aircraft that most air forces around the world were still reliant upon. The Bf 109 V2, along with the Heinkel He 112 V4, was not met with much in the way of enthusiasm from the pilots involved in the design contest. Despite the initial concerns of the pilots regarding the Bf 109 V2, it soon became one of the forerunners in the contest while the Arado and Focke-Wulf entries, merely back-up options, were totally outclassed.

Even though the Messerschmitt Bf 109 slowly began to win over the pilots, the real stick in the mud to the success of the Messerschmitt Bf 109 was Luftwaffe General Erhard Milch who was one of the decision-makers as to which aircraft would be selected for production. Milch had never forgiven Willy Messerschmitt for the loss of a dear friend in a Messerschmitt aircraft crash some years earlier. The Bf 109 design was saved by former First World War German 'ace'* Ernst Udet who was also a close friend of Hermann Göring and held a high position in the technical department. Whilst Udet understood little of the new technical aspects of aircraft design, he knew a good aeroplane when he saw one. Following a test flight in the prototype Bf 109, he jumped out of the cockpit with a huge smile on his face, assuring Messerschmitt that his was the best fighter design in the competition. The result would be the rapid evolution of the Messerschmitt Bf 109 into one of the Luftwaffe's primary frontline fighter aircraft. It was an airframe that would undergo

* Ace status was achieved after destroying 5 enemy aircraft

a series of design alterations and seven main variations, the A, B, C and D through to the later E, F and G marks.

Another aircraft which had rolled off the design board under the guise of civilian application was the Dornier Do 17 designed by Claudius Dornier. Due to its very slender profile, it became known as the '*Fliegender Bleistift*' or 'Flying Pencil'. The Dornier 17 came about as the German Ordnance Department's requisition for the construction of a freight aircraft for the German State Railways and a high-speed mail aircraft for the Lufthansa company. Work on the design for the aircraft began on 1 August 1932 at the Friedrichshafen factory.

The political events which followed favoured the Dornier. With the Nazis' ascent to power in 1933 and Hermann Göring appointed commissar for aviation with the former Deutsche Lufthansa employee Erhard Milch as his deputy, the Ministry of Aviation was formed. On 17 March 1933, just three months after taking up his appointment in the Ministry of Aviation, Milch gave the go-ahead for Dornier to produce prototype aircraft. At the end of 1933 the Ministry issued a further requirement for a high-speed aircraft with a twin-tail configuration and for a freight aircraft with special equipment. The reference to special equipment in Milch's specification was blatantly obvious: he was asking for a bomber. The Dornier Do 17 was first revealed as a full-size mock-up model in April 1933. The 'special equipment' required by Milch was absent from the mock-up but would be fitted later in order to disguise the aircraft's true purpose.

Despite all of this activity in the creation of the Luftwaffe, ripples of dissent were present. It was clear that the RLM wanted more control over the German aviation industry along with its individual companies. Few dared to complain about the degree of control the RLM was seeking apart from Hugo Junkers who was reluctant to allow the RLM to interfere with his company. Having refused to allow the RLM to effectively take over his company Junkers was now a 'marked man'. A short period after his refusal to comply with the RLM's wishes, Junkers was found dead in mysterious circumstances. The Nazi government then took possession of the company. This was typical of the fratricidal nature of the Third Reich.

Heinkel and Messerschmitt on the other hand fully complied with the RLM in anticipation of the unlimited funding which would be allocated to them. Despite the demise of Hugo Junkers, his company was responsible for the creation of two of the most notable German aircraft of the Second World War, namely the Junkers Ju 87 and Ju 88.

The Ju 88 was a fine aircraft that slotted into the role of a multi-role combat aircraft. First conceived as a fast bomber that was capable of outrunning any contemporary fighter aircraft, the Junkers Ju 88 had a troublesome start to what would become an admirable career. It was designed by Ernst Zindel, W. H. Evers and Alfred Gassner and was constructed by the Junkers Aircraft & Motor Works (JFM). It would become one of the most widely recognized Luftwaffe airframes after the fearsome Junkers Ju 87 and would prove to be one of the most versatile and respected of all the twin-engine light bomber designs to have been spawned in mid-1930s Germany. By the war's end in 1945, the Ju 88 would have served in almost every theatre of the Second World War and in almost every conceivable application from light bomber to dive- and torpedo-bomber, through to reconnaissance and night fighter.

Perhaps the most notorious of all the Junkers designs was that which also made its aerial debut in the year 1935, one that would perhaps illustrate Nazi terror more than any other. This aircraft became known the world over as the Junkers Ju 87 'Stuka'. The term *Stuka* is derived from the German word *Sturzkampfflugzeug* which means dive-bomber. It was designed by Hermann Pohlmann who later became Deputy Chief Designer at Blohm & Voss. Pohlmann's two-seat Ju 87 design was a radical concept featuring an inverted gull-type-wing configuration and fixed trousered undercarriage. On each undercarriage leg where the wing's leading edge met the top of the undercarriage leg was a propeller-driven siren. So when the Stuka went into a dive, the sirens would create the characteristic sound that would become the epitome of terror and the most powerful propaganda symbol of Nazi Germany. Unlike many aircraft designed by Germany in the mid- to late 1930s, the Stuka was from the outset designed as a weapon of terror. Several innovations were incorporated into the Stuka including an automatic pull-up dive-braking mechanism. The dive brakes were situated beneath the wings and would ensure that even if the pilot blacked out from the g-forces, the aircraft would not crash into the ground. It was an ingenious piece of engineering yet did little to allay the fears that some pilots had flying this aircraft. It required considerable courage and skill let alone a high degree of faith in the German engineering that had created it. It was Ernst Udet who again had a role in the success of the Stuka concept: while in

America in 1931, he was witness to the dive-bombing techniques being pioneered by US Navy pilots. It was Udet that would later demonstrate dive-bombing techniques in Germany. He also suggested the Luftwaffe utilize an aircraft classed as a kind of long-range aerial artillery piece that could assist the army on the ground and work as a spearhead for the ground forces alongside the Blitzkrieg strategy. The Junkers Ju 87 was the result and the aircraft first flew in April 1935 in the wake of the revelation of the new Luftwaffe to the world. The Stuka was large for a single-engine aircraft, possessing a sinister appearance even when static on the ground. Aviation historian William Green remarked upon seeing the Stuka for the first time: 'It is an evil-looking machine, with something of the predatory bird in its ugly contours. Its radiator bath and fixed spatted undercarriage resemble gaping jaws and extended talons.' To young Luftwaffe trainee Karl Voght, the Stuka was an awe-inspiring machine of war, recalling:

> I had made up my mind that joining the bomber forces was far safer an occupation than flying fighters. Though when I told my father of my plan to join the *Stukageschwader*, he asked me if I had gone mad. No, he wasn't happy about it at all, but I had made up my mind and after finishing flying school training I then went on to conversion training on the Stuka dive-bomber. It was hard work and not as easy as I first imagined it would be. There were times I felt I might get thrown off the course by my instructors and told to go and report to the army but, in the event, I passed through my training on this type of aircraft and was told I would soon be assigned to a unit along with the man who would be my rear gunner and companion for the most part; he was another young man the same age as me; his name was Siegfried Bech.

By the time the Messerchmitt Bf 110 twin-engine fighter concept had resulted in its first flight, the Luftwaffe was no longer a secret. In some ways the Bf 110 would enjoy a career of contradiction. It was referred to as one of the best and one of the worst Luftwaffe aircraft to have served in the Second World War and for differing reasons which will become clear later. It was Hermann Göring who had envisaged the power and superiority of having a force of twin-engine heavy fighter aircraft, or *Zerstörers* (destroyers). The merit of the whole *Zerstörer* concept was as inflated as Göring's waistline. While the Bf 110 would enjoy some success in Germany's early military campaigns, it would soon prove more a liability than an asset. The Bf 110 was designed to carry a heavy armament of four 7.92mm machine guns and two 20mm Oerlikon MG FF cannons mounted in the nose of the aircraft plus a rearward defensive machine gun operated by the second crewman. German fighter pilots such as Werner Mölders and Adolf Galland expressed their reservations over the twin-engine heavy fighter concept, but their misgivings fell on deaf ears.

In a letter to Adolf Galland in 1997 I asked him for his opinion as to the true value of the Bf 110 as a heavy fighter aircraft and he replied:

> The problem is a fighter aircraft is by its very nature a hunter; it has to be as light and as fast as possible and be able to compete in terms of manoeuvrability with the enemy. It was clear from the beginning that a two-engine fighter such as the Bf 110 would never be able to compete against a Spitfire or Hurricane in a dogfight. I expressed my opinions on this as did other fighter pilots, but our views were ignored. The Bf 110 was built with all good intentions of creating a long-range escort fighter for the bombers, but it was fatally flawed in being slow and lacking the agility with which to get out of trouble. It was an excellent ground-attack aircraft carrying heavy cannons and machine guns and in the early phases of the war in Poland and France it was good, yet beyond that it was a total waste of time and resources as a day fighter aircraft.

We will learn more about the Bf 110 and its baptism of fire later.

So, as we can see, the rearmament and remobilization of Germany under the leadership of Adolf Hitler and the Nazi Party, meant that all this new development in aviation and other key areas did so along the lines of the constantly evolving political dynamic in the country. If ever there had been a warning of what was to come, then it should have been obvious the moment Hitler began to establish his unchallenged powerbase in Germany. With the new Luftwaffe proudly showcased to the outside world on 26 February 1935, the Treaty of Versailles would soon be subject to open defiance and contempt.

The world appeared obstinately unwilling to act, Britain's Prime Minister Neville Chamberlain chose appeasement over confrontation with Germany, while the United States felt the problems were entirely Europe's concern and wanted no involvement. The French began to dig in and build fortresses for what they felt would be another static war if and when it came, and Germany's other immediate neighbours felt frightened and isolated. With hindsight, the apathy and lack of concern exhibited by the major powers would prove costly and embolden an evil regime with all the confidence needed to embark upon a worldwide campaign of terror, destruction and death. All facets of the Nazi war machine were complicit in this campaign and not even the Luftwaffe could be excused of an involvement.

By 1936 the output of the German aviation industry was rapidly outproducing that of Britain and America. Whilst Britain had produced 1,877 aircraft and the US 1,141 aircraft, Germany on the other hand had produced the alarming figure of 5,112 aircraft. The factories constructing these aircraft were built with war in mind, featuring protection for employees such as purpose-built blast protection walls and doors and well-dispersed production facilities to prevent any single air attack from destroying the entire facility.

The Heinkel and Messerschmitt companies were receiving such huge amounts of financial investment that both created housing estates complete with farms, medical and leisure facilities for their employees who saw themselves as the aristocracy of the German labour force. Of course, few understood at the time how all these perks were designed to create a subservient workforce that would become ever reliant upon the state.

This workforce was, however, more of a specific industry, almost a cottage industry, encompassing highly skilled individuals as opposed to a mass-production workforce of lesser-skilled individuals. It would be the latter who would produce the greater quantity of war supplies and aircraft to win the war. In parallel, the British car industry turned from building motor cars to building aircraft in order to increase its war production. This was a wise move and the production of military aircraft in Britain rapidly began to catch up with Germany's. By 1940, with Britain facing its most critical phase of the war, it had been mass-producing war materials and aircraft for four years. Mass production would be the key to winning the Second World War, yet Germany failed to grasp this crucial element which would prove just one in a catalogue of blunders.

# Chapter 2

# Developments in Luftwaffe Armament, 1935–9

Even by early pre-Second World War standards it should have been clear to many air forces around the world that rifle-calibre machine guns as a primary armament for the new breed of high-performance, all-metal-skinned monoplane fighter aircraft were obsolete. Although experiments had been conducted throughout the First World War exploring the feasibility of arming military aircraft with large-calibre, semi-automatic and automatic shell-firing guns of 20–37mm, few such installations that were trialled proved successful. Whilst the lethality of these heavy, cumbersome weapons was without question, their weight, coupled with the recoil they produced on firing, made them unpopular to say the least.

In Germany, the early marks of the Messerschmitt Bf 109 fighter were armed with the Rheinmetall-Borsig 7.92mm machine gun (*maschinengewehr*) 17 or MG 17, a design based on the older MG 30 light machine gun. The MG 17 was developed by the Rheinmetall company via its subsidiary in Solothurn, Switzerland, in 1934. This was a clever move which effectively circumvented the restrictions placed upon German arms developments through the Treaty of Versailles. The basic operating system of the MG 17 was the short recoil principle which utilized a rotating locking nut that held both the bolt and barrel together. It was a system originally adopted by the Austro-Hungarian army for a proposed infantry machine gun. In aircraft use the weapon was electrically fired and equipped with a belt-feed mechanism which could be adapted for either left- or right-hand feeding of the ammunition, and fed to the gun via a disintegrating metal-linked belt from a box magazine. The MG 17 was electrically fired yet was pneumatically cocked, accomplished through compressed air, the supply of which was stored in the fuselage of the aircraft. The MG 17 was extremely lightweight at just

10.2kg (22lb) with a length 1,175mm (46.3in) of which 600mm (24in) was the actual barrel. The weapon had the respectable rate of fire of 1,200 rounds per minute. When installed in the Messerschmitt Bf 109D single-seat fighter, a pair of MG 17 machine guns was mounted on top of the engine. These guns were synchronized and fixed firing forward through the propeller arc and fired at the lower rate of 1,000 rounds per minute, which was not unusual. The Bf 109D also had an MG 17 fitted in each wing just beyond the undercarriage wheel wells. These weapons, unhindered by the necessity for synchronization, fired at 1,200 rounds per minute. The guns required no coolant mechanism as they were cooled by airflow. On the contrary, problems were encountered with the guns freezing up at altitude which did occur. Another unforeseen issue experienced early on with wing-mounted guns was the tendency for ammunition belts to jam during air-to-air combat. This was more a consequence of the high centrifugal forces encountered as aircraft pulled high-g manoeuvres during dogfights. One of the methods pilots employed to combat this problem was simply to not fire the guns while engaged in tight turns. Many problems such as this would have to be resolved with a thorough understanding of the physics and of course through hard practical experience.

Experiments at mounting a centrally firing MG 17 fixed to fire through the propeller boss of the Bf 109D were carried out to ascertain its feasibility. This was by no means the first time that such an attempt had been made to utilize an engine-mounted gun firing through the engine centreline, though the problems encountered were obvious. Second World War fighter aircraft utilized geared propellers as it was discovered that it was more efficient to have the propeller blades rotating at a slower speed than the engine. The gearbox put the centre of the propeller in line with the cavity between the cylinder banks of a V-engine. Any V-engine intended to have a gun installed through the centreline, with the exception of radial engine,s had to be built with the necessary gap which in German fighter aircraft would allow for a 70mm-diameter steel sleeve in which a gun barrel could then be inserted. The Daimler-Benz 601, 605 and 603 series engines were fitted in an upside-down configuration which not only aided engine armament solutions but also controllability of the aircraft itself due to a counter-rotating crankshaft that relieved the problem some pilots encountered of roll and bank on accelerating during take-off. In simple terms, the gun would be in line with the middle of the propeller, coaxial to the propeller but not the engine. The barrel was adjusted among the cylinders and was not parallel with the upper crankshaft. For example, the gun on the Bf 109 was +3 /5° upward aligned, which solved any issues of upwarded aiming. The kill ratios achieved with the Bf 109 were testament to the fact that this theory worked rather well. That said, there could not be a more a hostile environment for an airborne gun than being mounted to fire through the engine itself. In this method of installation, the actual mechanics of the weapon were not in the engine itself, therefore not exposed to the extreme temperatures generated during flight. The breech of the weapon was situated well aft of the engine bulkhead, intruding into the cockpit and located between the pilot's legs and rudder pedals. Only the gun barrel itself ran through the engine with the muzzle exiting through the centre of the propeller boss. The ammunition boxes for the engine-mounted guns were also well aft of the engine for obvious reasons. Engine-mounted guns also relied upon the rush of airflow in flight to keep the barrel cool, particularly during firing. That said, during testing of the MG 17 in this configuration, it proved somewhat unreliable as the gun jammed at regular intervals and in static ground-firing tests the gun barrel inevitably suffered due to heat and vibration from the engine. The inflight firing testing proved erratic in nature too. Some firing tests were carried out where no problems or jamming occurred but in others the gun would jam or fail to fire either from a problem with the ammunition feed, firing mechanism due to excessive vibration or damage caused by heat from the engine.

The MG 17 utilized the standard 7.92mmx57R (Rimless) Mauser cartridge as used in the standard Heer rifle. The 7.92mmx57R reference refers to the military terminology for the metric designation of the cartridge, 7.92mm being the calibre of the bullet, 57 referring to the length of the cartridge case minus the bullet and 'R' to the fact that it is a rimless round, the cartridge case lacking the rim that can be found on some ammunition. This cartridge, known as the s.S Patrone (s.S ball cartridge), had been specifically designed for use in long-range machine guns. It was loaded with a 35.3mm- (1.39in-) long, boat-tailed s.S Schweres Spitzgeschoss (heavy pointed or Spitzer bullet), which was basically a lead core with a gilded metal-plated jacket weighing 12.8g (197.53 grains). The muzzle velocity attained with this round was a respectable 2,493 feet per second (ft/s) with an operating pressure rated at 46,412 pounds per square inch (psi). Although the general ballistic coefficiencies of this cartridge remain debatable, when fired at the typical muzzle velocity of 2,493ft/s from a barrel 600mm (23.6in) in length, the projectile retained supersonic velocity up to and beyond 1,094 yards (1,000m). Penetrative performance of this round was satisfactory and could penetrate 10mm (0.39in) of iron at 328 yards (300m), 7mm (0.28in) at 601 yards (550m), 5mm of steel at 109 yards (100m) and 3mm (0.12in) at 656 yards (600m). The muzzle energy (kinetic energy) attained with this round was 2,583 ft-lb (foot-pounds). Other 7.92mmx57R Mauser rounds developed for service use, apart from the standard ball, were the Phosphor 'B' cartridge and armour-piercing tracer (SmK L'spur or APT). The Phosphor 'B' cartridge was an incendiary round which contained a phosphorus pellet enclosed within the bullet itself. This was designed to ignite fuel, oil and any other flammable material upon penetration of the target. The armour-piercing tracer round contained steel, iron and later tungsten cores in an effort to improve penetrative performance and conserve lead resources. Tracer elements added to MG 17 Mauser ammunition came in two types, one for daylight use and the other for night use. For the cartridge casings most were initially produced from brass with steel casings being introduced later. The steel casings were often lacquered to assist in both the prevention of corrosion whilst in storage for long periods and to aid in the extraction process from the gun's breech after firing.

The prerequisite for machine guns designed as a defensive armament for the Luftwaffe's fleet of medium bomber aircraft was that the weapons should possess a high rate of fire. The idea behind this was purely to increase the hit probability when used as a countermeasure against fast-flying fighter aircraft.

One of the earliest defensive machine guns selected for use in German bombers was the 7.92mm MG 15 (Maschinengewehr 15) designed by Theodor Bergmann in the 1920s' Weimar Germany. The MG 15 saw service up until 1941 when it was replaced with the MG 81 and MG 81Z. The MG 15 was no lightweight, weighing in at 27lb fully loaded with gunsight and cartridge case bag fitted. It was fitted with a pistol grip and trigger mechanism and as such it possessed the appearance of a more conventional firearm one might encounter in army use on the ground. The trigger ring of the weapon was designed to be large enough to allow a gloved hand to squeeze the trigger. The MG 15 used the same 7.92x57mm Mauser ammunition as the MG 17 with a rate of fire of 1,000–1,050 rounds per minute with the very respectable muzzle velocity of 2,480ft/s. The MG 15 was fed ammunition via a seventy-five-round double-drum magazine. This arrangement fed rounds into the gun in an alternate fashion: one cartridge from the one drum and then a cartridge from the other and so on. This proved to be a more balanced system of feeding ammunition as each ammunition drum was emptied in turn, thus lightening the weight of the weapon evenly. Several preloaded ammunition drums were stored ready for use in the gunner's station. Once a drum magazine was empty, it was simply removed and another slotted into place. The MG 15 drum magazine was not interchangeable with the drum magazines of ground-based army weapons which were identical in most respects. The drum magazine for the army weapon had an angled feed chute where the drum was attached to the actual weapon whereas drum magazines for aircraft use were in parallel. Although the days of the machine gun as both an offensive and defensive weapon for use in aircraft were numbered, the MG 15 proved adequate for the task of defending early Luftwaffe bomber aircraft.

As much as the fighter pilot had to become both marksman and tactician, Luftwaffe airmen selected to become air gunners in bomber aircraft also had to attain a satisfactory level of marksmanship and proficiency at maintaining the weapon they were to operate before being allocated to the role. Much of the initial air gunnery training took place on the ground, starting in the classroom with general instruction into the theory and basic physics of ballistics. General marksmanship aside, of critical importance was also a degree of technical ability. The gunnery student had to be fully competent not only at aiming, firing and reloading his weapon but also being able to clear any 'stoppages' which were an inevitable occurrence at some point during operational flying. Most of the stoppages encountered with machine guns such as the MG 15 were either due to a faulty linkage in the ammunition magazine or a fired cartridge case or live round getting jammed in the breech of the weapon. A live round failing to fire and getting jammed in the breech is often referred to as a 'hang-fire'. A special tool was required and was included in the onboard gun toolkit, primarily for clearing a jammed case or live round from the gun breech. Mastering the art of clearing a jammed gun by using this tool was of course essential. Air gunners also had to learn to clear a jammed case or round from a weapon in near total darkness, as many Luftwaffe bomber operations took place at night. A proficient gunner could perform this task by feel alone and have his weapon cleared and reloaded in less than a minute. More serious gun malfunctions could mean the weapon having to be stripped down completely then checked for any damage before being reassembled and reloaded. A gun that still failed to fire after this procedure had been performed was likely to create major problems.

Being the defensive gunner of a Luftwaffe bomber, particularly those charged with guarding the rear of the aircraft from attack, was a perilous position. Rear gunners were often the main target for attacking enemy fighters: if the rear gun position was neutralized, it left the aircraft tail unit and rear of the engines vulnerable to close-in attack. In the event of a gunner being killed by fire from enemy fighters, it was not only difficult to extricate a dead or badly wounded gunner from his position but sometimes impossible for another crewman to take his place in the heat of an air battle or during a bombing run.

Claude Hunnemeyer who flew Heinkel He 111 bomber aircraft in 1940 recalled in an interview in 1997 how rear gunners suffered a high rate of attrition, particularly during the air campaign over Britain in 1940:

> We had flown our first six operations without serious incident when on the seventh we lost our rear gunner to enemy attack. He was killed instantly by machine-gun bullets from an RAF Hurricane fighter who attacked from directly above. The aircraft needed some light repairs to patch up the bullet holes and the blood and other mess was washed from the rear gunner's position. The replacement was this young fellow aged 21 whose name was Albert Goeshoff and he came from Leipzig. He asked about the marks on the seat in the gunner's position; I told him, 'Those marks were made by enemy bullets who killed our comrade that you are now replacing.' I was not the kind of man for beating around the bush or making excuses as I never saw the point in that. I took him aside and I told him, 'This is not the Hitler Youth, and this is not a training academy; men are being killed, check your gun, keep checking your gun, and most of all, you stay damn well alert at every moment that we are in

> the air.' He stared at me like a frightened child. I always remember that look on his face and I saw that same look on many young men's faces, some of whom who did not survive the 1940 air battles.

A number of Messerschmitt Bf 109 fighters armed with varying combinations of either 7.92mm MG 17 machine guns or 20mm MG FF cannons were sent to Spain during the Spanish Civil War for combat evaluation. Of all the Bf 109 models sent to Spain the only true cannon-armed variant was the Messerschmitt Bf 109E-3 which had a 20mm MG FF cannon fitted in each wing. It seems cannons had yet to be fully exploited by the Luftwaffe as a weapon for air-to-air combat. Among the first German military aircraft to be fitted with a 20mm cannon were medium bombers, most notable of which was the Heinkel He 111. It was designed to carry a manually operated 20mm Oerlikon cannon which was primarily fitted in the ventral position, though some were fitted in the glazed nose section of the aircraft. The 20mm Oerlikon cannon, a German derivative of the Swiss 20mm Oerlikon cannon, was designed mainly for the anti-shipping role. Some marks of the Dornier Do 17 were also fitted with this manually operated cannon, usually in the nose. Basically, this gun was the same weapon that would be fitted in the Messerschmitt Bf 109E-4, Messerschmitt Bf 110 and Focke-Wulf Fw 190 as the 20mm Oerlikon MG FF. The manually operated weapon as fitted in the Heinkel and Dornier was known as the 20mm Oerlikon FL. This weapon was fitted with handgrips and a shoulder stock and was quite distinctive in appearance, having a bulbous barrel-casing arrangement. The weapon was electrically fired by depressing the firing button located on the top portion of the right-hand grip. Cocking was accomplished manually and the firer had to simply pull back the bolt handle on the right side of the receiver to charge the weapon. The weapon was fed from a sixty-round drum magazine and fired the brass cased 20x80RB (Rebated Rim) series of ammunition which consisted of an armour-piercing shot and a high-explosive incendiary, both with tracer elements. Overall, this manually operated flexible version of the 20mm MG FF performed very well and was to prove a useful weapon in both anti-shipping and ground-attack roles. Later, during the Blitz, it was said that many a British searchlight had been extinguished by a burst of fire from one of these weapons.

It must be said that France, at least initially, led the field in research and development of having centrally mounted 20mm cannon fitted to fire through the centre of aero engines, and had encompassed these weapons in many of their fighter aircraft designs prior to the 1930s. In the First World War, the French Spad XII utilized a geared Hispano-Suiza engine to allow the fitting of a central-firing 37mm semi-automatic Puteaux cannon. In early 1940, the French Dewoitine D.520 fighter followed suit, having a 20mm Hispano cannon firing through the engine centreline. Britain opted to remain with wing-mounted rifle-calibre .303 Browning machine guns. At the time the British had no 20mm cannon designs of their own and had never experimented with any engine-mounted gun configurations. When 20mm cannons did become available to the British in the form of the French 20mm Hispano, Royal Air Force (RAF) fighter aircraft such as the Spitfire, which had never been designed with a cannon armament in mind, had to undergo some modification to take the heavier guns. The only feasible option of fitting 20mm cannon into the slender wings of a Spitfire was to have the cannon mounted on its side as opposed to the upright position. When trials began, it was soon discovered these early Hispano cannons were prone to jamming. If one 20mm Hispano wing cannon became inoperable, the one in the other wing would still fire but would create asymmetric interference through the recoil which effectively threw the Spitfire off course. These were all issues that would have to be overcome before the cannon became the potent weapon that it undoubtedly was (and still is today) in aerial warfare.

Germany, like the British, utilized the rifle-calibre machine gun for the early versions of the Messerschmitt Bf 109, but the Germans clearly understood the advantages of the destructive capabilities of the 20mm cannon, and by 1936 were working on their own design of the Swiss 20mm Oerlikon. The Luftwaffe carried out trials with engine-mounted Oerlikons but encountered numerous technical and reliability issues; the engine-mounted cannon in German fighter aircraft would not become a reliable option until two years into the Second World War, the reasons for which will be explained later.

The Luftwaffe bomber arm was also equipped with an extensive range of air-dropped ordnance and became increasingly innovative as the war progressed. The following are examples of the bombs carried by Luftwaffe bombers and fighter-bombers from the Spanish Civil War onwards.

To include a detailed technical specification on each particular bomb type listed is not possible within the context of this volume, but it is hoped that this brief overview will suffice. We will gain some understanding of the destructive capabilities of these bombs in the later chapters.

## General-Purpose Bombs

A general-purpose bomb (designation GP) was produced to find a compromise between the four factors of blast, fragmentation, penetration and incendiary effect in a single package. These types of bombs were effective against enemy troop emplacements, vehicles, aircraft (on the ground) and buildings. The thickness of the bomb casings varied from 7–8mm to over an inch (25mm), bearing in mind that some segments of the bomb, much as in the case of artillery shells, had areas where the casing could be several inches in thickness. With German bombs generally, the nose section was made up of the thickest metal for obvious reasons.

The letters SC in the list below refer to *Splitterbombe Cylindrisch* which translates to cylindrical fragmentation bomb.

- SC50 Bi. SC1000 'Herman'
- SC50 Grade 1
- SC1200
- SC50 Grade 2
- SC1800 'Satan'
- SC250
- SC2000
- SC500 Grade III
- SC2500

## Armour-Piercing Bombs

Anti-armour and armour-piercing bombs were weapons developed specifically for use against armoured enemy structures such as concrete bunkers and command centres, aircraft hangars, tanks and armoured vehicles or naval vessels. Generally, anti-armour and armour-piercing bombs had a heavy solid-steel pointed nosecone to aid penetration prior to detonation in armoured targets and the metal bomb casings were thicker than those of general-purpose bombs, the idea being that when the weapon exploded, the heavier thicker fragments would have a greater penetrative and destructive capability overall. I have seen some German anti-armour and armour-piercing bomb fragments that are almost three inches thick and weighing several pounds in weight. A missile such as this, even when travelling at relatively low velocity, could be lethal against exposed personnel and material for several hundred yards.

The term PC in the table below refers to *Panzerbombe Cylindrisch* which translates to cylindrical armour-piercing bomb. The term PD refers to *Panzersprengbombe Dickwandig* which translates to thick-walled armour-piercing explosive bomb and SB refers to *Spezialbombe* which translates to special bomb.

- PC500 (Anti-Armour)
- PC1000 (Anti-Armour)
- PC1400 'Fritz' (Anti-Armour)
- PC1600 (Anti-Armour)
- PD500 (Armour-Piercing)
- PD1800 (Armour-Piercing)
- SB1000. SB1000 Parachute Retarded
- SB2500

## Semi-Armour-Piercing Bombs

The fragmentation of semi-armour-piercing bombs offered a limited degree of armour penetration unlike the dedicated armour-piercing types, but they combined limited armour penetration with blast and incendiary effect. In the list below the term SD refers to *Sprengbombe Dickwandig* which translates to semi-armour-piercing bomb.

- SD1 Fragmentation
- SD2 Butterfly
- SD4 HL Hollow Charge
- SD10 Fragmentation
- SD10C Anti-Personnel

- SD50 Fragmentation
- SD70 Fragmentation
- SD250 Fragmentation
- SD500 Fragmentation
- SD500A Fragmentation
- SD500E Fragmentation
- SD1000 Fragmentation
- SD1700 Fragmentation

## Concrete and Converted Bombs

The reasoning behind the production of the concrete bombs used by the Luftwaffe was to serve two purposes. These bombs were designed as an adjunct to the SD series of semi-armour-piercing bombs. The term SBe refers to *Splitter Beton* which translates to concrete fragmentation bomb. The term 'concrete' is somewhat misleading and gives an impression that these weapons might not be as lethal as other bombs in the Luftwaffe armoury. However, concrete as a material was selected merely as a means of cutting costs and these weapons possessed considerable lethal power combined with good fragmentation and explosive effect at the target. In place of a thick steel bomb casing, a relatively thin layer of concrete was used. The concrete had scrap-metal fragments embedded in it and this in combination with blast and incendiary effect proved remarkably successful.

The SC10 bomb design was notably different from the other concrete-type bombs and came in two types. One was with a forged or cast steel casing with the base being an integral part of the bomb's construction. The second consisted of two steel casings approximately 0.1 inches thick which were welded together. The cavity between the two metal casings was filled with concrete which in turn had small steel projectiles embedded in it. The bomb was fitted with a screw-in Type AZC 10 (Hut)*(3) nose fuze

- SBe50 Concrete Fragmentation
- SBe250 Concrete Fragmentation
- SC10 Concrete Fragmentation
- SB15 Converted Projectile

## Smoke Bombs, Flares and Markers

Smoke bombs were and still are generally used for creating a smokescreen on the ground either to prevent an enemy seeing the movements of your forces or to provide a screen under which your forces can conduct tactical manoeuvres against the enemy or in cases where a retreat is necessary. Flares and markers basically serve the same purpose; a flare is often used for signalling or illuminating an area at night and to mark targets. The term NC refers to *Nebel Cylindrisch* which translates to smoke cylinder or cylindrical smoke bomb.

- NC50 Smoke
- NC50 WC D/SEE Smoke
- NC250 S Smoke

## Incendiary Bombs

The scourge of the London Blitz (parachute mines aside) were undoubtedly the fire or incendiary bombs deployed by the Luftwaffe. These types of bombs were rightly greatly feared during the German air attacks upon British cities. Again, there were a few variations in design, filling, weight and fuzing of these weapons. The first basic incendiary bombs were constructed of tubes of magnesium alloy filled with thermite explosive and fitted with an impact fuze. To accommodate both the fuze and fuze holder the tube was threaded internally at the nose.

The term B refers to *Brandbombe* which translates to incendiary bomb and *Flam* refers to *Flammenbombe* which translates to firebomb. Although both types of bombs served the same purpose, there were differences in the types of filling used. Most early Luftwaffe incendiary bombs contained phosphorus, a solid, highly reactive, poisonous non-metallic element which occurs naturally in phosphates, especially apatite, and exists in three allotropic forms: white (or sometimes yellow), red and black. Of the three types of phosphoric elements white was found to possess the greater incendiary qualities. When encased in a metal bomb casing the highly dangerous material remains in an inert or stable condition. When the material is released and exposed to oxygen, it will spontaneously ignite, reaching temperatures of 2,760°C (5,000°F) and is deadly poisonous not only to humans but to the environment too. Just one pellet of white phosphorus the size of a matchhead, if dropped into the open palm of your hand, would burn all the way through and out the other side. This is how dangerous white phosphorus is; it is still used today in military applications.

**B1 Series (1kg & 1.3kg types) B2EZ**

- B2EZ Incendiary Brand 10 Liquid-Filled Incendiary
- Brand C50 High-Intensity Incendiary
- Brand C50B High-Intensity Incendiary
- Brand C250B High-Intensity Incendiary
- Flam C250 Liquid Incendiary
- Flam KC250 Liquid Incendiary
- Flam 500 Liquid Incendiary
- Sprengbrand C50 Explosive Incendiary
- C500 Anti-Personnel Liquid Incendiary

Note: The *Flammenbombe* incendiary was withdrawn from the Luftwaffe armoury in January 1941 due to reliability issues.

## Submunition Dispenser/Containers

Air-dropped submunitions and the various containers used in their deployment were weapons which came to the fore in aerial warfare in the mid- to latter years of the Second World War. A submunition was generally a bomblet which was held in a container with a mass of others which on deployment separated and deployed over an area individually, the spread depending on the particular type of submunition in question. Some submunition weapons were designed to saturate a target area with anti-personnel, incendiary or anti-armour munitions, depending on tactical requirements. The submunition containers were set to release their payload at a predetermined time of fall from the aircraft. There were of course submunition-type containers used for dropping supplies to troops on the ground in much the same fashion as those used for offensive applications. The list below is accurate to the best of my knowledge as the primary types used by the Luftwaffe at various stages in the war. Further reading on these weapons, their fuzes and colour codings can be found in the relevant army technical manuals held by UK and US historical archives.

- AB23SD2 (Submunitions)
- AB24T SD2 (Submunitions /Drop Container)
- AB36-BSK36 (Submunitions)
- AB42 (Submunitions/Drop Container)
- AB70-1 (Flare)
- AB70- (Submunitions/Drop Container)
- AB70-D1 (Flare)
- AB250-1 (Submunitions/Drop Container)
- AB250-2 (Submunitions)
- AB250-3 (Submunitions/Drop Container)
- AB250KZ (Incendiary Container)
- AB500-1 (Submunitions/Drop Container)
- AB500-1B Submunitions/Drop Container)
- AB500-3A (Submunitions/Drop Container)
- AB1000-2 (Submunitions)
- ABB500 (Submunitions)
- BDC10 (Submunitions Container)
- BSB360, 7000 &1000 (Incendiary Container)
- Mk 70LK & Mk BK (Flare Container)
- Mk 250LK & BK (Flare Container)
- Mk 500 Boden Container-Streubrand C500 (Incendiary Container)

## Miscellaneous Bombs

- 1½kg Anti-Personnel Parachute
- SD1 Type Practice
- SD2 Type Practice
- ZC10 Concrete Practice
- ZC50 Concrete Practice

## Miscellaneous Bomb Equipment

The *Stabo* variant of Luftwaffe bombs had a threaded lug forged to the nose of the bomb that allowed the fitting of an 18.5in (470mm) steel spike 1.8in (46mm) in diameter which could then be secured to the lug. The idea of this application was to detonate the bomb before it could bury itself into the ground, typically at the height of an average person for maximum lethal effect. Anti-ricochet rings helped to prevent bombs from ricocheting, particularly off the decks of ships or when striking rail installations.

- Nose Stabo Spikes for SC50, 70, 250, and 500
- Anti- Ricochet Rings

# Chapter 3

# German Aero Engines

As early as 1933, the RLM, responsible for all design, development and production of both civilian and military aircraft plus associated resources, was too busy catering to the personal whims of the Reichsminister for Aviation, Hermann Göring, and others rather than focusing on the job at hand. This was a factor prevalent in the Third Reich's military and administrative infrastructures where individual offices appeared to be in competition with one another as opposed to working together as a single cohesive body. As a result of this, progress in many areas of the Luftwaffe's development was slower than what it should have been. The technological innovations achieved under the circumstances, particularly in the development of German aero engines, is therefore all the more quite remarkable

A detailed analysis of every German aircraft engine leading up to the Spanish Civil War and indeed up to the end of the Second World War is not possible here. However, we can briefly examine some of the more notable piston-engine powerplants as used in the frontline fighter and bomber aircraft from the Spanish Civil War through to the Second World War. The rocket and jet propulsion technology which had been in existence some years previous to the realization of its military value and therefore arriving late for operational service, will be discussed in Chapter 20.

Perhaps three of the most notable German aircraft engines of the Second World War (rocket and jet engines aside) were the Junkers Jumo, Daimler-Benz and BMW series of powerplants.

Contrary to popular belief, the Messerschmitt Bf 109D, the most useful version of the early Messerschmitt fighters to see action in the Spanish Civil War, was in fact powered by a Junkers Jumo 210D engine. The misconception that the Messerschmitt Bf 109D was fitted with the Daimler-Benz 600 engine came about as a result of pre-Second World War propaganda, and the showcasing of the DB 600-powered V13 at the Zurich Air Show of 1937. At the time, the plan was for the Messerschmitt Bf 109D to be powered by the DB 600 engine, yet a shortage of these engines meant the Jumo 210 was chosen as an intermediate choice until sufficient numbers of the DB 600 engine became available. Monica Vanessa Kieler Dorsche who served as a Luftwaffe ferry pilot late in the war recalled:

> In my personal opinion the shortage of the DB 600 engines amounted to incompetence and a lack of communication between the RLM and the manufacturers of these engines. There were staff in the RLM that were too busy pandering to the requests of others in higher offices of the state rather than getting on with their jobs and pushing forward. I think had those in the RLM hierarchy not been so distracted with the trivial tasks of keeping Göring happy, the 'E' series of the Messerschmitt Bf 109 could have been ready for the Spanish Civil War along with the Daimler-Benz 600 engine. That said, the Junkers Jumo was a good engine, not as good as the Daimler-Benz 600 but was sufficient for the task at that time as was the Bf 109D even though I never flew one of these. I flew the later 'G' types or Gustavs as they were known. I remember asking one of our pilots about the Bf 109s shortly before I began flying as a ferry pilot and he told me, 'A Messerschmitt is a Messerschmitt, and it is like a naughty child whose ear you have grasped in your hand. You have to keep a firm hold of that naughty child's ear otherwise it might kick you hard in the shins.'

The Junkers Jumo 210 was Junkers Motoren's first production inverted V12 petrol engine specifically developed for aircraft use. Developmental work began on the engine in 1931 under the designation L10. The L10 was one of Germany's first truly modern aircraft engine designs featuring three valves per cylinder, an inverted V layout, a supercharger as standard and a cast cylinder block. The configuration of the 210 engine was somewhat unusual in that the cylinders were machined into a block along with one side of the crank casing, the two components being bolted together side by side to form the engine. Normal construction methods usually consisted of three parts: two-cylinder blocks and a separate crank case.

Static engine tests were carried out on the L10 on 22 October 1932. The first series of tests were merely engine warm-ups designed to ensure all of the running components were seating in correctly. As engine testing progressed, the rpms were steadily increased up to full power. The designation 210 came about with the official formation of the RLM who proposed a series of numerical engine designations from which to identify manufacturers. Junkers received the '200 block', and so the L10 engine became the 210. Approval was given in March 1934 and the engine was first tested in the air installed in a Junkers W33. The engine performed satisfactorily, yet there was some disappointment with the power output of prototype engines. The Germans generally measured horsepower as the metric PS or *Pferdestrke* (literally 'horse strength'). Despite this, production began on the 610PS (602hp) Jumo 210A in late 1934. Development was a continuing process and in 1935 the 640PS (631hp) Jumo 210B and 210C were produced. Both possessed a new supercharger for improved performance, along with a dump valve arrangement to avoid over-boost occurring. The Jumo 210B had a propeller geared at 1:1.55 (propeller: engine rpm) for high-speed use, while the Jumo 210C was geared at 1:1.63 for slower flying speeds. In 1936, the new 670PS (661hp) 210D and 210E were introduced into service, which possessed the same gearing as the B and C but utilized a new two-speed supercharger specifically to increase take-off power and higher performance at altitude.

The Jumo 210G was designed with a direct injection system developed by August Lichte. The Jumo system used a small pump piston positioned beside each of the main cylinders, driven off the crankshaft. The injector used a simple check valve to prevent internal pressure from blowing back into the engine fuel line, and the pump was timed to inject at the proper point in the intake cycle. The injection system increased take-off power by approximately 20PS without increasing boost rates and also had the advantage of reducing fuel consumption. It is largely for this reason that most German aircraft engines were equipped with fuel injection systems. Fuel injected engines also possessed advantages in air-to-air combat as they would not cut out in certain flight profiles as did the early British Rolls-Royce Merlin engines which were fitted with carburettors rather than fuel injection.

Further developments of the Jumo 210 were planned, such as the Jumo 210F and 210H, yet these two versions were never built. In

1935, the Jumo 210H, with twin exhaust valves for each cylinder, was produced for the development of the Jumo 211 engine. The Jumo 210S was a special development engine comprising rotary disc valves, as used in KM-8 Kriegsmarine (German Navy) torpedo engines. Production of the Jumo 210 series engines came to a close around 1938.

The Bramo 323 Fafnir nine-cylinder radial engine as used by the Luftwaffe was conceived as a result of Siemens/Bramo's experience in the production of the British-built Bristol Jupiter engine which the company had built under licence. Manufactured by BMW, this particular powerplant saw limited use in the war, namely in the Dornier Do 17, Henschel Hs 126, Focke-Wulf Fw 200 and Blohm & Voss BV222. In all, the 323 was in many respects a modified version of the Bristol Jupiter design. The first modification carried out resulted in the Sh.20 and Sh.21 engines. The design was then bored out to produce the 950hp Sh.22 in 1930. The Sh.22 had the appearance more of an engine that might have powered a First World War biplane rather than a modern Luftwaffe monoplane: the antiquated appearance of this engine was more down to the prominent valve pushrods which protruded from the front of the engine. The RLM gave Bramo the 300-block number for this this engine, thus the Sh.14 and Sh.22 became known as the 314 and 322, respectively. The 322 was not a reliable powerplant in many respects and despite attempts at improvement, it remained what can best be described as immature. In fact, one German engineer tasked with the maintenance and 'complaints department' was heard to say that the 'Sh' designation stood for '*Schiesse*' (shit). In all, the Bramo 323 Fanir engine proved unpopular despite undergoing modification to increase horsepower. It still suffered from poor fuel economy; its most notable installation was in the Dornier 17 Z. The final versions, P, R and T, featured a two-speed supercharger for better all-round performance. This allowed it to generate 1,000PS at sea level as in the C and D models, but improved performance at altitude quite considerably, producing 940PS at 4,000 metres (13,000 feet). The R-2 subtype was fitted with an MW50 methanol water injection system for added low-altitude performance, boosting the power output to 1,200PS at 2,600rpm.

Perhaps one of the best German aero engines of the Second World War was the BMW 801 radial engine. Again, this was a German-manufactured derivative of a foreign powerplant. In the 1930s, BMW took out a licence to build the American Pratt & Whitney Hornet engines, and by the mid-1930s they had produced a much-improved version in the BMW 132, used most notably on the Junkers Ju 52 transporter which utilized this type of engine for the entirety of its existence.

In 1935, the RLM allocated finance for two prototype engines which were much larger than the BMW 132. One of the prototypes came from Bramo in the guise of the Bramo 329 and the other from BMW in the BMW 139. BMW utilized many of the existing components of the BMW 132 to create a two-row radial engine with fourteen cylinders, producing some 1,550PS (1,529hp). Following BMW's purchase of the Bramo company in 1939, both projects were merged into what became the BMW 801. The merger of the two separate technical projects proved to be a fairly smooth transition and advantages were that any shortcoming in the two engines had already been revealed and could readily be addressed. The BMW 139 was initially proposed as a powerplant for bomber and transport aircraft, but midway through the development programme the chief designer at the Focke aircraft company, Kurt Tank, suggested the engine be selected for what would be a revolutionary new fighter aircraft, the Focke-Wulf Fw 190. At the time the departure from conventional aircraft engines to that of radials was considered odd in many European aircraft designs. The reason behind this train of thought was the fact that radial engines were considered to have too great a frontal area which was detrimental to good aerodynamics and would be wholly unsuitable for high-speed aircraft especially fighters. Kurt Tank was of the opinion that attention to detail could result in a streamlined radial that would not incur undue drag and would prove competitive against the more standard inline aero engines.

The crucial issue with the big BMW 139 engine was that of keeping it cool during operation. It was necessary to keep a cooling airflow over the cylinder heads to prevent overheating. This was generally remedied by having a large opening at the front of the aircraft whereby cooling air was ingested into the engine bay. Kurt Tank's solution to this problem was an engine-driven cooling fan behind an oversized, flow-through, hollow propeller spinner which was open at the extreme front, blowing air past the engine's cylinders, with some of it being drawn through S-shaped ducts over a radiator for oil cooling. As simple as the solution appeared, there were numerous problems when the theory was put into practice, especially in the case of the Focke-Wulf Fw 190 fighter programme. The problems of overheating were not impossible to fix yet BMW considered the engine an already outdated powerplant in terms of design and in 1938 the BMW company proposed an entirely new engine specifically designed for fan cooling that could quickly be brought into production.

This new design was given the name BMW 801 (the BMW company had been given a new block of '109-800' engine numbers by the RLM following their merger with Bramo). The BMW 801, although a completely new motor, retained the BMW 139's older-style, single-valve intake and exhaust, while many inline engines of the day had moved to either three or four valves per cylinder. A number of small technical advances were assimilated into the design, which included the use of sodium-cooled valves and the fitting of a direct fuel injection system that was manufactured by Friedrich Deckel AG of Munich.

In early models of this powerful motor the supercharger was somewhat basic, utilizing a single-stage, two-speed design directly geared to the engine (unlike that of the DB 601's hydraulically clutched version) which led to a rather limited altitude performance, in keeping with its intended medium-altitude application. One of the key advancements made with the BMW 801 was the use of a *Kommandogerat* (command device), which was a mechanical–hydraulic unit that automatically adjusted engine fuel flow, propeller pitch, supercharger setting, mixture and ignition timing in response to a single throttle lever. This simplified the whole process of engine control and management thus reducing the pilot's resource management. The *Kommandogerat* could even be considered a forerunner to the engine control units used for many vehicle internal combustion engines of the late twentieth and early twenty-first centuries. Such things are a true measure of German technical ingenuity of the time and the brilliant scientific and technical minds brought together in many such military programmes throughout the 1930s and 1940s.

BMW had carried out an exhaustive series of wind-tunnel testing on the new engine and designed a forward engine cowling which incorporated the engine's oil-coolant system. The tests carried out at the Luftfahrtorschungsanstalt (LFA, the Aeronautical Research Institute also known as the Hermann Göring Research Institute) led to the conclusion that it was perfectly feasible to reduce drag equivalent to 150–200hp and also to maximize the use of positive air pressure to aid cooling of the cylinders, heads and other internal engine components.

The first of the BMW 801A engines was running by April 1939, some feat considering the design had only been submitted some six months previous; production began in 1940. The BMW 801B was in most respects identical to the 801A apart from the airscrew, which normally rotated to the left, being altered to rotate counter-clockwise or the opposite direction as seen from the pilot's view behind the engine. This motor also utilized a different gearbox to the 801A model. The 801A and 801B model engines were specifically designed for use on twin-engine aircraft, whereby they cancelled out net torque, creating greater stability and handling of the aircraft in the process. However, there is little evidence to suggest that the 801B engine was anything more than a prototype and it did not go into production. Both engines produced 1,560PS (1,539hp) for take-off. The BMW 801A/L engine was the powerplant selected for variants of the Junkers Ju 88 and Dornier Do 217. In every respect the 801A was an excellent powerplant, both reliable and powerful.

BMW also produced the 801C, developed primarily for single- and multi-engine fighter aircraft. This model utilized a newly designed hydraulic propeller control unit; various changes were made to combat the problem with cooling, with measures including 'gills' on the engine cowling behind the engine in place of the original slot configuration. The 801C was used mostly in the early variants of the Focke-Wulf Fw 190A series fighters. The BMW 801L was basically an A model engine with the hydraulic propeller control mechanism combined into the 801C engine. Subsequently, both the C and L models of this engine produced the same power output as the original A model.

Development of the BMW 801 engine continued at a fairly rapid pace as did the 801D-2 series of powerplants, with work beginning on these in early 1942. This engine was fuelled by C2/C3 100 octane fuel in place of the A/B/C/L's B4 87 octane fuel. This new mixture boosted take-off power to 1,700PS (1.677hp). The BMW 801G-2 and H-2 model engines were merely D-2 engines which had been modified for use in bomber aircraft. These had lower gear ratios to accommodate the driving of the larger propellers, both clockwise and counter-clockwise respectively. The 801H-2, like the 801B, was not developed beyond the prototype stage.

The BMW D-2 engines underwent testing with an emergency boost system known as the MW50 methanol/water injection system. This boost system enabled the pilot to inject a 50/50 mix of water and methanol into the supercharger (primarily for its anti-detonation effect), allowing the pilot to increase boost pressures in any situation where he required an emergency power increase. Upon testing it was found that the disadvantages of MW50 outweighed the advantages. The use of MW50 reduced the service life of the engine due to the increased pressure its use placed on the internal components of the engine. The MW50 system was replaced by one which injected fuel rather than methanol/water into the engine and became known as the C3-injection, a unit used up until 1944 when fuel shortages forced a retro step back to the MW50 injection system. It was noted that with the MW50 boost activated for take-off, the engine power increased to 2,000PS. Much work was also conducted on the supercharger fitted to the 801 series engines.

With fighter and bomber aircraft operating at ever-increasing altitudes, especially fighters, a number of technical improvements were proposed to improve what was the limited performance of the original supercharger. Basically, the job of a supercharger on any engine is to consume air via a duct at the front of the engine facing into the airflow. In turn the supercharger acts as an air compressor forcing air into the engine at high pressure. This gives each intake cycle of the engine more oxygen, which in turn enables the engine to burn more fuel, which in turn produces more power. It all sounds simple enough, yet supercharging and correct engine tuning was something of an art for the mechanics tasked with the job of maintaining these engines and their high performance. The BMW 801E, a modification of the D-2, adopted different gear ratios of 6:1 at low speed and 8.3:1 at higher speeds, which in turn tuned the supercharger for the higher altitudes.

The E model also served as the basis for the design of the BMW 801R engine, a more complex beast which included a powerful two-stage, four-speed supercharger along with diecast hydronalium cylinder heads, strengthened crankshaft and pistons, along with chromed cylinders and exhaust valves. It was predicted that this fine example of German engineering would produce over 2,000PS (1,973hp) to 2,600PS (2,564hp) when used along with the MW50 methanol/water injection boost system. Despite the technical improvements, this E model motor was not widely used. The Luftwaffe were content with improving on the basic E model which led to the BMW 801F, a motor which offered a very substantial increase in performance in all areas. With a take-off power increasing to 2,400hp, this model of the 801 series engines became the only German aero engine of an existing type that had a producible subtype in existence that could break the 1,500kW top output barrier. This engine was proposed as the powerplant for all late marks of the Focke-Wulf Fw 190 fighter aircraft, yet the war came to end before production of this mighty new powerplant could go ahead.

No study on German aero engines, however brief, would be complete without a look at perhaps the most notable German aircraft engines up to and throughout the whole of the Second World War. The Daimler-Benz series of aero engines certainly qualify for this honour, powering some of Germany's most famed combat aircraft in the process.

Daimler-Benz began producing aircraft engines for the Luftwaffe following a requisition from the Reichverkehrsministerium (Reich Ministry of Transport) in 1930 for an aero engine of the 30-1itre (1,800-cubic-inch) displacement class. The engine would be a liquid-cooled inverted V twelve-cylinder piston engine designated F4. By 1931 two prototypes had been built and underwent tests on a static engine test bench. The prototypes proved highly satisfactory during the tests and a further engine was developed as a result, the F4B, which was an improved version of the basic F4 engine. It was the F4B that became the prototype for the Daimler-Benz 600 engine which, as with other high-performance German aircraft engines, became subject to continuous development, remaining at the cutting edge of piston engine technology.

It was in 1933 that Daimler-Benz was finally awarded a contract to develop its new engine and, as a result, six examples of the DB 600 were built. Over the following year the DB 600 was the only German aircraft engine in the 30-litre class. In total some 2,281 DB 600 engines were produced.

The DB 600A-1 engine was conceived through the success of the DB 600 and came with a mechanical direct fuel injection system which was quite unique for an aircraft engine of its day as many other countries were still building aircraft engines with carburettors as opposed to fuel injection. As with all DB 601s, the engine had a 33.9-litre displacement. The first prototype of the DB 601-A engine, designated F4E, was subject to test-running in 1935. Following satisfactory test results in February 1937, an order was placed for 150 of these engines. Serial production of the engine began in November 1937, ending in 1943, after some 19,000 units of all types had been produced. The variants of the DB 601 engine are listed here:

**DB 601A-1**

Up to 1,100PS (1,085hp) at sea level at 2,400rpm, up to 1,020PS (1,006hp) at 2,400rpm and 4,500 metres (14,800 feet) altitude using B4 fuel.

**DB 601Aa**

Up to 1,175PS (1,158.9hp) at sea level at 2,500rpm, up to 1,100PS (1,085.0hp) at 2,400rpm and 3,700 metres (12,000 feet) altitude using B4 fuel.

**DB 601B-1**

Same as BD601A-1 for use in Messerschmitt Bf 110 and/or bomber aircraft. This motor had a different propeller/engine ratio of 1:1.88 instead of 1:1.55.

**DB 601Ba**

This powerplant was identical to the Aa model and was for use in the Messerschmitt Bf 110 and/or bomber aircraft with different propeller/ engine ratio, 1:1.88 instead of 1:1.55.

**DB 601M**

This model of engine was fitted to the Heinkel He 100D, rated at 1,175PS (1,158.9hp).

**DB 601N**

This engine produced 1.175PS (1.158.9hp) at sea level and at 4,900 metres (16,100 feet) altitude with 2,600rpm, using C3 fuel, and up to 1,270PS (1,252.6hp) at 2,100 metres (6,900 feet) altitude with 2,600rpm.

**DB 601P**

Same specification as the DB 601N for use in the Messerschmitt Bf 110 and/or bomber aircraft, again with different propeller/engine ratio, 1:1.88 instead of 1:1.55.

**DB 601E**

This engine produced 1,350PS (1,331hp) at sea level with 2,700rpm, up to 1,320PS (1,301.9hp) with 2,700rpm at 4,800 metres (15,700 feet) altitude using B4 fuel, and up to 1,450PS (1,430hp) at 2,100 metres (6,900 feet) altitude with 2,700rpm.

**DB 601 F/G**

Basically, the same specification as the DB 601E for use in the Messerschmitt Bf 110, Messerschmitt Bf 210 and/or bomber aircraft with different propeller/engine ratio, 1:1.875 (601F), 1:2.06 (601G) instead of 1:1.685.

**DB 606A/B**

This was the overly technical and much-maligned specification created in February 1937 that was specifically developed for use in the experimental single-propeller monoplane, the Heinkel He 119. It utilized a new concept of a mated engine configuration. This powerplant was basically a twinned-up pair of DB 601A or DB 601E engines coupled to run off a single propeller shaft. The weight of this installation was colossal at some 1.5 tons (3,000lb). This engine was also chosen for the Messerschmitt Me 261 (twin DB 606) and the concept proved satisfactory during the testing of the prototype aircraft. However, the first military application of this engine was as the standard fit in the Heinkel He 177As. The engine was rated at 2,700PS at sea level using a mirror-imaged starboard component engine supercharger. Even Göring derided this dangerous powerplant in August 1942 when he remarked they were little more than 'welded together engines'.

The engines made the Heinkel He 177A one of the most dangerous aircraft in the Luftwaffe inventory. Despite being a pointless concept, they were a totally unnecessary and overengineered waste of not only resources but aircrew's lives. These engines were prone to catching fire and detonating in flight. The faults were blamed largely upon inadequate installation design yet the whole concept was a waste of time when four separate engines could have done more or less the same job and not risked the lives of the crew flying the aircraft.

**Alfa-Romeo R.A.1000 R.C 41-I Monsone**

Licence-built version of DB 601A produced by Alfa Romeo in Italy.

**Aichi Atsuta**

Licence-built version of DB 601A produced by Aichi in Japan.

**Kawasaki Ha-40**

Licence-built version of the DB 601Aa produced by Kawasaki in Japan.

# Chapter 4

# The Spanish Civil War

Some military historians are of the view that the Spanish Civil War (*Guerra Civil Espanola*) which broke out on 17 July 1936 was in a sense a dress rehearsal for the Second World War. The political, social and religious factors behind the conflict certainly bore some resemblance, yet while the Spanish Civil War was primarily a socio-political religious conflict, the war the Nazis would later instigate in Europe and beyond was more orientated towards racial, ideological and territorial gains as opposed to any specific social, political or religious squabblings.

The civil war in Spain came about as a result of Spanish Republicans' alliance with anarchists of the communist anarcho-syndicalism movement. These were individuals who accepted the anarchist school of thought that viewed revolution, industrial unionism and syndicalism as a method for workers in a capitalist society to gain control of an economy, thus controlling influence throughout the broader society. Both the Republicans and communist/anarchists were loyal to the left-leaning Second Spanish Republic, a form of government that had existed in Spain from 1931 to 1939. The Second Spanish Republic was proclaimed on 14 April 1931 after the deposition of Alfonso XIII, yet it would enjoy a painfully brief and bloody existence.

The Spanish Nationalist faction led by the fascist General Francisco Franco Bahamonde who opposed the Republicans was composed of a variety of right-wing fascist political organizations that supported the Spanish coup of July 1936, a nationalist/military uprising designed to overthrow the Second Spanish Republic, which in turn precipitated full-scale civil war. The Nationalists expected to achieve their aims rapidly. The civil war that ensued, from 17 July 1936 to 1 April 1939, a total of two years and eight months (two weeks and one day), would prove a beneficial experience to the new Luftwaffe of Nazi Germany. However, the Spanish Civil War would be remembered for the social and political divisions caused in Spanish society and the atrocities that were carried out. Mass executions were commonplace in both Nationalist- and Republican-controlled areas and in many cases the local authorities were complicit in these executions.

The world was forced to take sides yet many nations including the United States and Britain opted to remain neutral, such was the nervousness of another full-scale war in Europe. There were, however, volunteers from various countries including Russia and America who joined the Republican International Brigade to fight the fascists. The Russian-built Polikarpov 1-15 and 1-16 single-seat fighter aircraft formed the backbone of the Republican air arm and would give a good account of themselves during the battles to come.

Nazi military aid to General Franco's nationalist forces was almost guaranteed. At the time fascism was a relatively small club on the European stage, principally Italy and Germany. Though other countries on the European map adopted many of the political characteristics of fascism, it was yet to become the political and social wildfire of the late 1930s and 1940s.

In the wake of the July 1936 military coup, the Nationalists requested military aid from both Italy and Germany. The request for the assistance of the Luftwaffe was made on 22 July, barely five days after the coup. This was primarily for ten transport aircraft which Hitler agreed to, yet Hitler was at the same time wary of provoking what could become a Europe-wide war. However, he had several motives for allowing German involvement in the Spanish conflict: it would prove something of a distraction from German remilitarization which was gathering momentum at the time; he also viewed the war as a means of stopping the spread of communism in Western Europe; and lastly, he wanted a state friendly to Germany with a view to the contesting Anglo-French influence.

The Luftwaffe contingent sent to Spain to aid Franco's fascists was known as the Condor Legion and was placed under the command of Generalfeldmarschall Hugo Sperrle. Luftwaffe aircraft that would take part in the fighting consisted of the following:

- **Henschel Hs123**
  Single-seat single-engine biplane dive-bomber and close-support attack aircraft that proved a durable, robust and

effective combat aircraft with a top speed of 212mph (341kph). It was armed with a pair of 7.92mm MG 17 machine guns (later two 20mm MG FF cannons) and up to 450kg (992lb) of bombs.

- **Junkers Ju 87**
  Two-seat single-engine dive-bomber and ground-attack aircraft. The Ju 87 or 'Stuka' as it was known became the terror of the skies and made its debut with the Condor Legion in Spain. The Ju 87 had a maximum speed of 238mph (370kph) at 13,410 feet with a cruising speed of 130mph (209kph). The Stuka carried two 7.92mm MG 17 machine guns, one in each wing, and a 7.92mm MG 15 machine gun operated by the rear gunner. The Ju 87 could carry up to 1,100lb of bombs in various combinations or a single air-dropped weapon such as the 500kg bomb.

- **Junkers Ju 86**
  The Junkers Ju 86 was a monoplane bomber employed both as a civilian airliner which could carry up to ten passengers and in the offensive role with a crew of four. It had a maximum speed of 260mph (418kph) which was respectable for an aircraft of its type. Its offensive armament consisted of various combinations of bombs plus defensive 7.92mm-calibre MG 15 machine guns. It saw limited service in the war and during one of the first sorties one was shot down by Republican fighters with the loss of three crew killed and one captured. A replacement aircraft was dispatched from Germany but, in the summer of 1937, another was lost in an accident and the three remaining Ju 86s were sold to the Nationalists.

- **Heinkel He 111**
  The distinctive form of the Heinkel He 111 was another contributor to the Nationalist air forces and overall gave a good account of itself, proving far superior as a bomber than the Junkers Ju 86. The variant of the He 111 which saw service in Spain had an open retractable ventral gun turret mounting a 7.92mm MG 15 machine gun whereas later

marks had an enclosed ventral 'bathtub' gondola mounting a 7.92mm MG 15 machine gun in the forward position of the gondola and a flexible 20mm Oerlikon MG FF in the rearward position. The He 111 also had a 7.92mm MG 15 machine gun in the nose and dorsal position of the aircraft for defence against enemy fighters. The He 111E-1 production aircraft could carry a bomb load of 12,000kg (4,400lb) and possessed a top speed of up to 270mph (418kph) with a crew of five.

- **Dornier Do 17**
  Often referred to as the '*Fliegender Bleistift*' ('Flying Pencil'), the Dornier Do 17 was designed as a lightweight *Schellbomber* (fast bomber) with a crew of four, that in theory was capable of outrunning any enemy fighters. Like the Heinkel He 111, the Dornier Do 17 formed the nucleus of the Luftwaffe bomber fleet in 1939/40. With a top speed of 255mph (410kph) and an armament of up to six 7.92mm MG 15 machine guns all mounted in the cockpit area (a heavy armament for a Luftwaffe bomber of the period) and bomb capacity of 1,000kg (2,205lb), the Dornier Do 17 was an excellent and versatile bomber. One later version was fitted with a flexible 20mm Oerlikon MG FF cannon in the nose.

- **Heinkel He 51**
  The Heinkel He 51, although unusual in being a biplane configuration that would not have been out of place in the First World War, was an aesthetically pleasing aircraft. Although its career as a fighter in Spain was short-lived due to the quality of Republican fighters such as the Soviet Polikarpov 1-15 biplane and the new Polikarpov 1-16 monoplane fighter which soon arrived in service on the Republican side. It proved its worth as an excellent ground-attack and close air support aircraft. With a crew of one and top speed of 210mph (338kph), it was armed with two 7.92mm MG 17 machine guns fixed above the engine to fire through the propeller and could carry up to six 10kg bombs for the ground-attack close air support role.

- **Heinkel He 112**
  Another aircraft developed as a single-seat monoplane fighter, the Heinkel He 112 also had a lacklustre career in the Spanish Civil War. One version armed with 20mm Oerlikon MG FF cannons was shipped to Spain and assigned to Versuchsjagdgruppe 88, a unit of the Condor Legion where new aircraft were combat-tested. Wilhelm Balthasar (a later Luftwaffe Battle of Britain ace) attacked an armoured train in the cannon-armed He 112 followed by an armoured car with good results. An engine seizure and a crash caused the aircraft to be written off. Despite a top speed of 303mph (488kph) and punchy armament of two 7.92mm MG 17 machine guns mounted in the sides of the nose firing through the propeller and two 20mm Oerlikon MG FF cannons (one in each wing), the He 112 remained inferior even to the early marks of the Messerschmitt Bf 109.

- **Messerschmitt Bf 109**
  For the early marks of the Messerschmitt Bf 109 the Spanish Civil War served as the proving ground. Whilst there were still many technical bugs to be ironed out of the initial design before the Bf 109 would emerge as the all-conquering Luftwaffe fighter of the early phases of the Second World War, it was clear that the Bf 109 was an excellent basis for development. Lightly armed with up to four 7.92mm MG 17 machine guns, the Bf 109, although not having everything entirely its own way in Spain, was more than a match for any aircraft in the Republican inventory and inflicted heavy losses on the Soviet Polikarpov fighters of the Republican air force. Variants available for combat evaluation in Spain were the A, B, C and D models. At the close of the Spanish Civil War, of the 136 Bf 109s sent to Spain, some forty-seven B, D and E models were retained by the Spanish air force. It is quoted that some twenty Bf 109s was either shot down in air-to-air combat or lost to ground fire. Much valuable tactical experience was learned by Luftwaffe pilots, tactical experience that would prove vital in the war that loomed on the horizon.

- **Heinkel He 70**
  An aircraft similar in design to the Heinkel He 51, albeit in a monoplane configuration, the He 70 was intended as both an auxiliary bomber and reconnaissance aircraft. By 1933 the He 70 had set eight world speed records. Twenty-eight He 70s were sent to Spain where the aircraft quickly gained the nickname of the '*Rayo*' which is the Spanish term for 'lightning'. Used primarily in the fast reconnaissance role, one of the major flaws in construction was that parts of the airframe were manufactured from an extremely flammable magnesium alloy known as Elektron, though the majority of the aircraft's monocoque fuselage was made from duralumin. Elektron was a lightweight, strong material yet burned fiercely when ignited and the resulting fire was very difficult to extinguish. Non-self-sealing fuel tanks located in each of the wings of the He 70 only served to exaggerate an already hazardous airframe structure. It was noted that even a single bullet from a light machine gun or rifle was capable of setting the entire aircraft ablaze. Thus, the He 70 did not enjoy a long or successful career in the Luftwaffe or the Hungarian air force which adopted the type (He 70K) for a relatively short period in 1941/2

- **Junkers Ju 52**
  One of the most easily distinguishable of all Luftwaffe airframes, the Ju 52 was initially conceived as a civilian passenger aircraft and was easily adapted as a military transport and bomber aircraft. It was unique in having a corrugated duralumin metal skinning plus three engines, one mounted on the nose and one on each wing. In the military role it was fitted with a defensive armament of two 7.92mm MG 15 machine guns operated by the crew, one in the dorsal position of the aircraft and the other in a retractable 'dustbin'-type ventral turret. In the bomber role the Ju 52 could carry a useful payload of 1,500kg (3,300lb). The Ju 52 has the distinction of being one of the first aircraft types to be delivered to the Nationalist air force. It was used in almost every major engagement in support

> of the Nationalist forces, gaining a fearsome reputation in the process, particularly as a participant in the controversial bombing of Guernica. Although considered obsolete by 1937, the Ju 52 would serve the Luftwaffe throughout the entirety of the Second World War.

Kampfgruppe 88 (Battlegroup 88) of the Condor Legion was equipped with three squadrons of Ju 52 aircraft operating in the bomber role, while Jagdgruppe 88 (Fighter Group 88) was equipped with three squadrons of Heinkel He 51 fighters. At this stage it is clear that both Kampfgruppe and Jagdgruppe 88 were merely experimental wings equipped with largely untested prototype aircraft in the combat sense. The Spanish Civil War would prove of immense military value to the Germans: aircraft were tested in an operational environment and pilots gained valuable combat experience.

New aircraft could be rotated in and out of the theatre of combat as the Germans desired. Typically, the Luftwaffe fighter contingent was organized into what was known as a *staffel*. A *staffel* consisted of twelve aircraft, much the same as an RAF squadron. Yet, although the Germans were committing some of the most modern combat aircraft to the Spanish campaign, they were not as yet the polished products of the 1940s and despite their technological advantages, did not have it all their own way.

Generalleutnant Hugo Sperrle was given overall command of the Luftwaffe contingent with Oberst Wolfram Freiherr von Richtofen as his chief of staff. Richtofen was the cousin of the First World War fighter ace Manfred von Richtofen, best known as 'The Red Baron'. The Condor Legion was keen to exploit methods of strategic bombing and to observe the effects on the civilian population. Even at this stage in the Luftwaffe's development there was the understanding that if one could break the will of the civilian population through bombing then that particular conflict might be brought to a rapid conclusion. In fact, the Luftwaffe would implement the first of what became known as terror bombing during the civil war. General Franco did not share the same enthusiasm as the Germans for bombing cities before allowing ground forces in, but clearly Franco was not calling the shots.

The first major challenge facing the Germans in Spain was the 20,000 Nationalist troops stranded at their outpost in Morocco, their movement prevented by a Spanish Republican naval blockade. In a quite remarkable operation for its day, the Luftwaffe succeeded in evacuating by air the confined Nationalist troops, something which had never been done before. The troops were flown to Seville with the loss of only one Junkers Ju 52. It led US General Hap Arnold to comment later that this action was ‘the most important development in air power of the inter war period’.

Following the evacuation, the Luftwaffe concentrated its efforts on harassment raids against the Republicans and conducted ground-attack missions in support of Nationalist troops. With these early operations the Germans initiated both strategic and tactical bombing sorties against the Republicans. While many military thinkers of the time were still contemplating the validity of aerial bombing, the Luftwaffe in Spain was fine-tuning the art and gaining valuable practical experience of ground and air forces working in a cooperative manner in order to achieve an objective. This was the template for the later Blitzkrieg method of attack that would prove so devastating throughout Europe in the Second World War.

As Soviet aircraft began arriving on the Republican side in October 1936, the Luftwaffe began the use of tactical bombing to weaken enemy troops ready for assault by the ground forces. In Bilbao, in the north of Spain, saturation bombing was used to destroy what was termed as the Republican ‘Iron Belt’ – a twenty-two-mile-long line, leaving holes open for exploitation. This action also prevented Republican reinforcements from plugging the gaps.

It was, however, strategic bombing that attracted the most attention. At first the methods employed were crude: German bomber crews were using tourist maps to help locate their targets, but soon the attacks became routine. Despite this, there were no repercussions as many theorists had anticipated. In fact, civilian resistance and resolve on both sides appeared only to strengthen. One British observer was heard to comment on the situation ‘that the Spanish would blacken every balcony so as to get a good view of bursting shrapnel’.

Of all the air raids carried out by the Germans, the bombing of Guernica, a city in the north of Spain, came to best illustrate the horror and destructive nature of aerial bombing. Guernica was the epicentre of Basque identity and culture. The parliament building and an oak tree under which Basque leaders annually swore an oath to uphold the liberties of the people were the symbol of Basque identity. On 26 April 1937, aircraft of the Condor Legion in the space of just three hours dropped 100,000lb (almost 50 tons) of bombs onto the city. German aircrews are also said to have been guilty of indiscriminate machine-gunning of fleeing civilians. A typical example is that given by José Marguerass, passed down from his great-grandfather, Aranzana:

> The German planes rained down death on the city with bomb after bomb falling from the air. The sounds of the explosions, buildings collapsing and people screaming were ones I can never forget. As the planes finished dropping their bombs they came back around, swooping down to low level where they machine-gunned anything or anyone that moved. I saw the bodies of men, women and young children who had been murdered in this way; that is what it was, it was plain murder. I saw a young child crying hysterically over the body of her dead mother, she was shaking her mother as if to attempt to wake her from some kind of deep sleep, but the mother would not wake up. Upon realization that her mother was never going to wake up again the, little girl began screaming out loudly, '*Muerta, muerta*' ('Dead, dead'). I felt only anger and hostility towards the Germans after that. They had brough death and destruction to our country; they were criminals and devils with their machines of death. I hated them from that day onwards.

Generally, historians agree today that the casualty figure for civilian deaths at Guernica was actually between 170 and 300 people, not the overtly exaggerated claim of 1,700 as originally mooted. This revised figure by no means serves as any excuse for what was a deliberate terror attack on a civilian populace, yet it was a tactic the Luftwaffe would employ repeatedly in future campaigns.

Germany was eager to send only its most promising officers and aircrews to Spain, where they would remain for between three and seven months so as many as possible gained combat experience. When these men returned to Germany, they were employed to pass their experience on through training establishments and flying schools.

As mentioned, the Germans did not have everything entirely their own way and, on 13 November 1936, the appearance of twelve short, stubby-looking monoplane fighter aircraft caused quite a stir among the Nationalist pilots during a bombing raid over Madrid. The aircraft in question were Soviet Polikarpov 1-16 fighters known as *Rata* (rat) by the Germans and flown by Soviet pilots. The Polikarpov 1-16 carried a potent armament of two 7.62mm ShKAS machine guns and two 20mm ShVAK cannons. By the time the twelve Republican fighters turned for home they had downed four of the Nationalist raiders; two Heinkel He 51 pilots were reported as being killed. On the Republican side the group commander collided with one of the enemy machines and another 1-16 pilot was forced to crash-land after sustaining damage. The Polikarpovs were far superior to the Heinkel He 51 and Arado Ar 68 biplanes of the Nationalist air force and enjoyed air superiority until the arrival of the Messerschmitt Bf 109 fighters.

German fighter pilot Ernst Willi Gabel, who flew Heinkel He 51 biplanes against the Polikarpov fighters, recalled the struggles they faced in the air at that time of uncertainty:

> To suddenly find oneself at a disadvantage in the air is very disheartening and bad for morale. I was an experienced pilot and I had flown biplane aircraft and monoplane aircraft prior to joining the new German air force. The problem was the Heinkel He 51 was representative of the old German air force; it was a lightly armed biplane and not particularly fast either. When the Russian-supplied Polikarpovs first appeared, we had no easy answer to combatting them. In some ways the slower He 51could be used against them provided you saw them coming first. When attacked you could if the situation permitted use your slower speed as an advantage. I would turn in to the attacking enemy before diving for the ground, I would let him pass and then I would turn into him and fire my machine guns. The problem was even if you scored hits with just two machine guns, you could barely inflict enough damage to achieve a victory. You would try to fire head on at them into their propellers and engines where they were most vulnerable. The Polikarpov had two machine guns at first like our He 51s, yet they

> later fitted 20mm cannons in the wings to improve their armament. Yes, we suffered losses and lost the momentum, and we were consigned to aerial manoeuvring rather than aerial fighting and shooting down the enemy; it was a case of survival as we could not compete equally with the Polikarpov. It was an immensely frustrating time. Only the delivery of the Messerschmitt Bf 109 saved what was an impending disaster in the air. With that point made clear, the Heinkel He 51 was an excellent aircraft when used solely in the ground-attack role in support of our ground forces. It was obsolete as a fighter by the 1930s and as good as it was against other biplane fighters and as a utility aircraft, it could not compete with the all-metal monoplane fighters which began to enter service.

The Polikarpov 1-16 was not an easy aeroplane to fly. The type had poor visibility and the cockpit canopy was prone to fouling from engine oil and the moving section of the canopy tended to slam shut and then open during hard manoeuvres. The frontal section of the fuselage where the engine was located was too close to the centre of gravity and the pilot's cockpit too far to the rear. Pilots also noted that the Polikarpov possessed insufficient longitudinal stability and was impossible to fly 'hands off'. However, it was a better aeroplane than many of those in Nationalist service until the arrival of the Messerschmitt Bf 109B and the subsequent overwhelming numbers of Nationalist fighters. The Polikarpov 1-15 and 1-16s soon suffered heavy losses at the hands of the Luftwaffe.

The Messerschmitt Bf 109 proved an essential component in returning dominance of the air over Spain to the Nationalist forces. There was not an aircraft on the Republican side that could compete with the Bf 109 which was superior in every aspect to anything the Republican air force possessed. When the first Bf 109s arrived in Spain, they were quickly sent into action and soon proved their worth against the Polikarpovs. The air war suddenly became a very one-sided affair. Soviet machine-gun technician Viktor M. Sinaisky recalled the Bf 109:

> It was a very well-designed aeroplane. Firstly, it had an engine of an inverted type, so it could not easily be knocked out from below. It also had two water radiators with a cut-off

> system: if one leaked you could fly on the second or close both down and fly at least five minutes more. The pilot had good armour protection from the back, and the fuel tank was also behind armour. Our aircraft had fuel tanks in the centre of their wings; that's why our pilots ended up being incinerated. What else did I like about the Bf 109? Well, it was highly automatic and thus easy to fly. It also employed an electrical pitch regulator, which our planes didn't have. Our propeller system with variable pitch was hydraulic, making it impossible to change pitch without the engine running. If, God forbid, you turned off the engine at high pitch, it was impossible to turn the propeller and was very hard to restart the engine again. Finally, the fact that the Bf 109 was fitted with an ammunition counter was also very good.

The Messerschmitt Bf 109's participation in the Spanish Civil War is both notable and confusing. Over the years it has been difficult to clearly ascertain the exact number and types of Bf 109 that served in the Condor Legion. The confusion appears to originate from the lack of available documentation for those Bf 109s sent to Spain, along with the lack of any clear and authentic photographic evidence. For example, the Bf 109 A, B, C and D models were all externally identical to one another and identifying the different models even through photographs is not the easiest of endeavours.

This is an area of study which would run to many pages; however, below is a list of types of Bf 109s known to have been sent to Spain for combat evaluation with the Legion Condor:

- **Bf 109A**
  Fitted with the Jumo 210D engine and two-blade wooden fixed-pitch propeller. Armament consisted of two 7.92mm MG 17 machine guns.

- **Bf 109B**
  Fixed-pitch propeller replaced by a variable-pitch Hamilton propeller fitted to aid the accommodation of a 7.92mm MG 17 machine gun firing through the centre of the engine to augment the two synchronized MG 17 machine guns mounted in the nose firing through the propeller blades.

- **Bf 109C**
  Fitted with the Jumo 210 Ga engine incorporating direct fuel injection (giving increased high-altitude performance). The armament configuration for this model was increased to four 7.92mm MG 17 machine guns with the addition of an MG 17 in each wing just outboard of the undercarriage wheel wells. The gun muzzles were enclosed in the wings.

- **Bf 109D**
  This model reverted to the Jumo 210D powerplant (not the Daimler-Benz 600 series powerplant as commonly believed) and included the additional two wing-mounted 7.92mm MG 17 machine guns.

- **Bf 109E-1**
  Fitted with the Daimler-Benz DB 610 powerplant utilizing a three-blade propellor that made the profile of the nose of this model distinctive from earlier types.

- **Bf 109E-3**
  This version saw the introduction of a heavier armament where the two wing-mounted 7.92mm MG 17 machine guns were replaced by two 20mm Oerlikon MG FF cannons, each with sixty rounds of ammunition. The wing-mounted cannon muzzles protruded beyond the wing leading edges.

There were many technical and structural differences between the models but what is clear is that with the introduction of the Bf 109 into the Spanish Civil War, the type rapidly regained the initiative for the Nationalists. The Bf 109 was far superior to any aircraft in the Republican inventory and was pivotal in achieving ultimate victory. However, success in the air over Spain relied much upon tactics and experience as it did having a better aeroplane than the opposition. Tactics devised relied on altitude, speed and surprise and were the main elements of attack. Only around twenty Messerschmitt Bf 109 fighters were lost over Spain, shot down by Republican fighters or ground fire.

German fighter ace Johannes Trautloft was among the first German aviators to volunteer for service with the Condor Legion. Writing to Johannes in 1988, I asked if he had any particular memories of his service in the Spanish Civil War, to which he replied:

> We were fortunate in having the better aeroplane and I myself shot down five enemy aircraft in Spain. I claimed my victories between the months of August and December 1936. My first victory was the shooting down of a Breguet 19 light bomber aircraft, this enemy aircraft crashing into the ground in the vicinity of Colmenar Viejo. In fact, this I believe was the first enemy aircraft to be shot down in Spain. I shot down a Potez 540 which was an antiquated-looking, French-designed reconnaissance aircraft. This enemy fell easily to the guns of my Heinkel 51. Five days after I had achieved this victory I myself was unfortunate enough to be shot down. My aircraft became totally unresponsive due to the damage inflicted by my opponent and I was forced to bale out, thankfully over Nationalist-held territory. In December my unit, Versuchsjagdgruppe 88, received its first Messerschmitt Bf 109 aircraft for evaluation and I was chosen as one of the pilots to fly one of these. I was even given a personalized aircraft bearing the 'Green Heart' motif of Thuringia, which was quite an honour for me back then as a young fighter pilot. I was asked my opinion of the Bf 109 after flying the type for several more operations over enemy territory. By 2 March 1937 I was on my way home back to Germany with a total of five victories and the fact I was now considered something of an expert fighter pilot. This was not the end of my career as a fighter pilot but merely the beginning. I learned that in order to be successful against an enemy in the air you needed to gain the advantage of height in order to see your adversary before he saw you, attack out of the sun wherever possible using the speed of your aircraft, hit your enemy in one vicious swipe and then use your superior speed advantage to dive and climb back to altitude to leave the battle as the situation dictated. Often our enemy never saw us coming until they were falling in

> flames. The Bf 109 gave us the edge as it did so throughout what would be the Second World War. It was not always the best aircraft by late-war standards, but I can say with a good pilot at its controls, aware of the tactics you could employ to aid your survival, the Bf 109 always gave you a fighting chance. It was a very good aeroplane.

German fighter pilots with the Legion Condor who returned to Germany as ace fighter pilots were greeted as heroes. They enjoyed an almost celebrity status, capturing the imagination of all. Listed here are the German flying aces of the Spanish Civil War:

- Hauptmann Werner Mölders 14 victories
- Hauptmann Wolfgang Schellmann 12 victories
- Oberleutnant Harro Harder 11 victories
- Leutnant Peter Boddem 10 victories
- Leutnant Otto Bertram 9 victories
- Leutnant Wilhelm Ensslen 9 victories
- Oberst Herbert Ihlefeld 9 victories
- Oberleutnant Walter Oesau 9 victories
- Major Reinhard Seiler 9 victories
- Hauptmann Herwig Knuppel 8 victories
- Oberleutnant Hans-Karl Mayer 8 victories
- Hauptmann Wilhelm Balthasar 7 victories
- Oberleutnant Kraft Eberhardt 7 victories
- Generalmajor Walter Grabmann 7 victories
- Leutnant Horst Tietzen 7 victories
- Hauptmann Rolf Pingel 6 victories
- Oberfeldwebel Kurt Rochel 6 victories
- Unteroffizier Herbert Schob 6 victories
- Unteroffizier Georg Braunshirn 5 victories
- Oberst Gotthard Handrick 5 victories
- Hauptmann Wolf-Heinrich von Houwald 5 victories
- Oberleutnant Wolfgang Lippert 5 victories
- Hauptmann Günther Lutzow 5 victories
- Major Joachim Schlichting 5 victories
- Unteroffizier Willi Szuggar 5 victories
- Oberleutnant Hannes Trautloft 5 victories

The Spanish Civil War ended on 28 March 1939 with the Republican surrender of Madrid and an overwhelming victory for General Franco and his Nationalists. Up to a million lives were lost during the conflict, the most devastating in Spanish history. The war would have far-reaching ramifications, creating all manner of political and social divides in Spanish society. The Germans on the other hand had gained valuable military experience both in the air and on the ground. They were able to go away and with the lessons learned make improvements to their military hardware and develop further the tactics they had used so effectively in Spain. The Spanish Civil War had also proved highly beneficial to Hitler and his generals for their future aspirations in Europe, despite the fact that they left Spain with the blood of thousands on their hands. The Luftwaffe, even at this early stage of its development, was now tainted by accusations of war crimes through the application of the indiscriminate terror bombing of civilians. Yet the free world was content to stand idly by, the repercussions of which would soon return to haunt it.

Franco himself had much to thank Hitler for: the military assistance that Nazi Germany provided ensured that he remained dictator until his death in 1975, thirty years after Hitler's. Today the Spanish Civil War remains a suppurating sore on the Spanish national conscience.

# Chapter 5

# Air Sports

The Flieger Hitler Jugend (Flying Hitler Youth) came about as a result of boredom infiltrating a youth movement that was weary of the stale routine of sporting activities and political indoctrination. The Hitler Youth (HJ) leader, Baldur von Schirach, was quick to react. He understood that in order for the Hitler Youth movement to remain relevant and fresh and to keep its members focused on their duties, he needed to introduce newer, more exciting programmes into the organization. The Flieger HJ was thus formed in 1937 and not only served to reinvigorate a somewhat ailing Hitler Youth movement but also to help meet the requirements of the rapidly expanding Germany military machine. Although the Nationalsozialistisches Flieger Korps (NSFK, the National Socialist Flying Corps) had been in existence since 1932, it was primarily a tool for promoting interest in aviation and flying throughout the country as opposed to recruiting manpower to meet Germany's future military aspirations.

Christoph Oegen was 18 in 1939 and one of many boys in the new Germany who had followed the progress of the Condor Legion in Spain and was thus inspired to become a flyer with the Luftwaffe.

His ambition to become a pilot was cemented by his joining of the newly formed Flieger Hitler Jugend in 1937. He explained the allure of the Luftwaffe:

> To be a flyer was seen as the best; all the boys in my Hitler Youth group aspired to become fighter pilots. They had no interest in becoming bomber crews, just fighter pilots; that's where the prestige lay in our minds anyway. I remember at school learning daily the exploits of our armed forces in the struggle against the Republicans in Spain and of course how German might, particularly air power, overcame them and

secured a Nationalist victory. We understood that Franco could have only ever succeeded with help from Germany, that was how great a nation we had become. We had gone from Versailles to having the best army and air force the world had ever seen, we thought we were invincible, and we all wanted to play this part even if only in a small way, but the Spanish war had ended and as it drew to a close, we felt a sense of dejection at having missed it through not being old enough, yet we possessed much admiration for those who had taken part in it.

It was thrilling when one of our pilots, Werner Mölders, came to one of our Hitler Youth meetings to give us a talk about his flying experiences. We sat there mesmerized by what he told us, yet he also outlined that the fighter pilot lived a very precarious existence, he relied constantly not only on the abilities of the machine he was flying, but also on his wits, his sixth sense and also his natural instincts. He told us a good pilot starts from nothing, he starts with his feet on the ground, learning all the facets of aero dynamics, how an aeroplane works, the tactics a good fighter pilot relies upon and the weapons he has. He explained the transition into the air as something which has to be mastered incrementally and asked all those in our group, 'Who wants to become a fighter pilot?' Nearly all the boys thrust their hands eagerly up into the air in response. He then held up a model of the Messerschmitt Bf 109 fighter and pointed out the tactics used in air combat and the various characteristics of the aircraft itself. The time seemed to literally fly by and soon he had to leave. Before he left, he signed autographs for us and shook our hands and said, 'Maybe someday one or two of you here will be flying in one of my wings, maybe even under my command.' The prospect for us was so enthralling. Mölders left to rousing applause from everyone until our leader called for silence.

Our leader explained that many of the present-day Luftwaffe fighter pilots had gained their positions through flying gliders as youngsters. These operated under the guise of air sports and soon the opportunities were there for us to join gliding clubs to get a taste of flying. The Hitler Youth operated many glider clubs for young lads who wanted to become pilots. I desperately wanted to fly though my parents were apprehensive about it; they felt I might have an accident and get myself killed or something, but I persisted and, in the end, they agreed I could forward a membership request to one of the local glider sporting clubs. I first had to pass a medical where I was declared fit without any problems. It all started for so many by building flying models of gliders, learning all about aero dynamics and how glider aircraft use thermals to gain height. We would spend much time just sitting in the cockpit of a glider aircraft, where you imagined yourself soaring high into the skies and full of wonder for what it was like. There was a lot of theory to digest as one had to gain a thorough understanding of how a glider, which had no engine, was controlled and how you could get into problems and how these problems could sometimes be resolved. Any form of flight was dangerous, and one could not just jump into a glider and take off. So, there was a lot of classroom work mixed with just sitting in the open cockpit of a standard glider, learning what the controls did and how they should be used. There were even girls who wanted to learn to fly gliders but as girls they were discouraged from doing so by those in charge, who would say, 'Flying is not a job for a woman, it is a man's job; now go home to your mother,' though some girls did end up flying gliders in some of our clubs.

Once you had passed a series of very thorough tests on the ground, they would tether a glider to a vehicle with a short tow rope. You would be asked, 'Are you ready?' You would give them a hand signal and they would accelerate until the glider began to lift of the ground. At first it was just a short distance, maybe ten or fifteen feet from the ground, to give you a feel of the controls and see if you were steady enough to go any further. I loved it; it was an amazing experience and I couldn't wait to get back home to tell my parents all about it. I remember seeing one boy crash his glider. I don't know how it happened or what he did wrong, but he came down rather abruptly, damaging the nose of the glider; he walked away a little scared and pale with a few bruises for souvenirs, but he never came back again; it wasn't for everyone, I guess. They always used to say accidents happen and you have to put them to the back of your mind and get back on the horse; don't be a coward, you have to be man to fly an aeroplane.

We also operated balloons which took us very high off the ground. Again, this was not for everyone. There were those who loved it and those who suddenly realized they had no taste for heights and wanted to get back down on the ground. Most of us as boys had no rational sense of fear back then and most of those I began flying club with entered the Luftwaffe later.

I settled down and took over the running of my father's butchery shop. I didn't relish the job but by mid-1943 the Luftwaffe was crying out for young men, even ones with no flying experience at all to enrol for flying training. I have to admit I failed my first attempt and they advised to me to go for a ground job, as they put it, but I was persistent and finally entered the war flying the Bf 109G in the autumn of 1944. My parents were not happy about this at all and my younger sister Irene had to take responsibility of the shop when I left to join the Luftwaffe. I was 23 years of age, a good average for a Luftwaffe fighter pilot at that time.

As already mentioned by Christoph, girls did join the Flieger HJ foundation, many of them proving to be very good glider pilots. Monica Vanessa Kieler Dorsche was one young girl born with flying in her blood and she recalls of her experiences:

My father had been a military aviator in the First World War, so the fascination for aircraft and flying was certainly in my blood, yet there was this chauvinistic attitude, particularly among the old Weimar government regarding women and flying. Yes, we could participate in the various sporting and gliding clubs, but these were very much male-run affairs, and they made all the decisions. I had no end of frustration with these flying clubs, and I got into arguments with those in charge which didn't go down very well at all. They told me to 'Go home and do something useful'. In fact, they banned me from most of them, telling me I had a bad attitude.

In the end my father got me what you'd call private flying tuition; he paid for me to have lessons and that way I could learn without interference. I don't think for one minute he had any idea of what I would go on to do in the future. If he had, he may not have paid for my lessons [she laughs]. I think my father felt it might just be a fad, that I would get bored with it all, but I didn't. I learned to master the art of flying a glider which was a weird experience as there were no engines and you were totally reliant on the thermals generated by the environment around you. You could only fly in good weather conditions, so the club I joined was closed for the much of the winter. The people around me were mostly adults just flying gliders for their own recreation. I saw it not as a hobby but as a means of going on to powered aircraft. Yes, I wanted to fly proper aeroplanes with engines and maybe make a career from it; that was my plan. I was a very determined, headstrong young girl back then and I was totally focused on what I wanted to do, despite the men thinking they should do the flying, not us. I wasn't interested in war and while we all followed what was happening back home, I never thought I would ever fly a military aeroplane.

I moved to powered aircraft and flew monoplanes and twin propeller planes doing mostly mail drops to remote areas. When things began to deteriorate in Europe, I was in Africa where I often took wealthy photographers on flights to photograph the herds of elephant, giraffe and buffalo over the plains. There was very good money to be made from these wealthy great white hunter types as they were back then, and I lived very well over in Africa and Egypt and thought how good life was and how far I had come.

It was my father who called me back home as the situation back in Europe began to deteriorate. He told me it looked as if Germany was soon going to be involved in

> war; it didn't look good and he wanted me to come home as soon as I could. I worked the remainder of my contract for the mail company and completed my last two bookings for photographic flights and then I returned home to Germany. In a matter of just months Germany invaded Poland. I couldn't get any work flying; it felt as if I were a square peg in a round hole all over again; no, I wasn't happy, I was fucking raging with anger. Why does Hitler have to go to bloody war again? Have we all not grown sick of fighting wars? That was my feeling at the time.

Michael Ott was another young man encouraged into a career with the Luftwaffe via the Flieger HJ Foundation. Michael's son, Bernhard, recalled:

> They [the Nazis] needed a good supply of cannon fodder; this was very clear. The Nazi orientation towards war had been very clear also for many years prior to 1939. Through Spain they learned that air power was the greatest new weapon of all, that the bomber was a crucial element in crushing obstinate enemy nations. My father Michael wanted to study to become a doctor as helping people, not killing people, was his passion. The Hitler Youth took that away from him; they brainwashed him into notions of joining the German air force. They told him, 'First we conquer all of Europe, then you can go back to your studies, but the Reich and the Führer's wishes must come first and all the Hitler Youth must obey.' At the time he must have thought it a very important thing to honour these Reich duties and as such he did as he was told.
>
> He was seduced by the feeling of flying gliders, but I don't think for one minute he really thought about the horrors these simple gliding aeroplanes were going to lead him to witness. The Nazis knew exactly what they were going to do: they were going to start a war with the world which they felt they had every chance of winning. They seduced the young with tales of heroism and conquest through these Hitler Youth flying clubs. This was of course

before the youth had seen dead and dying airmen being pulled from their bullet-riddled aeroplanes, or seen their comrades falling from the sky in flames with no hope of escape and hearing their screams over the communications.

My father entered the Luftwaffe in August 1944, aged 21. Before the end of the war, he would be crippled and wheelchair bound, and both my mother and I were left to care for him because he couldn't even go to the toilet himself. His hands resembled chicken's feet from the burns he had received when his aircraft was shot down. It was a very undignified end for what had been a very fit, good-looking and proud young man who just wanted to become a doctor.

Another former member of the Flieger HJ and Luftwaffe, Gottfried Urquhart, recalled:

The Hitler Youth was becoming boring for us young lads at the time. To be honest, we were bored with the boxing matches, running races, being told what to do all the time and the endless political rhetoric. Of course, you couldn't speak out and say this, but it was felt by our superiors indirectly. That is one of the reasons the Hitler Youth flying corps was created, to give us something more exciting to go for, to aspire to.

Flying had figured very prominently in Germany post-1918 under the guise of being a sports activity. It was one area of the military the powers that be sought to hang onto; this became very obvious throughout the 1930s when our country began to rebuild its military. The new Luftwaffe would need a steady flow of recruits. Our nation was gearing up towards war and war takes lives as we all know; those killed in combat or accidents would need to be replaced and the Hitler Youth was the ideal solution. Give the Hitler Youth a taste of flying and they would want more as it was all very exciting, and, combining this with the ethos of struggle and defending the nation, it was very easy to convince boys to volunteer to attend flying academies. Throw in a nice uniform and the prestige that went with it and it was all very easy.

I myself got involved in the Hitler Youth flying corps, and the more I got involved the more I wanted to be a pilot. Yes, they used to say to us back then, 'Being a flyer with the Luftwaffe is the ultimate achievement. The Luftwaffe is invincible and it's a lot safer than the job of a soldier on the ground.' That's what they told us and of course they were very wrong: the Luftwaffe was by no means invincible; it would suffer losses on all fronts and steadily it would become ineffective both as an offensive air force and a defensive one too. The problem was at the time we never imagined what the outcome was going to be. We were utterly convinced through the propaganda and the early successes that we were unstoppable, that we alone could win the war for Germany.

Flying a glider in peacetime over the quiet hills, woodlands and valleys of our communities was nothing like flying a high-performance fighter or bomber aircraft in a war situation. In the days where we flew our gliders and gained confidence to go onto the flying training schools, we had no one shooting at us. I think many joined up with the Luftwaffe with the mentality that it would all be very easy if and when we went to war.

For Christoph, Michael, Monica and Gottfried the coming war that would unfold with the German attack on Poland in 1939 would have mixed fortunes, as it would for all those entering the aerial fray with the Luftwaffe. We will examine more of their personal stories later.

# Chapter 6

# Blitzkrieg on Poland

The Blitzkrieg on Poland which began during the early hours of 1 September 1939 was the catalyst for the outbreak of the Second World War. Poland was to symbolize more than anything else the evil which had been permitted to take root in Europe throughout the 1930s. The political cancer of Nazism had spread throughout Germany and spilled over beyond its borders, its leaders making non-aggression pacts where it saw fit, pacts which were not worth the paper they were written on. The attack on Poland saw the use of the Luftwaffe once again. The Luftwaffe was the spearhead, the aerial artillery component of the Blitzkrieg, or lightning war, where both land and air forces worked together as a cohesive and devastating weapon.

The one aircraft in the Luftwaffe inventory which would come to symbolize the terror of Nazism to the outside world like no other was that of the Junkers Ju 87 'Stuka', an abbreviation of *Sturzkampflugzeug* or dive-bomber. The main air units assigned to the invasion of Poland were Luftlotte 1 and 4 with some 1,302 aircraft between them. It has often been stated that the valiant Polish Air Force was annihilated on the ground in just three days during the initial stages of the invasion, yet this is not true. Much of the myth regarding the Luftwaffe's campaign against Poland was concocted by the Nazi propaganda machine. It is true that the Polish Air Force was both outnumbered and outclassed, their aircraft were antiquated machines in comparison to the modern equipment the Luftwaffe had at its disposal. What the Polish Air Force lacked in technical finesse was more than made up for by their sheer grit and determination to fight back against all the odds. Polish pilots inflicted surprisingly high losses on the Luftwaffe, especially during the early days of the campaign. Warsaw's air force fought the Luftwaffe for one week and, at a reduced level of capacity and personnel, continued to meet the Germans in the air for over two weeks – hardly the resounding defeat that the Nazi propaganda proclaimed. The Luftwaffe knew that it was most effective against an enemy if he could be caught on the ground as opposed to in the air. The Polish Air Force as with the Luftwaffe had been conceived primarily with the view towards supporting its ground troops. The Poles had one independent fighter group with fifteen *escadres* (squadrons) and one bomber brigade of nine *escadres*, spreading the remainder of its resources in mixed detachments assigned to the Polish ground forces. The main adversary of the Messerschmitt Bf 109 in the skies over Poland was the PZL P.11 which in 1931 was a state-of-the-art gull-winged monoplane fighter armed with two rifle-calibre machine guns. By 1939 the P.11 was several generations behind anything the Luftwaffe had in its arsenal and 100mph slower than the Messerschmitt Bf 109. The Polish Air Force was also equipped with thirty of the older P.7 fighters. It had attempted to acquire Hawker Hurricane and M.S.406 fighters from Britain and France respectively yet at the outbreak of war these aircraft were awaiting final assembly and forward shipment in Rumania, an ally of Poland. Had the Polish Air Force received these aircraft, they would have most certainly inflicted greater losses on their enemy in the air war over their territory.

With these factors in mind, it is no wonder the Luftwaffe attacks on Poland were carried out with a high degree of confidence that all would result in achieving a quick victory. Yet the Luftwaffe assault was hardly a surprise to the Poles. Tensions between Germany and Poland had been significant enough to warrant a high state of readiness in Poland and Polish Air Force units were mobilized prior to the outbreak of war. As war broke out the Polish squadrons scattered to a series of secret satellite airfields, carrying out hit-and-run attacks on German aircraft and armour from their hidden bases whenever opportunities arose.

The first aerial victory of the Second World War was claimed by Luftwaffe pilot Franck Neubert (Stukageschwader 2 Immelmann,) flying a Ju 87 Stuka. The unfortunate victim was Captain Mieczyslaw Medwecki of the 2nd Krakow Air Regiment who was attempting to take off in his P.11 when Neubert dived in behind and opened fire with his two wing-mounted MG 17s. Ironically, as with the fortunes of war, Captain Medwecki's wingman, Lieutenant Władysław Gnyś, shot down two Dornier 17s, achieving the first two Allied aerial kills of war.

Meanwhile, a bigger aerial scrap broke out in the skies over the outskirts of Warsaw. A large formation of Heinkel He 111 bombers from Kampfgeschwader (KG) 27 (27th Bomber Group) escorted by Messerschmitt Bf 110 twin-engine fighters of 1/LG 1 were intercepted by Polish fighters. In what was a well-executed attack by the Poles, six Heinkel He 111s were shot down for the loss of one Polish P.11c, which crashed during a forced landing. *Der Spaziergang Uber Warshau* or 'Stroll over Warsaw' turned out to be anything but a stroll. It was during the fighting that Polish fighter pilot Second Lieutenant Borowski of Polish fighter wing 113 Eskadra claimed a Messerschmitt Bf 109, the first Bf 109 to be shot down in the Second World War.

However, the secret airfields the Poles were operating from did not remain secret for long and on 2 September, a pair of Messerschmitt Bf 109s on a patrol flight spotted a camouflaged airfield near Lodz. The two Bf 109s made several passes over the airfield, strafing several aircraft parked on the ground and shooting up a fuel storage facility, setting it ablaze. This incident, far from deterring the brave Polish fighter and bomber crews, raised the alarm and allowed the majority of Polish combat aircraft and their pilots to avoid destruction on the ground. On 3 September, the Luftwaffe attacked the Polish airfield at Malaszewicze three times in succession, destroying its aircraft hangars and most of the bombers of the resident training cadre. Two days later five Bf 109s shot down three P.11s attempting to take off and two more in aerial combat near the airfield at Widzew.

Warsaw bore the brunt of the Luftwaffe offensive and was bombed continuously from the start of the invasion. Polish fighter units managed to deter a force of eighty Heinkel He 111 bombers as they headed for the Polish capital. In the fight that ensued seven German aircraft were shot down for the loss of four Polish P.11s. Polish Colonel Leopold Pamula shot down two German aircraft and rammed a third with his P.11 before baling out to safety. Oddly enough, this would become a tactic used by the Luftwaffe during the final days of the air war over Germany itself. It is also worth noting at this point that although loathing of the German invader was tenacious in respect of the fighting, the Poles did not resort to shooting German pilots as they parachuted to safety. One Polish pilot, Lieutenant Skalski, brought down a Luftwaffe Hs 123 bomber then landed nearby to ensure his wounded opponent received prompt medical attention. Most Luftwaffe pilots also believed that chivalry should be observed in the air but not all adhered to this principle. There were confirmed reports of several Polish pilots being machine-gunned as they hung helplessly in their parachute harnesses. Their bodies were found riddled with bullets. The criminal act of shooting pilots while attempting to parachute to safety became prevalent as the war dragged on and nearly all sides admitted to doing this in some context.

The Poles, despite their deficiencies, also took a heavy toll on German armour. A number of sources have concluded that Polish bombers accounted for the majority of the 600 or so German tanks destroyed during the campaign. What can be confirmed is that the advance of the German XVI Panzer Corps was stalled for two days at Radomsko as a result of bombing attacks by Polish Air Force P.23s and at Czestochowa the 4th Panzer Division was attacked repeatedly by Polish P.37s, subsequently losing 28 per cent of its strength.

To summarize, the German campaign against Poland was not the easy victory many were later led to believe. In the first six days of battle the Polish Air Force shot down 105 German aircraft for the loss of seventy-nine of its own. It also dropped 200,000 pounds of bombs on German targets. Whilst the Poles fought fearlessly, it was merely a matter of time before they had to consider their options. German armoured columns were advancing deeper into Polish territory along with thousands of troops. While some Poles had no option other than to surrender, others made good their escape via Rumania and the Black Sea and some would later rejoin the fight against the Germans with the French Air Force and Britain's Royal Air Force where Polish 303 Squadron would be credited with shooting down more German aircraft than their British counterparts. It is sad that few of these remarkable Polish fighter pilots ever received the recognition they so deserved.

Unteroffizier Karl Voght was just one component of the Luftwaffe spearhead against Poland. He had seen service in the Spanish Civil War and recalled his experiences in Poland:

> I flew with the Stukageschwader 77. In Poland we were in action against almost every conceivable target. We bombed targets in Lodz, Wielun, Radomsko, the Pilica River and Warsaw. The operations included bombing in support of our ground forces; in effect these were close air support missions. We also attacked railway networks, and anything felt to be enemy traffic which our ground or air reconnaissance observed on the roads. There was virtually no danger from

Flak [anti-aircraft fire] and the Polish fighter aircraft posed no real threat, even to a Stuka.

I flew with the same rear gunner for each mission as successful Stuka operations relied on the two crew being familiar with one another, a good idea and very sensible in many aspects. The first rear gunner I had guarding my aeroplane's arse was a young man named Haustoff. He was fresh out of training school and quite useless and I lost my temper with him on a few occasions. Before his first operational flight with me I told him, 'If you see anything flying up behind us that does not have black crosses on its wings you shoot it down, now do you understand me?' He nodded and said 'Yes sir' in affirmation. The lad was quite pale and shaking in his flying boots. I told him to relax, do the job they had trained him to do and leave the rest up to me. It was while we were dropping bombs on targets around the city of Wielun in central Poland that things went a little askew with this young man. He alerted me to the fact he could see two aircraft approaching us from the rear; it annoyed me as I was trying to focus on the target and was preparing to put in my attack dive. I shouted at him, 'Are they enemy or are they ours? You should know this.' He did not reply so I shouted again, 'Are they enemy or are they ours? Answer me now.' He then replied, 'They are enemy' to which I again shouted, 'Well, fucking shoot them, you fool.' I heard the rattle of the machine gun and glanced quickly over my right shoulder to see what he was doing and saw that he was shooting rather wildly. I then instructed him over my radio, 'Brace yourself, we are going in now.' I rolled the aircraft to the port and went into a steep dive. Over the radio I could hear him whining like a girl. I know he must have been very scared, though the only noise you could hear was the rush of the wind over the aircraft as we dived in to drop the single bomb. I could clearly see the target below and released the bomb. The Stuka pulled out of the dive and I began to level the aircraft out. That was the most nerve-wracking part of it; you had to have faith that the aircraft would automatically pull out of the dive which of

> course it did. When we landed back at our airfield, I cursed the young Haustoff, 'Don't ever do that again. You can tell a Bf 109 from a P.11 easily; look at the profiles. Have you not taken notice of what you have been taught?' He stood in silent dejection as I berated him. I later complained to my commander and another gunner was appointed to fly with me. I never saw this young man Haustoff again and I believe he was transferred to ground operations. Poland was not that bad at all compared to where we would be fighting in future.
>
> The Stuka worked well throughout the Polish campaign because we had no real opposition in the air and little threat from Flak to worry about. If a young airman couldn't cut it in Poland, then he was no good and would only end up endangering his comrades. Before we left Poland for a rest period, we were allocated to attack what was described as a concentration on a road out of Warsaw. When we arrived over the target area, I could see a long train of people. They looked like mostly civilians to me, yet the flight leader said there were soldiers amongst them. We dived in dropped our bombs and I watched as all these bodies scattered like ants. Some took refuge in the ditches either side of the road. We came back and fired our machine guns along the road. I saw the dust flying up as my bullets hit the road, then I turned for home with the others. I didn't feel good about this particular event as I was sure the target was not military but fleeing civilians, but orders were orders, I could not have argued about this.

I could find no other Luftwaffe veterans who fired on Polish civilians. However, one such account stands out above all the others: the one captured by the American photographer Julien Bryan. Although Bryan did not witness the actual attack on a group of seven Polish women who were out digging potatoes in a field just outside Warsaw, he photographed the aftermath and recalled the scene:

> As we drove by a small field at the edge of the town, we were just a matter of minutes too late to witness a tragic event, the most incredible of all. Seven women had been out digging

> potatoes in a field. There was no flour in their district, and they were desperate for food. Suddenly two German planes appeared from nowhere, dropping two bombs which fell on a small house only two hundred yards away. Two women inside the house were killed instantly. The seven women out in the potato field dropped flat on the ground, hoping they would not be noticed. After the bombers had gone, the women returned to their work as they had to have some food. The Nazi fliers were not satisfied with their work. In a few minutes they came back and swooped down to within two hundred feet of the ground, this time raking the ground with machine-gun fire. Two of the seven women were killed. The other five escaped somehow. While I was photographing the bodies, a 10-year-old girl came running up and stood transfixed by one of the dead. The woman was her older sister. The child had never before seen death and couldn't understand why her sister would not speak to her. She looked at us in bewilderment. I threw my arm around her and held her tightly, trying to comfort her. She cried. So did I and the two Polish officers with me broke down and cried too.

The 10-year-old child in question was Kazimiera Mika and the images captured by Julien Bryan that day shocked the world and illustrated perfectly the savagery that the Germans were capable of. The most likely culprits of the attack as documented by Julien Bryan were Ju 87 Stukas. When I put the question of the killing of these seven women to Karl Voght, he could not give me a clear answer. He simply remarked: 'If you're asking if it was me or something then I can tell you it most certainly wasn't, and I don't know who the aircrews involved in this incident were either. They were not aircrews of my unit as far as I know. That is all I can tell you, sorry.'

Such accounts are not rare and would surface again and again wherever the Luftwaffe was in action. However, it would be wrong to suggest that all Luftwaffe airmen participated in such deliberate, criminal attacks upon civilians.

Unteroffizier Ernst Willi Gabel, another Luftwaffe veteran of the Spanish Civil War, had a slightly less than enthusiastic view of the German campaign against Poland:

I had undergone conversion training on the Messerschmitt Bf 109 and we knew war was not far away as we were ordered to transfer to an airfield at Gutenfeld in eastern Prussia under the command of Oberleutnant Günther Scholz. There were three fighter groups in all: ours plus two others under the command of Oberleutnants Eggers and Schneider. We were flying the Bf 109D. I remember as we waited for news to go into action; every time the phone rang, we would gather round in anticipation that this was it, we would be going into action. Finally, when the order to 'go' came, it was a little of an anti-climax for an eager young fighter pilot with experience of his craft. I was disappointed as we met no real opposition as such. The Polish fighters were really no match for the Bf 109D although the Polish had some excellent pilots and we lost quite a few aircraft to them. I personally did not encounter that many Polish fighter aircraft. It was not always a target-rich environment and the Poles were very crafty. They used hit-and-run tactics against our bombers. Sometimes by the time you had got to where the trouble was, they had run away and landed at airfields we knew nothing about. After some initial frustration I shot down two P.11 aircraft. The first one I overshot twice before I could get a good burst of fire on him; sometimes the slower aeroplane had the advantage of being able to perform manoeuvres that you flying your Messerschmitt at much faster speed could not perform. That first P.11 was no real threat to me; it was like a cat with a mouse as I slowed down and hit him from directly behind with my machine guns and that was it – there was a big puff of smoke and he headed towards the ground. I saw the pilot jump out and his parachute deploy. The pilot was later captured and taken prisoner by our ground forces. That was my first aerial victory. My second didn't even see me bearing down on him. I scored several hits in his engine and the cockpit area. He turned over onto his back and crashed into the ground where he burned fiercely. Later on, I thought to myself, *I shot an enemy aeroplane down, but I also killed someone*. I had not killed before and somehow it felt odd. Another pilot told me, 'Never focus on the enemy pilot, focus your thoughts on his machine – you are killing his machine not him. That's the way to look at it; don't go getting sentimental now, Gabel.' I never forgot those words and they came from a man who did not survive the Second World War. He vanished without trace after taking off for an operation over the Eastern Front in 1942 and was never seen again.

Gefreiter Ernst Heinrich Husse flew the Messerschmitt Bf 110 twin-engine heavy fighter in the Polish campaign and recalled:

As part of Luftflotte 4 I flew several ground-attack missions against Polish forces. We were assigned targets such as communications centres, logistical supply lines and enemy troop emplacements. The Bf 110 was an ideal aircraft for this task. For most of these missions we used the four machine guns and two 20mm cannons that our aircraft was armed with. When you spotted the target, you would swoop in on it and fire, and the aircraft behind you would do the same; you would then make a second pass to observe if damage had been done. If the target was not completely destroyed to our satisfaction, then we would go in again until it was destroyed or until we had exhausted our ammunition. My most memorable moment was an attack against a Polish ground communications post. It was relatively small and surrounded by what looked like sandbags. As I headed in for the attack, I fired all six guns at the target in my gunsight. The tracer ammunition helped me ensure I was firing properly and hitting the target. As I fired a large cloud of dust obscured the target for a few seconds. As I turned around for a second pass, one of the other Bf 110 aircraft of my flight was going in and firing and I saw small figures running away from the communications post. Soon they disappeared too in a cloud of dust as other aircraft in the flight opened fire upon them. They were the enemy and they were fair game as military personnel. I did not have any problems sleeping over this; in war you have to kill the enemy sometimes, that's how it is. By the time we had

> finished our attack the communications post was on fire and several bodies lay around the site. Our cannon shells had the effect of hand grenades, there was not much left of the bodies and even from the air I could see that the cannon fire had ripped them apart.

As the Blitzkrieg gathered momentum, attacks against the Polish Air Force increased significantly and the Luftwaffe inexorably secured air superiority. Low on supplies, 98 per cent of the Polish air crews fled into neutral Rumania. Their strength had been reduced to the extent that they could no longer offer effective opposition, yet they had shown that the Germans were by no means invincible. However, the lessons Germany's future enemies might have learned from the invasion of Poland were never fully digested. No written history could ever illustrate fully the ferocity of the fighting on the ground and in the skies over Poland or the savagery in the way that Poland was eventually crushed.

# Chapter 7

# The Fall of France

Having conquered Poland, Hitler now turned his attention west, particularly to the old enemy, France. He was desperate for revenge against the French whom he viewed as the prime mover of Germany's humiliation following defeat in the First World War. He hoped for another quick and decisive victory in his drive west to conquer France and the Luftwaffe would again play a vital role in securing victory. Along with Britain, France had declared war against Germany on 3 September 1939 as a consequence of Germany's invasion of Poland.

*Fall Gelb* (Case Yellow) was the name for the first phase of the conquest of France, the invasion of the Netherlands and Belgium. The Germans had rightfully predicted that the French and the British Expeditionary Force (BEF) would advance into Belgium in an attempt to counter the threat. The main blow would then be delivered as German armoured divisions cut through the Ardennes and crossed the Meuse, effectively cutting off the Allied forces in northern France and leaving the remainder of the country defenceless.

The Luftwaffe's commitment to the battle for France consisted of the following: Luftflotte (air fleet) 2 (Kesselring), with Fliegerkorps (air corps) I and IV subordinated and including the sea-mining Fliegerdivision 9, supporting the operations of Army Group B under Generaloberst (Colonel-General) von Bock to the north. Generalfeldmarschall (Field Marshal) Gerd von Runstedt's Army Group A, in the Ardennes sector, was supported by Luftflotte 3 (Sperrle) which consisted of Generalfeldmarschall Wolfram Karl Ludwig Moritz Hermann Freiherr von Richtofen's Fliegerkorps VIII and Generaloberst Bruno Loerzer's Fliegerkorps II. Against the defences of the French Maginot Line, to the south, Army Group C was supported by Generalfeldmarschall Robert Ritter von Greim's Fliegerkorps V, operating under the control of Luftflotte 3.

Luftwaffe units ranged in the west for *Fall Gelb* consisted of 1,120 bombers, half of which were Heinkel He 111s, drawn from *Kampfgeschwader* (bomber wings) KG 1, KG 2, KG 3, KG 4, KG 26, KG 27, KG 51, KG 53, KG 54, KG 55, *Kampfgruppe* (battle group) KGr.100, *Lehrgeschwader* (training wings) LG 76 and LG 77, and the mine-laying unit KGr.126. The Junkers Ju 87B-1 and B-2 dive-bombers were concentrated in Fliegerkorps VIII, consisting of Stab (staff) I, II, III/StG 2 (S*tukageschwader*) with 1/StG 76 and Stab I, II/StG 77 with IV (Stuka) LG 1, numbering some 380 aircraft. Also, in this command was II *Schlachtergeschwader* (close air support/assault group)/LG 2 equipped with Henschel Hs 123A biplanes. The single-engine fighter force was drawn from *Gruppen* (groups) of *Jagdgeschwader* (fighter wings) JG 1, JG 2, JG 3; JG 21, JG 26, JG 27, JG 51, JG 52, JG 53 and JG 54, numbering a total of some 860 Messerschmitt Bf 109E-1 and E-3 fighters. The *Zerstörer Gruppen* (heavy fighter groups) were I and II/ZG 2, 1/ZG 1, I and II/ZG 26 and I (Zerst)/LG 1 with 355 Messerchmitt Bf 110C-1s and C2s. The long- and short-range *Aufklarungsgruppen* (reconnaissance group) had a total strength of 640 aircraft at its disposal. For logistics and paratrooper operations there were 475 Junkers Ju 52/3M transport aircraft available plus 45 DFS 230 gliders subordinated to Fliegerkorps zbV (under General Putzier), drawn from four *gruppen* of KGzbV 1, and four *gruppen* of KGbV 2, with KGzbV 101, 104 and 106.

The Germans had learned from the Polish campaign that no enemy should be underestimated. The Luftwaffe did not enter the campaign with the view that it could destroy the French and British air forces exclusively on the ground, though the commander of Luftlotte 3, Albert Kesselring, hoped that this could be achieved against the Dutch and Belgians. The Armée de l'air, or French Air Force, had some 1,562 aircraft at its disposal while the RAF commitment stood at 680, including 392 aircraft of Bomber Command.

Over a period of six weeks, from 10 May 1940, the Wehrmacht swept aside Dutch and Belgian resistance and soundly defeated the French armies and BEF in a ferocious, asymmetric, yet highly mobile, military operation.

Karl Voght was once again off to war after a brief period of leave to visit his family in Germany. He recalled:

> We were called back for duty as we were told we were to be briefed for a series of operations which must conclude in

the destruction of the French. Again, we were to cooperate closely with the forces on the ground, flying ahead of them and hitting our assigned targets which had been located through reconnaissance flights and spies on the ground.

We went through Belgium and the Low Countries and these parts of the overall campaign were of no real concern to us as our ultimate prize was the French. Securing victory for our Führer was the ultimate prize: yes, what nationally minded German did not want to play a part in hammering the French for humiliating Germany at the end of the First World War? When it came to bombing the French, we understood that the British were also there fighting alongside the French; we couldn't understand how fellow Anglo-Saxons could do such a thing, but if they were there with the French, they were going to be bombed with them too. When we took off on missions against the French, we flew with a good fighter escort. Most of our operations were again in support of our army on the ground. We ran into British and French fighters a few times, but our stronger numbers of determined fighters drove them off. Again, we hit communications sites, artillery and troop emplacements and airfields as we pushed further into French territory. Our ground forces had entered France in the most unlikely of places – through the Ardennes. The Ardennes were so thickly wooded that they [the French] never expected our ground elements, particularly the armour, to be able to negotiate the terrain, but they did, and that was their secret weapon. As we flew ahead bombing targets, our tanks, artillery and infantry followed closely behind. It was a marvellous symphony of the harmonics of war, how war should be fought.

For the French it was a real shock to suddenly find our Stukas screaming down on them. We once targeted an anti-aircraft emplacement; as we dived into the attack, we saw the French gunners running away in panic from their guns instead of shooting at us. Well, of course we were pleased as it made our job of destroying their weapons easier. The British didn't go down without a fight though; they had these 40mm anti-aircraft cannon that fired high-explosive

> shells rapidly. These were very dangerous to us at low to medium level. The fighters would attack these with their 20mm cannons to neutralize their effect as we went in to attack. I recall diving down with shells popping all around me; one hit my aircraft and it made a loud tearing sound as it tore a hole the size of a medicine ball in my starboard wing. The round hit and exploded, and pieces of shell came out through the upper surface of the wing and some struck the cockpit just aft of my compartment. My gunner shouted, 'Fucking hell, that was a close one, Karl. Watch out!' As we climbed to get away from the Flak, my gunner saw our 50-kilogram bombs as they struck home, exploding in and around the gunpit. He said later, 'Karl, the crew manning the gun were blown several hundred yards away from it as our bombs detonated; it was just arms and legs that I saw'. The whole site was shot up and bombed until we were happy that it was out of action. We also attacked retreating French and British soldiers as they flooded the roads heading west, away from our forces.

There was also a degree of German ineptitude during the invasion of France. On 10 May, a force of ten Luftwaffe bombers was assigned to bomb the French airfield at Dijon-Longvic yet managed to drop their bombs some 140 miles away on Freiburg in south-west Germany, killing fifty-seven civilians and injuring a hundred more. It was an embarrassing fiasco for the Luftwaffe to say the least.

The largest single raid carried out by the Luftwaffe during the French campaign was against airfields, railways stations and factory units in the Paris area on 3 June. Three hundred Luftwaffe bombers carried out sorties which destroyed sixteen French aircraft on the ground plus seventeen which were shot down by escorting Messerschmitt Bf 109E fighters. Several railway stations were damaged yet quickly repaired by the French. The Citroën automobile factory was worst hit, and a major fire broke out at the plant. A figure of thirty-two French military personnel was quoted as killed in this raid while 195 civilians were listed as being killed. There is much debate as to the effectiveness of the French Air Force and why they failed against the Luftwaffe throughout the invasion period. The answer is relatively simple: while shortages of men and materials have been cited as one factor, a lack of leadership, along with a misunderstanding of how best to utilize their resources, were the most likely causes.

The commonest French fighter that took off to engage the Luftwaffe was the Morane-Saulnier M.S.406 that packed a punch with its central-firing 20mm cannon and two 7.5mm machine guns, yet it had the disadvantage of being slower than the Messerschmitt Bf 109E. At the time of the invasion, this single-seat fighter was regarded as an obsolete type awaiting replacement, yet French fighter pilots scored a total of 250 kills in this type during the invasion of France. One Allied fighter pilot, Robert Williams, shot down three Luftwaffe Bf 109Es, followed by three Ju 87 Stukas in an M.S.406, all on the same day of 8 June 1940.

It was also on 8 June 1940 that fledgling Luftwaffe fighter pilot Heinz Gunsche experienced his first and last combat mission as a fighter pilot with the Luftwaffe. Heinz recalled:

> I had not long been out of training school but had done very well in all of the disciplines and passed with a very good grading which many of my friends I had made at training school were envious of. I had never expected to get hurt on my first mission against what was described as inferior opposition. On the day in question, I had engaged an M.S.406 from the rear and fired shots into his aircraft; there was a puff of smoke as my cannon shells found their mark, then from nowhere I recall this bright flash right before my eyes and a loud crash. A piece of metal from my own control panel entered my right eye and I immediately lost the use of it. My front screen had a small crack to its right-hand corner but was not broken into pieces. There was a hole in the top right where the frame met, and air was rushing in through it. I felt so much pain from my eye it was as much as I could do to see to turn away from the fight and return to my airfield. My Bf 109 still seemed to be responding so I turned back to the airfield, but I was in considerable pain with my eye. The goggles were broken and had almost torn my face off and I knew I was hit bad as I could feel warm blood running from my eye down my cheek and down my neck. I was able to get the 109 down safely but remember little else as I must have passed out.

I later woke up in a hospital bed with my right eye covered and heavy bandage around my head. They had to take my right eye out as it was completely damaged by the fragment of metal. I was told I had been incredibly lucky as a French 20mm cannon shell had detonated against the top right of my cockpit. The fragment of control panel that had entered my eye was placed on a small dish at my bedside. I told them I didn't wish to keep this souvenir and one of the doctors took it away. They then told me that I would never be able to fly again as I would never have proper eyesight, flying with one eye being prohibited.

So that was it for me: one mission, I get hurt then end of flying. I was angry about it for a while. I had not seen the enemy aircraft that fired on me; maybe it was a lucky shot, I don't know. My parents were relieved as when they were first told the news they must have been hysterical. I spent six weeks recovering from my wound and returned to the Luftwaffe to a desk job. Not much to really boast about but these are the fortunes of war. You can be fine one minute then dead or injured the next. I later considered myself one of the lucky ones.

Werner Mölders, who became Germany's first fighter ace to reach 100 aerial victories, was stationed with his unit in the west protecting Germany's border in the Mosel–Saar–Pfalz region. Flying the Messerschmitt Bf 109E-4, Mölders' flying career was almost brought to an abrupt end when, on 8 September 1939, his Bf 109 experienced an engine failure. Mölders later recalled of the event:

My aircraft suffered a complete engine failure; it began to splutter, and I felt the instant loss of power and knew I was going to have to crash-land. I looked around for a suitable location, somewhere that appeared relatively flat, for me to get the aircraft down without too much risk to myself. I attempted to belly-land the Messerschmitt which flipped over onto its back. In the resulting crash I received an injury to back, but luckily for me it was not serious. On that occasion I was lucky.

Mölders returned to flying on 19 September and the following day claimed his first kill of the war. There is some dispute as to whether Molders' victim was a Curtiss P-36 or a French Hawk H-75As of Groupe de Chasse 11/5 piloted by Sergeant Queginer who baled out safely. Molders filed the following report:

> I took off with my *Schwarm* [a tactical formation of four aircraft in two pairs] at 1427 hours to intercept a small formation of six enemy aircraft reported south of Trier. As we flew over the river Saar near Merzig at 4,500 metres altitude, six machines were sighted south of Conz flying at 5,000 metres. I climbed above the enemy aircraft in a wide curve to the north and carried out a surprise attack on the rearmost enemy machine. I opened fire, close, at approximately 50 metres, whereupon the Curtiss began to fishtail. After a further lengthy burst, smoke was observed coming out of the enemy machine and I could see individual pieces of wreckage flying away from it. I then observed as the enemy aircraft tipped forward into a steep dive and then I lost sight of it, as I had to defend myself against other enemy aircraft which had begun to arrive on the scene.

On 22 December 1939, Mölders, along with fellow Luftwaffe fighter pilot, Hans von Hahn, earned the distinction of being the first German pilots to shoot down an RAF Hawker Hurricane.

Günther Rall was another young Luftwaffe fighter pilot who experienced his first air combat during the invasion of France. Rall, a man I had the pleasure of meeting and talking with on a number of occasions during his visits to the UK, survived the war after becoming the third highest-scoring Luftwaffe ace. Rall's career as a fighter pilot was perhaps unique as he flew virtually every mark of the Bf 109. In fact, his impressive tally of 275 victories was attained while only flying the Bf 109. Rall reflected upon his affection for the Bf 109 and what was for him a largely quiet affair during the invasion of France:

> The 109 was in my opinion a great aeroplane and I have to say that to me as an individual pilot, it grew on me and I grew with it, if you understand. You become accustomed

to its faults and learn to master it. For example, one of the big problems with the 109 was its undercarriage. The undercarriage was very high and narrow so you had to be very cautious when accelerating on take-off; when you pushed the throttle lever forward, the 109 would gather speed very rapidly, you would feel the tailwheel leave the ground but then you had the negative effects of the torque produced by the engine. When this occurred, you had to give instant opposite rudder; failure to do so could result in the loss of your tailwheel – yes, it would get broken off and in more serious situations the 109 would pitch violently and roll over onto its back. Many of our pilots were lost in such accidents. It was something you had to understand, a feature of the aircraft that you had to master. Once used to it after a few flights, you didn't even think about it as everything came automatically.

The 109 was very small overall and the cockpit was a tight fit, and not all of the pilots liked this. The weapons, particularly on the E-4, were very good: the two 20mm cannons arranged one in each wing had good stopping power. When the war broke out, I considered myself ready; there was no fear as such as we considered ourselves a professional and highly technical force. There was more excitement than actual fear at that time anyway. Where France was concerned, we all felt the same way: 'Let's get on with the job we have to do.' Our commanding officer at the time was a Captain Schumann who sadly got killed later in the war. By January 1940 we were at a state of high alert, yet I did not see any combat until our ground forces entered the Netherlands and Belgium then France. We had carried out a lot of training up until this point which put us all in a pretty good position.

My first ever action came against the French Air Force and took place on 12 May 1940. We had been ordered to escort a Heinkel He 111 operating in the reconnaissance role and to basically protect it on its flight back to Germany. We took off from the airfield as a formation of ten aircraft. We operated in two flights, utilizing the figure-four formation with two Bf 109s flying top cover above us. The figure-four formation was a tactic created by Werner Mölders in the Spanish Civil War. I was leading the second flight of four Bf 109s. We made contact with the Heinkel which was heading in an easterly direction back to Germany. Some distance behind the Heinkel we noted twelve little specks tailing behind. We accelerated and dived down to investigate the pursuing aircraft to find that they were French Curtiss P-36 Hawk fighters. At that moment the fight began. I flew into the second flight of P-36s and as I performed a high-g turn, the slots on the leading edges of my Bf 109's wings came out; this was a common thing that had the effect of slightly stalling your aircraft. This did not prevent me from shooting one of them down as he came across my line of fire right in front of me. He caught fire and I watched him fall from the sky in flames. My aircraft had received hits; you know when you have been hit as the sound of bullets against your aircraft makes a very distinctive sound. It is like someone throwing stones against your car while you are sitting inside; yes, my aircraft had been hit by machine-gun bullets. Luckily, we had the two Oerlikon 20mm cannons which were far more destructive than machine-gun bullets, as they fired explosive and armour-piercing shells. Had I been hit by 20mm cannon fire I may not have been here now to tell you this story [he laughs]. Then I realized I was lost and somewhat disoriented from the fighting. I made the decision to go to Mannheim and land there. By the time I got the 109 down the sun had almost set. How did I feel having scored my victory? I felt excited as I understood that both me and my aircraft could do the job; I could do the job I had been trained to do, so yes, I was happy. Part of the success in air combat is down to psychology along with the tactics you have learned and the aircraft you have learned to fly in.

By the second phase of the Blitzkrieg against the French, known as *Fall Rot* (Case Red) which began on 5 June 1940, the French and BEF were already facing an untenable position from a defensive perspective. The

Heer had suffered heavy casualties and was struggling to get to grips with the French, particularly in the fighting to cross the river Aisne. In the face of stubborn French resistance, the Luftwaffe was called in time and again to neutralize French artillery concentrations around the Aisne as Stuka pilot Unteroffizier Karl Voght recalled:

> The French guns were causing our forces a great headache. The commanders on the ground were frustrated by the sheer resistance of the French around the Aisne sector. In fact, one of the commanders was heard to say, 'For God's sake, where are our fucking Stukas? We need Stukas, as many of them as we can bring to bear.' I think the officers on the ground were growing angry over French stubbornness, seeing droves of wounded men being brought through on stretchers, broken and dripping with blood. That sort of thing is bad for morale, so we were called in again to bomb enemy artillery concentrations in and around the Aisne area.
>
> We took off and with expert direction from our forces on the ground, we picked out the French artillery and hit them as hard as we could with various types of bombs, mainly high-explosive fragmentation types, designed for maximum blast effect and to rake the target area with razor-sharp steel splinters. The French artillery could not counter us and we simply picked them out from above, dived on them, released our bombs onto them and then climbed high to observe the effect. If a target was not hit, we would call to a comrade who would be standing by to go in and hit it again. Once the bombs were gone, we flew down and machine-gunned the bombed-out positions to ensure any gunners were dead and knocked out of the fight.

As the fighting grew in intensity casualties mounted steadily on all sides. The French and British contingent found themselves increasingly outnumbered, outmanoeuvred and outgunned on the ground and in the air. When the BEF was given orders to withdraw, it was an order met with some consternation as the British felt that they were holding their own against the Germans. The point was that while soldiers of the BEF were doing well in some areas of the front, those holding their own were unaware of the deteriorating situation elsewhere. It was pretty clear that France had become untenable, and it was a just course of action by BEF commander General Viscount Gort to order the evacuation of whatever was left of the BEF. To this end Gort saw the best solution was to withdraw to the small French port of Dunkirk, the closest port he saw fit whence to launch his evacuation plan. As both British and French forces fell back on Dunkirk, they were under almost constant attack from the Luftwaffe who now had total control of the skies. There was much scorn poured upon the RAF and their noticeable absence in the skies above Dunkirk. This was not down to the fact that Britain's air force was not active over the Dunkirk front – quite the contrary: the RAF had been engaging the Luftwaffe some miles inland of Dunkirk where the air battles were out of view of those trapped on the beaches, giving the impression to the BEF troops that they had been abandoned. Unteroffizier Anthony Scholl recalls an engagement with the RAF some twenty-five miles inland from Dunkirk. He recalled:

> It was our first experience of combat with a mixed bag of Spitfire and Hurricane aircraft. We were flying a patrol and spotted the enemy fighters below us. We dived in to introduce ourselves and they spotted us and immediately broke formation. Four of them turned directly in towards us, climbing very fast. We fired at these aircraft which broke left and right as we came through them. I caught a glimpse of that famous wing plan that made the Spitfire silhouette so easily recognizable from any other aeroplane. He was attempting to come around to my left and meet me as I crossed his path. I accelerated into a fast climb and I saw him following me. My wingman, Unteroffizier Troth, was on his tail already and fired on him, forcing him to break off right. Troth attempted to follow his line but lost him. I looked all around me and there was nothing. I saw two of our Messerchmitts heading for home but no Spitfires or Hurricanes and no sign of any aircraft having been shot down. I checked for smoke on the ground but nothing. Troth informed me through my radio that our enemy had run for home. I circled the area alone for around two minutes before turning for home. I had wanted to continue fighting as I felt

> we had the measure of them. I felt no fear whatsoever at that moment. I noticed the Bf 109 was much faster in the climb and dive than the Spitfire, though the Spitfire could get out of trouble very easily and could out-turn us. We looked forward to meeting them again, yet they failed to materialize.

The lack of RAF presence after this particular incident may well have been down to Fighter Command's steady withdrawal of its aircraft from France. It was clear the battle for France would soon be over and every single Spitfire and Hurricane fighter would be required for the defence of British skies in battles yet to be fought. In all, this was a logical decision based upon the dire situation of the time.

At Dunkirk the beaches were packed with men and equipment who were now surrounded. German ground forces could have been ordered to attack, yet they were ordered to halt as it was thought the Luftwaffe were more than up to thc task of finishing the job off. It was this oversight that led to the BEF escaping Dunkirk in the miraculous Operation *Dynamo*. A flotilla of every conceivable ocean-worthy vessel was commandeered by the Royal Navy in an effort to cross the English Channel and rescue the besieged BEF from the beaches of Dunkirk. Operation *Dynamo* was a tremendous effort and despite being under constant air attack from the Luftwaffe, it was a success.

I asked Karl Voght of his experiences as he was sent to drop bombs on the trapped soldiers on the beaches of Dunkirk. He recalled:

> Yes, we were in action over Dunkirk, and we would fly over the target area and if a ship presented itself, we would try to sink it. Soon there were many ships and smaller boats coming across the English Channel. I recall hitting one with a cluster of 50-kilogram explosives, but they failed to sink it. With my bombs gone, I returned to the airfield to rearm. As I touched down, I told the armourer's 'For God's sake, give me something that will sink a ship, not those fucking things.' I pointed to a crate of 50-kilogram bombs. There was some argument with my armourers over this. I needed a heavier bomb and eventually I took off with a 550lb bomb beneath my aircraft. Had I used an even heavier bomb

I would have had to take off without my gunner and I was not prepared to tempt fate on this occasion.

Back over the beaches we saw no RAF fighters but lots of ships and small boats were visible and these were either coming in or going back out. I could see trails of men heading out into the water to meet the ships. I picked out a target and climbed steadily, and as I did so I could see other aircraft of my flight either diving down to attack or climbing after dropping their bombs. A hit was registered by shouts of 'Yes, I've got one'. After climbing to altitude, I told my gunner, 'Watch our arse, stay alert, we're going in.' I levelled out as I was at 15,120 feet altitude; my target had moved a bit so I flew on slightly ahead of him, reduced my throttle and looked down at him for the right moment to attack. I noticed some light Flak popping below but nowhere near us, then I pushed the control stick forward and began my dive attack. My airspeed indicator moved rapidly; again, the only sound was that rush of air over the entire aircraft. I remained fully composed and committed to my attack and soon we were diving at over 300mph; no doubt the enemy below were already cowering from the scream of our Stuka. At 1,000 feet above the target, I released the bomb; through the small window in my cockpit floor I could see the bomb slung down then fall. As the aircraft pulled up out of the dive, I felt myself slammed into my seat; for a few seconds I must have blacked out, but it was just a couple of seconds. My view had changed from the sea to the sky again and I looked down to the left over the wing of my aircraft and saw that I had scored a hit on the target ship. I shouted over my radio, 'Yes, we've got him, a direct hit.' My gunner also saw all of the action from his seat in the rear of the aircraft and was also elated, shouting, 'Yes, yes, good work, sir.'

We turned for home as the remainder of the flight dropped their bombs; we had Bf 109s providing cover as we made good our escape through some determined yet relatively light Flak coming up from the beaches. One of the flight decided to dive down and give them some machine-gun fire. We were all a bit like loose cannons back at that time and it was nothing out of the normal for one of our aircraft to break off and do something like that on occasion. He went down low and fired his machine guns at soldiers on the beach and received some damage in the process. It was nothing much and he made it back to the airfield, yet the Stuka could not be fixed and had to be returned to Germany for repairs and the crew in question got a new aircraft.

We expected to be in action again yet were then told to stand down and await further orders. Other units continued bombing attacks until the beaches of Dunkirk were empty of the enemy. We then asked the question why the tanks and troops did not go in and capture the trapped enemy forces? Why did the German army let them get away? We felt some dejection at this but were soon happy when we heard that military operations in France were now over with the total defeat of the French by 25 June 1940.

After Dunkirk most of our time was spent relocating our units closer to the English Channel. It was hoped that we could avoid further confrontation with the English, that they would sue for peace with us rather than continue a war against us. For the time being, until further orders, we were given leave to recover, replace men and aircraft lost over the past months and of course go home and visit our families. I received notice that I was to receive the War Merit Cross 1st Class. This was the first decoration I was to receive in my military career. I was presented my award by the unit commander, Gunter Schwartkopf, who congratulated me for my destruction of a notable enemy vessel during the operations at Dunkirk. Yes, I was proud of the medal and pinned it to my tunic and could not wait to show it to my family back home. Some of our unit, mostly the single men, remained in France and they had a whale of a time with all the wine and beer commandeered from French cellars and public houses. France was a nice place for a single guy back then, but I went home to see my parents and get away from it all for as long as I could. I had the feeling we would soon be involved in some sort of action before long, so I was determined to get some decent rest and recharge my batteries, as we say today. When I returned home, I was greeted like a hero by all of the people from my neighbourhood; yes, it felt great.

The Luftwaffe lost a total of 1,236 aircraft during the invasion of France with 1,129 airmen killed. While these figures are nowhere near the astronomical losses of men and material experienced during the last two years of the war, the reality was they were losses that the Luftwaffe could ill afford, and which surely impacted on the Luftwaffe capabilities in the forthcoming Battle of Britain.

With the battle for France over, many new and established Luftwaffe fighter pilots could reflect on the whole experience. For some it had been a learning curve while for others a chance to top up their scores of aerial victories. Below is a list of Luftwaffe fighter aces from the battle of France. Their rank, name, unit and victory tally are indicated:

| | | |
|---|---|---|
| • Hauptmann Wilhelm Balthasar | JG 1 | 23 |
| • Hauptmann Werner Mölders | JG 53 | 16 |
| • Hauptmann Adolf Galland | JG 26/27 | 14 |
| • Leutnant Helmut Wick | JG 2 | 12 |
| • Oberleutnant Lothar Keller | JG 3 | 10 |
| • Oberfeldwebel Werner Machold | JG 2 | 10 |
| • Feldwebel Erich Rudorffer | JG 2 | 10 |
| • Oberleutnant Gert Framm | JG 27 | 9 |
| • Leutnant Ludwig Franzisket | JG 1 | 9 |
| • Major Hannes Gentzen | ZG 2 | 9 |
| • Feldwebel Hans Golubinski | JG 53 | 9 |
| • Oberleutnant Gerhard Homuth | JG 27 | 9 |
| • Hauptmann Günther Lutzov | JG 3 | 9 |
| • Oberleutnant Heinz Nacke | ZG 76 | 9 |
| • Leutnant Heinz Hoffmann | JG 2 | 8 |
| • Oberleutnant Hans-Karl Mayer | JG 53 | 8 |
| • Leutnant Friedrich-Karl Müller | JG 53 | 8 |
| • Leutnant Joachim Müncheberg | JG 26 | 8 |
| • Leutnant Roloff von Aspern | JG 76 | 7 |
| • Leutnant Hans-Joachim Jabs | ZG 76 | 7 |
| • Leutnant Heinz Kunert | JG 53 | 7 |
| • Leutnant Hans Philipp | JG 76 | 7 |

- Oberleutnant Wolfgang Redlich JG 27 7
- Hauptmann Wolfgang Schellmann JG 2 7
- Oberfeldwebel Johann Schmid JG 2 7
- Oberleutnant Gustav Sprick JG 26 7
- Oberfeldwebel Max Stotz JG 76 7
- Oberfeldwebel Max Bucholz JG 3 6
- Feldwebel Wilhelm Hermes JG 2 6
- Leutnant Otto-Heinrich Hillecke JG 26 6
- Oberleutnant Dietrich Hrabak JG 76 6
- Oberleutnant Wolfgang Lippert JG 53 6
- Feldwebel Hermann Neuhoff JG 53 6
- Hauptmann Rolf Pingel JG 53 6
- Oberleutnant Josef Priller JG 51 6
- FeldwebelKarl Schmid JG 51 6
- Leutnant Helmut Tiedmann JG 3 6
- Oberleutnant Walter Adolph JG 1 5
- Unteroffizier Hugo Dahmer JG 26 5
- Hauptmann Karl Ebbighausen JG 26 5
- Leutnant Heinz Ebeling JG 26 5
- Oberfeldwebel Franz Gotz JG 53 5
- Oberleutnant Karl-Heinz Greisert JG 2 5
- Oberleutnant Hans von Hahn JG 53 5
- Oberleutnant Hans Hahn JG 2 5
- Feldwebel Georg Keil JG 2 5
- Oberleutnant Walter Oesau JG 20 5
- Leutnant Gerhard Sprenger JG 3 5
- Leutnant Anton Stangl JG 76 5
- Leutnant Werner Tismar LG 2 5
- Hauptmann Alexander von Winterfeldt JG 2 5
- Leutnant Igor Zirkenbach JG 27 5

# Chapter 8

# The Battle of Britain

There have probably been more books written on the Battle of Britain than any other aspect of the Second World War. As the focus of this work is primarily the Luftwaffe's perspective in the aerial conflict of the Second World War, I will endeavour to stay with this theme rather than risk going off at a tangent which might end up leaving the reader confused.

In brief, having conquered France and the Low Countries, Hitler had hoped that Britain, faced with the threat of imminent invasion, would sue for peace. The primary objective given to the Luftwaffe by its commanders was to secure air superiority of the skies over southern England which in turn would permit the proposed seaborne invasion which was given the codename *Seelöwe* (*Sea Lion*). *Seelöwe* had been initiated as early as 1939, yet disagreements between factions within the Heer and Kriegsmarine proved detrimental to the overall planning. Economic strangulation of England had been given serious consideration by the German high command, yet the prospect of having to wait a protracted period of time for economic measures to take their full effect was unfeasible. Hitler viewed *Seelöwe* as little more than a large-scale river crossing wherethe RAF and Royal Navy (should they materialize) would be simultaneously engaged and destroyed by the use of air power. The German invasion plan proposed the establishment of bridgeheads in Kent and Sussex plus numerous others to the west, culminating in a drive northward. The Germans felt once the majority of southern England had been taken that resistance would then collapse. However, these were of course the best-laid plans of mice and men. It is highly unlikely that the British would have given up so easily and it is almost certain that fierce resistance would have continued long after any invasion.

As already noted, it has been said that the first major task facing the Germans was that of securing air superiority over southern England.

It was believed that invasion would only be possible if the RAF was swept from the skies and the threat of Royal Naval intervention removed. The Royal Navy was denied access to the narrow strip of water that is the English Channel, having been removed from their normal patrol zones to safer areas, just as the Luftwaffe and U-boat threat had forced the Admiralty to relocate the Home Fleet from Scapa Flow some months earlier. The battleships, cruisers and destroyers required to repel a German invasion force were hundreds of miles away safely anchored in the Clyde. Had the German invasion taken place, the Royal Naval would have needed many hours' sailing time to reach the English Channel, by which time they may well have been too late to affect the outcome. Then one also has to ask the question: did the Luftwaffe actually need total air superiority in order to invade England? Karl Voght reflects on this question:

> No, I don't think we would have needed to secure total control of the skies over the proposed invasion area. Had the invasion gone ahead at the most critical point in the Battle of Britain and this was when the British were at their most stretched, I feel a seaborne invasion could have succeeded. It would have meant that we, the Luftwaffe, would have had to throw absolutely everything in the pot for one final great effort, but I think it was feasible at that point, around mid- to late August 1940.

It was the view of the Luftwaffe high command that control of the air over southern England could be achieved within four weeks. Despite the large volume of German landing craft arriving in the Pas de Calais in preparation for Operation *Seelöwe*, there are many who have concluded that Hitler was already losing interest in England, looking more towards his ambitions in the East. Karl Voght addressed this issue:

> I think both Hitler and the Luftwaffe high command were totally serious about invading England. I do however firmly believe that as the struggle known as the Battle of Britain continued on beyond the few weeks that Hermann Göring had predicted he would secure victory, I seriously think Hitler grew both tired and impatient of Göring whom he

> now viewed as incompetent and not up to the task. I think at that point Hitler got distracted by his ideas of invading Russia. England was at that time not on the offensive and was viewed as little more than a nuisance dog yapping away in his backyard; maybe he believed that that nuisance dog could be kept at bay until a later date, I don't know; only he knows that answer and as he is dead, we will never know for sure, will we? This was the impression that I got anyway.

The Luftwaffe order of battle for the campaign against Britain comprised the aerial resources of Luftflotten 2 and 3 as follows:

- Medium bombes: Heinkel He 111, Dornier Do 17 and Junkers Ju 88. Total 1,200 of which 69 per cent were serviceable as of 20 July 1940
- Dive bombers: Junkers Ju 87B. Total 280
- Single-engine fighters: Messerschmitt Bf 109E. Total 760
- Twin-engine fighters: Messerschmitt Bf 110. Total 220
- Long-range reconnaissance: Dornier Do 17, Messerschmitt Bf 110, Junkers Ju 88. Total 50
- Short-range reconnaissance: Henschel Hs 126, Dornier Do 17, Messerschmitt Bf 110. Total 90
- **Total strength: 2,600 aircraft**

In addition, Luftflotte 5 with Fliegerkorps X subordinated, retained a force of 130 Heinkel He 111s and Junkers Ju 88s, 30 Messerschmitt Bf 110 long-range fighters and 30 long-range reconnaissance aircraft. While this force would play virtually no part in the actual battle, it offered a valuable diversionary role, forcing the RAF to retain fighter defences in the north of England.

As this formidable force was gathering momentum across the Channel, the intervening weeks prior to operations commencing were put to good use by the RAF who were busy bringing their squadrons back up to full strength, along with rebuilding reserves in readiness for the German assault which was to come. There was an eerie period of quiet immediately prior to the Battle of Britain, leading many to question, 'Where are the Germans, why don't they come?' Hearing of this, Hitler retorted, 'When the people of England nosily inquire "Well, why isn't he coming?" Calm yourselves, he is coming, he is coming!'

In theory one can be forgiven for thinking the advantage lay with Germany; after all, the Germans had swept all before them. Yet, for the first time since Poland, the Luftwaffe would be operating independently without ground forces and armour, for obvious reasons. The Luftwaffe would be taking the battle to the British across the twenty-six-mile expanse of water that is the English Channel, a natural barrier that has proved a challenge for potential invaders for centuries.

Having conquered France, the Luftwaffe brought its fighter and bomber units forward to within striking distance of England. Many of the fighter groups took over airfields in the Pas de Calais region in readiness for operations over southern England.

16 October 1939 was an ominous day for young Luftwaffe pilot Leutnant Horst von Riesen of I/KG 30 as it was on this day that the RAF's new frontline fighter aircraft, the Supermarine Spitfire, went into action for the first time, and the young Leutnant Riesen would be on the receiving end. He recalled what happened:

> We were based at Westerland on the island of Sylt [in the Frisian archipelago in the North Sea], and at that time we were the only unit to be equipped with the new, fast, long-range dive-bomber, the Junkers Ju 88. Initially our activities kept us well clear of the British defences. But on the morning of 16 October, one of our reconnaissance aircraft spotted the battlecruiser HMS *Hood* entering the Firth of Forth. We were given the order to attack her, if we could catch her in open water; at that stage in the war both sides were trying hard to avoid causing civilian casualties and we had the strictest orders that if she was in harbour, we were to either attack warships outside or return with our bombs. Nine of us took off, but when we arrived over Rosyth, we found the *Hood* safely in dock where we were not allowed to harm her. Just to the east of the Forth Bridge there were some small warships, however, and I decided to attack one of these. I selected one and carried out a dive attack but registered only a near miss. Then, as I was climbing away, my radio operator suddenly shouted over the intercom that

there were several fighters about two kilometres away, diving on us. I looked where he was pointing and as soon as I saw them, I knew that I would need all the speed I could possibly squeeze out of my Junkers if we were to escape. I pushed down the nose and opened the throttles fully and dived for the sea. This was no good. The Spitfires – we soon recognized them – had the advantage of speed and height from the start and they soon caught up with us. As I sped down the Firth of Forth just a few metres above the surface, I could see clearly the splashes of the shells from the shore batteries as they too joined what was an unequal battle. At this point I thought we were finished. Guns were firing at us from all sides, and the Spitfires were taking it in turns attacking us. I think they were surprised by how fast our Junkers was as I was doing more than 250mph, which must have been faster than any other bomber they had trained against at low level and of course I jinked the Junkers from side to side to make their aim as difficult as possible. At one stage in the pursuit, I remember looking down and seeing what looked like raindrops hitting the water. It was all very surreal. Then I realized what they were: those raindrops were bullets from the Spitfires who were firing at us from above. Our only ally in this situation was time. Every minute the Junkers kept going meant another seven kilometres further out to sea and further away from the Spitfires' base. They could not continue to chase us much further, and I had far more fuel to play with than them.

Finally, however, the inevitable happened; after a chase of more than twenty minutes there was this loud and sudden *phoof* and my starboard motor suddenly disappeared from view in a cloud of steam. One of the enemy bullets had pierced the radiator, releasing the vital coolant and without this the motor was finished. I had no alternative but to shut it down before it burst into flames. My speed dropped to 112mph which was almost on the stall for the Junkers when flying asymmetrically – and we were only a few metres above the waves. I remember thinking how we were now a sitting duck. Yet when I looked around expecting to see the Spitfires closing in to finish us off, there was no sign of them. They had turned and gone home. Even so, we were in a difficult position. At that airspeed we were looking at some four hours of flight if we were to get back to Westerland. During our training we had been told that a Junkers 88 could not maintain altitude on one engine – and we were barely holding our altitude. Should we ditch there and then? I thought, no; it was getting dark; nobody would pick us up and we would most certainly drown or die from exposure. One alternative was to turn around and head back to Scotland and crash-land there. One of my crew suggested this but one of the others – I don't remember who – shouted over the intercom, 'No, no never! If we go back, the Spitfires will certainly get us!' He was right. The thought of going back into that hornet's nest horrified us so we decided to carry on and take our chances in the Junkers. We preferred the risk of drowning or the cold, rather than having to face those Spitfires again. Gradually, as we burned our fuel and the Junkers became lighter, I was able to coax the aircraft a little higher. The remaining engine, though pressed to its limits, continued running and finally we did get back to Westerland. That was how I survived my first encounter with Spitfires. I would meet them again in the Battle of Britain, over the Mediterranean and during the Battle of Sicily and I can tell you now that it was never a pleasant experience on any of those occasions.

Karl Voght returned to his unit refreshed from his period of leave and recalled:

I arrived at the airfield located at Cherbourg and the place was a hive of activity and excitement. I was assigned yet another new rear gunner which, at first, I was not happy about. He was a 21-year-old named Herman Hoth. Hoth had been through Poland and France with our group (StG 77) but was in another squadron. I was assured he would be fine but only after meeting Herman Hoth was my mind put at rest. I could see he was a good man, well presented, conscientious and committed. It was quite amusing when he strode up to me, stood rigid to attention and said, 'I am Hoth, sir, reporting to you' before giving a loud 'Heil Hitler' and thrusting out his right arm. I held my hand out to him and we shook hands and then discussed our experiences of warfare in the Stuka. I felt this was important, that we should understand if we had any particular weaknesses or dislikes before we took off on operations; it was good to clear the air in that way. I was immediately reassured by Hoth's attitude that he was a good man to be guarding the rear of our Stuka. It didn't take a fool to realize that we would be flying to England alone if orders to attack came in. Tanks, artillery and infantry cannot move on water. We would be reliant more on fighter escort this time and the vigilance of our rear gunners. I told Hoth if we had to go to England, we would be going into a hornet's nest, for sure, a hornet's nest of the unknown too. When briefings began for our role in the attack on England, we were all quite surprised that Allied shipping in the English Channel was to be our first objective. This was the phase of the battle known as the *Kanalkampf* (Channel battle).

Our war really began to get hot from July 1940. On 9 July, Hoth and I were one of twenty-seven of our group being led by Hauptmann Friedrich-Karl Lichtenfels. We had an escort of the twin-engine Bf 110 heavy fighters, or destroyers as we called them. The target was the naval base at Portland which we attacked with bombs. We came under attack from defending fighters and I recognized some of them as Spitfires. I told Hoth to be on his guard as we went in to attack one of the large buildings visible on the base. I was relieved to get the bomb away and turn for home as I heard the rattle of Hoth's machine gun firing at several enemy aircraft heading into us from astern. The enemy fired at us and I saw tracers streak past, just missing the surface of our right wing; the enemy fighters were very fast as they broke away hard to the right but Hoth maintained his fire, only stopping to change his magazines.

> Sadly, Hauptmann Lichtenfels got into some trouble and both he and his rear gunner were shot down and killed. We also lost one of our escorting fighters, a Bf 110 which also fell to the enemy. For damaging one vessel we had lost four airmen. This was a sobering experience, the loss of Lichtenfels in particular as he was no novice pilot and had received the Knight's Cross of the Iron Cross, one of our highest honours. As we returned home, we did so with mixed thoughts about how the attack had gone. We had hoped to inflict greater damage on the enemy, yet what we had done was merely a pinprick. I commented later to Hoth that if only we had some heavy bombers.

It is ironic that some Luftwaffe aircrews should question the tactics and the viability of their attacks at such an early phase of the battle. Both Voght and Hoth both concurred that the job they were doing, although moderately successful, would have been better carried out by heavy bombers, not single-engine dive-bombers or even light/medium bombers. Karl Voght continued with his reflections:

> I feel our Stukas were adequate for attacking shipping in the Channel, but not for the bigger land targets such as bases and other infrastructure. When used against targets that required that edge of precision, one or two bombs or clusters of lighter bombs to get the job done was fair enough. The fact we lost Lichtenfels played heavily on my mind too; he was an experienced Stuka pilot. If he fell at this very early phase of the fighting, what hope was there for us less accomplished airmen to survive. I guess something twigged in my mind after that. I began writing letters home far more frequently than what I had done in Poland and France. I made arrangements in case I did not come back home too. I even penned a letter to my parents which should only be opened in the event I failed to return from an operation. It was one of the hardest letters I have ever had to write. Can you imagine having to write to your mother and father from a dead man's perspective? What should I write, what words could possibly be said to comfort them?

The Battle of Britain officially began on 10 July 1940, so the loss of the aircraft as reported in the raid carried out by Karl Voght and his comrades of 9 July was not officially recognized as being the first Luftwaffe aircraft shot down in the battle. The first Luftwaffe aircraft to be claimed by the RAF as pointed out by aviation historian Bob Collis was a Dornier 17 Z of II/KG 3 which was a shared victory between three Spitfire pilots of the Coltishall-based 66 Squadron. The Dornier crashed into the North Sea twenty miles off the coast of Norfolk; the crew were observed swimming clear of their aircraft, one surrounded by a very conspicuous green marker dye used to alert the German air sea rescue service, the Seenotdienst, to their plight. One of the RAF pilots radioed in the position of the three visible Dornier crew in the water. Despite efforts to save the German airmen, all four perished and were never seen again. This was a fate that would befall many more Luftwaffe bomber and fighter airmen by the end of the Luftwaffe's aerial campaign against Britain.

Karl Voght recalled the fear of being shot down over the North Sea or English Channel:

> The prospect of having to bale out either over the North Sea or the Channel was too dreadful to comprehend. It mattered not what time of the year it was, the waters of the English Channel and North Sea were always freezing cold. We were not stupid; we understood that the chances of rescue once down in the water were slim. If you were lucky the British would come and get you and pull you out. Our own air sea rescue service was wary about flying into hostile airspace as they too faced the possibility of ending up in the drink alongside those they were trying to rescue. So, more often than not, any pilot ending up in the sea was finished and many were never seen again after parachuting into the English Channel or the cold waters of the North Sea. I always had a small pistol with me which I carried in the right pocket of my flying suit. I always said to myself, *Voght, if you end up in the drink with no hope of rescue, you can always shoot yourself rather than suffer death by hyperthermia or drowning*. Yes, that was a real thought and a real danger during the Battle of Britain especially.

Many other pilots experienced what became known as Channel Fever. The moment the order to take off was given, you would start to tremble and sweat, not a hot sweat but more a cold, chilling one; your throat would go dry, and your head began to pound. If you got back home, you were thoroughly mentally exhausted through the stress and fear, and the thought of having to do the same again the next day and the day after that and so on broke some of the crewmen. They just couldn't deal with it anymore and had to be withdrawn from flying and sent to sanatoriums back home.

Unteroffizier Ludwig Werner was the pilot of a Dornier Do 17 Z with I/KG 3 based at Le Culot, Belgium, and recalled his arrival there:

> It was all very nice touching down on this grass airfield surrounded by trees and the pleasant countryside. Our accommodation was far from that of a first-class hotel in the beginning, but it was adequate, and both the days and nights were getting warmer, so it wasn't a problem really. Some of us were billeted in tents, others had brick buildings which were hastily turned into mess rooms and sleeping quarters. It didn't take long for us to settle in and while we awaited further orders, we could go off into the nearby town to see the sights and admire some of the pretty Belgian girls there. Some of them were stunners but we had been warned against taking local girls out by our commanding officer. There was the risk that they could be spies and that harm could come to us as individuals or the whole unit. So, I'm afraid most of us had to stick to the rules, but there were brothels available to us, places where we could go and do the deed and walk away afterwards.
>
> We began operations a day after the French surrender. Our first loss came on the night of 23 June. One of our aircraft, a Dornier 17, did not return to the aerodrome and all four crew were never seen again. Reports were sporadic when they trickled down to us; they didn't want to tell us much about losses as obviously it was not good for morale. A comrade told me later that Oberleutnant Scharpkowski and his crew had gone down into the sea.

On 9 July, it was our turn as we took off for a night raid on central England [West Midlands]. For the most part the operation went to plan; it was just like the training, only we were now carrying live bombs. The flight was mostly textbook as you say, boring if anything. When we arrived over the target area there was no intense ground fire. We dropped our bombs and got out of there and returned home unscathed. The daylight operations were the worst, although our fighters ranged ahead of us and tackled any enemy fighters sent up to intercept us. The Messerschmitts did not carry sufficient fuel to be able to escort us back home, which was a huge problem. The Messerschmitt Bf 110 had the fuel capacity but was no match for the Spitfire and Hurricane fighters; it was quite ridiculous.

Our bomber groups pushed on in a battle that steadily grew in its intensity. We were attacked by Hurricanes on one occasion; it was like someone had struck a wasp's nest and all the wasps were chasing us. The enemy was a determined foe, and it was as much as our poor gunners could do to keep them off us. The Dornier 17 Z, which the British nicknamed 'The Flying Pencil' due to its shape, was a light bomber and its controls were highly responsive so luckily for us we jinked and weaved and got through the constant fighter attack by the skin of our teeth. Our bombs hit part of a radio station and once the bombs were gone, we turned and I set the controls at full throttle to get away. We had been hit by machine-gun bullets and to hear them strike your aircraft for that first time is terrifying; you realize someone is shooting at you, trying to kill you. When we landed back at Le Culot, we all breathed a sigh of relief. Yes, we were frightened by the experience and when I got out of the aircraft and saw the state of the rear fuselage, I thought to myself, *How the hell did we get away with that?* There were bullets holes in the metal, all over the place. We were very lucky they were small-calibre machine-gun bullets and not cannon shells; had they been explosive cannon shells like what our Messerschmitt fighters were armed with, they would have blown off the rear fuselage of the aircraft and

> we may have been forced to take to our parachutes or worse still, killed.
>
> The next problem was our machine that when inspected had some structural damage. It was not major damage, just pieces which had been severed by bullets. The aircraft could not be repaired properly at the airfield, so it had to be sent back to Germany; this was ridiculous. There was not one person who could carry out repairs in the field at that time.
>
> As we were expected to continue operations, sometimes a crew would land after flying a mission, their Dornier would then be refuelled and rearmed and we would get on board and fly it on the next mission while they had a rest. Just because our aircraft was sent off to be fixed did not mean we got out of flying missions. It was crazy and I began to lose heart at that point in how our planners were conducting things. It didn't seem organized at all.

From the 10 July 1940, the air war against England steadily intensified with the Luftwaffe mounting ever-larger bombing raids, especially against the RAF airfields in the south of England. The fighter pilots of the Luftwaffe would trail the bombers at medium and high altitudes on what were known as *Freie Jagd* (free hunt) missions. These missions were deliberately intended to draw out the RAF Spitfire and Hurricane fighters. Of course, the RAF obliged, only to find themselves at a serious tactical disadvantage against the Bf 109s. As the RAF fighters climbed to intercept, the Bf 109s would dive upon them and this is where many of the RAF fighter losses occurred. Luftwaffe fighter pilot Adolf Galland recalled of the RAF's predicament at the time:

> Our bomber force would take off first, as we were so much faster than them. We would give them an allotted time in which to take off and head out across the English Channel, then we would take off and position ourselves above and behind the bombers. As the bombers approached the south coast, the RAF would be alerted, but their ground control system did not allow for the time that they needed to climb to a useful altitude with which to engage us. Yes, this gave us the advantage that the fighter pilot always seeks, having

altitude and the opportunity of not only seeing the enemy but in a position to initiate the attack on him. We knew the Spitfires and Hurricane would come and we would see them straining to get height up to our bombers. Our task was then to fall on them using our high speed. You would select a victim in your gunsight and if you made just one good pass you could destroy him using fire from the two machine guns and the two 2cm cannons. After the first attack we would climb as fast as possible and make another attack on the enemy fighters.

Yes, I encountered the Spitfire on many occasions and it was a very good aeroplane. You avoided getting into a turning fight with them where you could end up in their gunsights; instead, you dived for the ground to shake them off, then climbed back to altitude where you as a pilot could assess your position and make the decision to either single out an enemy to attack or return home.

Often low fuel was a serious problem for us, as it was all too easy to get carried away in the fight where there were aircraft all over the place flying in this deadly ballet, with shot and shell flying everywhere. There would sometimes be hundreds of aircraft all over the sky for as far as the eye could see, but you would have to turn back and head home or you might end up having to crash-land in the sea on the way home, which was never a good prospect.

That was the only problem with our Messerschmitt Bf 109 – we had the firepower and the advantage of speed in the climb and the dive – it was the low fuel capacity that was a serious hinderance when the enemy was around and you could not engage him for any useful length of time. In all we had ten minutes of combat time, fifteen at the very most, and that was pushing things. The further inland we penetrated the less combat time we had; yes, it was a problem for us fighter pilots.

The shortcomings of the Messerschmitt Bf 110 also quickly became apparent as the Battle of Britain intensified. While the Bf 110 carried a heavy punch in terms of firepower and possessed the fuel capacity to range further into southern England, it was however totally outclassed in the one-to-one dogfights with the Spitfire and Hurricanes. The Bf 110 simply lacked the aerial agility to get out of trouble against the nimbler fighters of the RAF. The Bf 110 pilots devised tactical measures such as flying in a defensive circle, so each aircraft could defend the others from fighter attack. In more extreme circumstances the Bf 110s needed the protection of the Bf 109s. Fighters that required a fighter escort themselves made little tactical sense and it was testimony to the failed *Zerstörer* concept. The much-vaunted Ju 87 Stuka was also to prove a liability and following the slaughter of the Stuka dive-bomber unit StG 77 on 18 August 1940, the Stuka was withdrawn from the order of battle. Karl Voght the Stuka pilot who flew with StG 77, recalled that last action of the once-legendary Stuka.

> I don't know where it all went wrong but from 13 August, which we called *Adler Tag*, or Eagle Day, it went askew. On the 13th, it was certainly an unlucky day operations-wise; poor communications and bad weather caused hell. There were fifty-two Stukas involved in the operation to bomb the RAF airfield at Warmwell. We couldn't locate the target and our bombs were jettisoned quite indiscriminately. We were getting tired from the intensity of the operations too.
>
> On 18 August, 109 of our Stuka force attacked the English and our targets were RAF Ford, RAF Thorney Island where there was a naval air station, and Littlehampton. We took off and an escort of some 150 fighters joined us. As we arrived over the target area and began to make our diving attacks, that's when the Hurricanes attacked us; the Bf 109s were too far away to intervene and keep the Hurricanes off us. Hoth did his best to machine-gun the Hurricanes as they came in, but he was hit as we went in to drop our bombs. I called after him over the intercom and asked him if he was alright; he failed to answer and just groaned, so I asked him again, 'Hoth, are you alright?' He then reassured me he was okay and to get on with the attack. I put my Stuka in a steep dive and aimed my bombs at a cluster of buildings or huts, whatever they were; as I released them, I was sure of scoring good hits, as the bombs looked to be right on target.

As we pulled out of the dive with that force that slams you back so hard into your seat you almost black out, my eyes closed momentarily, feeling slightly nauseous, then we were level again with tracers flying all around us and the sound of bullets hitting our aircraft. I could see smoke rising from where my bombs had fallen so I was happy that I had done my job. I turned for home but was pursued for some miles by Hurricanes and I had to jink the aircraft constantly to avoid their tracers. Despite my best efforts our aircraft was damaged and began to smoke.

As we flew out over the sea again, I just hoped the engine would survive long enough for us to at least reach the French coast and safety. I called Hoth again on the intercom but there was no answer, so I called again, 'Hoth are you alright back there; what are your injuries?' As he failed to reply that second time, I looked over my shoulder and could see he was slumped in his seat or rather his head was slumped down as if unconscious or something. I couldn't do anything until I got the aircraft down on the ground. As we neared the French coast, I decided to make an emergency landing in one of the fields. My engine had held out and was showing no signs of immediate distress but with a wounded man on board, I decided I needed to act for his sake more so than mine. I saw several of our unit flying on above and I radioed to tell them my position, that I was going to make a forced landing and that Hoth was either seriously wounded or dead. The Stuka was big for a single-engine aircraft, but I shut off the power to the engine, feathered my prop and levelled her out and just let her gently glide down onto the field. There were some cows grazing in the field and they shot off in all directions as I bore down upon them; the last thing I wanted was a collision with one of those beasts. As the wheels touched down on the rough grass it was pretty hairy as the Stuka bumped around a bit and, for a moment, I thought she would turn over on me but she came to a stop some 200 yards away from a very large cattle water butt. Good job really, as if I had hit that we could have been in some trouble. I unstrapped myself from my seat and immediately began the process of getting Hoth out of the aircraft and onto the grass. Our arrival had not gone unnoticed and soon several Heer soldiers came running over to us, then another four appeared carrying stretchers and other equipment. I told them I was fine but Hoth looked in a bad way. I hadn't thought to check to see if he was breathing and one of the Heer medical officers checked and then told me, 'I'm very sorry, your friend is dead. There is nothing we can do for him.' A guard was placed on the aircraft; poor Hoth was covered in a blanket and his lifeless form carried away on a stretcher. I was taken to the local army headquarters and given some hot coffee and offered some food. Their medical officer checked me over but I was fine; I just felt really bad for Hoth as he was a good young man. I knew that his mother and father were going to receive one of those dreadful notices. I didn't wish to experience anything like this again, but I knew all too well that I would return to our unit and we would probably be thrown straight back into the battle. I enjoyed the hospitality of the Heer for what remained of that fateful day and they drove me back to my unit the following day where there was some dismal news.

We were simply told we were no longer participating in the battle against England. It soon transpired that we had lost a lot of our aircraft and crews on that mission of 18 August which had turned into a turkey shoot despite our substantial escort. There were a lot of empty seats in the mess on my return; it was not a good omen at all. Twenty-six airmen were killed that day, six taken prisoner and another six wounded. It was not completely over for us as later that year we were involved a few anti-shipping attacks, mostly against supply convoys coming into the Channel.

Even amongst the Luftwaffe ground crews there was a growing sense of frustration at the sheer lack of progress the previously unbeatable Luftwaffe was experiencing against the RAF. Ground crewman Rolf Ickert, in his own words a 'weapons mechanic' (armourer) attached to the 3rd Staffel of the KG 26 bomber group, recalled:

I recall after a raid on the city of Newcastle on 15 August 1940. an incident I wrote down in my personal diary. On that day it just felt that when the aircrews returned, they vented their wrath on us. We were merely the pleb element of the force and the fact that crews came back all shot up with dead men inside the aircraft, somehow made us feel we were at fault. I recall one such Heinkel of our staffel landing in a bad way; the nose was all shot up and the nose gunner was lying dead in his position. The pilot was an Oberleutnant Frisch; as soon as the aircraft was still, he leapt out and began cursing and swearing loudly. The body of the dead man was carefully extricated from the Heinkel; another crewman was also injured but not too badly. It was not a very pleasant sight at all. The dead crewman was riddled with bullet holes and you could clearly see these blood-soaked holes in his flying suit. As the wounded man was helped into a waiting ambulance Oberleutnant Frisch continued with his rage. We were working on another crate [slang for aircraft] when he shouted across to us, 'Hey, you three, get over here now, there are some things I want doing.' We stopped what we were doing and trotted over to him and I asked politely, 'Sir, what is it you need us to do?' Frisch then pointed to the shattered nose of his Heinkel and said, 'These fucking things, they are death traps! I want you to move that 2cm [hand-operated 20mm Oerlikon cannon in the ventral bay]; it is useless where it is. Have it taken out and put it in place of the nose machine gun in that crate over there.' He pointed to a fresh Heinkel several hundred yards away. 'You can do this on my authority.' He then went on to explain that 'if the British fighters try to attack us head on again, we will have a surprise waiting for them'. So, we did as we were told and removed the 2cm cannon and between us we put it into the nose position of the other aircraft. A lot of adjustments had to be made as the 2cm gun gave more recoil than the MG 15 machine gun which it was replacing, but we managed to do it after working quite late into the night. We did the work yet there were no thanks for it. We began to feel very dejected, treated like dogs sometimes.

> We understood the frustration of the airmen, but it wasn't our fault if they could not do the job their boss [Göring] had boasted they could.

Mounting losses, particularly amongst the bomber crews, brought about direct intervention from Hitler himself who made the decision that the fighters should stay closer to the bombers, an order which effectively rendered the fighter arm incapable of doing the job it was intended to do: range ahead and destroy RAF fighters. This would be just one of many tactical blunders which contributed to curtailing the Luftwaffe fighters' effectiveness in the battle.

Adolf Galland recalled a frontline officer briefing on Luftwaffe tactics with an enraged Luftwaffe chief Hermann Göring. Göring was unhappy with the mounting losses in the bomber groups. Galland recalled:

> He had come not so much to discuss tactics as I had already made my personal opinion on this clear. All Göring did was to personally criticize me and the other squadron leaders and insinuate we were cowards. We could not achieve air superiority over the south of England using the tactics he himself was forcing upon us under orders from Hitler. The task of staying closer to the bombers and having to escort the Bf 110s made our position as fighter pilots untenable. Göring should have known better being a former fighter pilot himself. He was being unnecessarily disrespectful and sarcastic to me. His attitude was an affront to all those German pilots who had given their lives in the fighting to that point. I could not let him get away with it. He stood there and said, 'Look, what can I do to help you? What is it that you need?' So, I told him, 'A squadron of Spitfires!' Of course, I preferred my Messerschmitt to a Spitfire, but I had made my point [he smiles]. My remark touched a nerve and he soon stormed off in a huff. When he had gone, some of my pilots were being less polite about Göring. They stood around in groups discussing what Göring had said to us and I heard one remark, 'Maybe they should give Fatty a Messerschmitt. Let's see how long it takes for him to get his fat arse shot up over there [England].' Seriously, it was not

> good, that one careless ill-thought remark from a leader who should have known better did little to improve the morale of the squadron. I will say that the Spitfire was a much better defensive fighter aircraft as it possessed superior manoeuvrability over the Bf 109. I personally preferred the Bf 109 as it was a better fighter for offensive sweeps over enemy territory.

13 August saw the launch of *Adlertag*, or *Eagle Day*. On this day the Luftwaffe flew 1,485 sorties against England. The immense scale of *Adlertag* is somewhat misleading: in order to accomplish this high rate of sorties, the fighter and bomber crews had to fly multiple missions and while they undoubtedly strained the RAF to its very limits, these proved detrimental to the Luftwaffe crews as one young bomber crewman, Fritz Herbert Scholle, recalled:

> We would take off and head out in formation across the English Channel. The fighters had been ordered to stay closer to the bombers, and while this was some small comfort to those of us flying in the bombers, it did not help the overall situation; if anything, it made things worse. We would go in and drop our bombs and fight our way out through the defensive attacks of the Spitfires and Hurricanes which we had been told were close to being defeated. The problem was they were always there, ready to meet us. How could this be the case? which is what many of us began to think. Those of us who made it back home then had to immediately prepare to take off again for another sortie to England. I know some crews flew three to four missions on 13 August; it was ridiculous to expect the aircrews to do that. We were getting to the point of exhaustion and losing faith in our leadership.

On 15 August 1940, the Luftwaffe was again expected to exert maximum effort against the RAF. On this day they flew 2,000 sorties, and again, many aircrews were expected to fly multiple times to attack targets across the Channel. On each occasion the RAF was there in force to meet them. It was clear at this point that the Luftwaffe had lost the initiative in the air war against Britain. From 19 August heavy night-bombing raids were carried out against ports and industrial cities, including the suburbs of London.

On the night of 24 August 1940, a disorientated Luftwaffe bomber crew flew off course and inadvertently dropped their bombs on central London. It was an event that would initiate a five-year campaign of destruction. For Britain's RAF this blunder could not have come at a more crucial time. RAF Bomber Command retaliated with a bombing raid on the Reich capital, Berlin. An enraged Hitler demanded that London and other British cities be razed to the ground in a sustained and indiscriminate campaign of bombing that became known as the Blitz. With the onset of the Blitz, Luftwaffe attention was diverted away from their primary task of attacking the RAF, its infrastructure and airfields, effectively giving the RAF time to regroup, reequip and recover from the previous months of battle.

## Luftwaffe Casualties in the Battle of Britain

The Luftwaffe lost 1,700 aircraft during the Battle of Britain along with 2,662 airmen either killed, wounded or taken prisoner. These losses included many experienced pilots and crews and were losses the Luftwaffe could ill afford and would never recover from.

## Luftwaffe Aces of the Battle of Britain

| | | |
|---|---|---|
| • Oberleutnant Helmut Wick | I/JG 2 | 42 |
| • Major Adolf Galland | III/JG 26 | 35 |
| • Hauptmann Walter Oesau | III/JG 51 | 34 |
| • Major Werner Mölders | JG 51 | 28 |
| • Oberleutnant Hermann-Friedrich Joppien | I/JG 51 | 26 |
| • Oberleutnant Herbert Ihlefeld | I/LG 2 | 24 |
| • Hauptmann Gerhard Schopfel | III/JG 26 | 23 |
| • Oberfeldwebel Siegfried Schnell | II/JG 2 | 18 |
| • Hauptmann Horst Tietzen | II/JG 51 | 18 |
| • Oberleutnant Hans Hahn | III/JG 2 | 17 |
| • Leutnant Erich Schmidt | III/JG 53 | 17 |

| | | |
|---|---|---|
| • Hauptmann Heinz Bretnutz | II/JG 53 | 16 |
| • Oberfeldwebel Werner Machold | I/JG 2 | 16 |
| • Oberleutnant Arnold Lignitz | I/JG 51 | 15 |
| • Oberleutnant Hans Philipp | II/JG 54 | 15 |
| • Oberleutnant Hans Ekkehard Bob | 111/JG 54 | 14 |
| • Major Karl-Heinz Leesmann | I/JG 52 | 14 |
| • Oberleutnant Joachim Müncheberg | III/JG 26 | 14 |
| • Oberleutnant Josef Priller | II/JG 51 | 14 |
| • Oberleutnantt Heinz Ebeling | 111/JG 26 | 13 |
| • Major Erich Groth | II/ZG 76 | 13 |
| • Hauptmann Hans-Karl Mayer | I/JG 53 | 13 |
| • Oberleutnant Hans-Joachim Jabs | II/ZG 76 | 12 |
| • Hauptmann Hans Wiggers | I/JG 51 | 12 |
| • Oberleutnant Helmut Bennemann | I/JG 52 | 11 |
| • Oberleutnant Erich Hohagen | II/JG 51 | 11 |
| • Oberleutnant Gustav Sprick | III/JG 26 | 11 |
| • Feldwebel Heinz Bar | I/JG 51 | 10 |
| • Oberleutnant Kurt Brandle | II/JG 53 | 10 |
| • Oberleutnant Josef Foz• | II/JG 51 | 10 |
| • Hauptmann Dietrich Hrabak | II/JG 54 | 10 |
| • Leutnant Rolf Kaldrack | III/ZG 76 | 10 |
| • Oberleutnant Karl-Heinz Krahl | I/JG 2 | 10 |
| • Leutnant Erich Leie | I/JG 2 | 10 |
| • Oberleutnant Gustav Rodel | II/JG 27 | 10 |
| • Oberfeldwebel Erich Rudorffer | I/JG 2 | 10 |
| • Feldwebel Walter Scherer | III/ZG 26 | 10 |
| • Leutnant Heinz Tornow | II/JG 51 | 10 |
| • Leutnant Eduard Tratt | I/Erp.Gr.210 | 10 |
| • Hauptmann Wolf-Dietrich Wicke | III/JG 53 | 10 |

## Factors in the Defeat of the Luftwaffe in the Battle of Britain

There were a multitude of factors as to why the Luftwaffe failed in their objective of defeating the RAF in the Battle of Britain. As with the Third Reich in general, the Luftwaffe's command infrastructure was poor and Luftwaffe chief Herman Göring's failure to grasp modern aerial warfare strategies proved a further hinderance. The Luftwaffe had only really evolved along the lines of an aerial utility of the German army, a close air support facility unused to offensive operations where it acted independently under its own initiative. Hitler himself felt obliged to intervene in Luftwaffe matters, making irrational decisions that often put Luftwaffe aircrews at a disadvantage. The lack of forward repair facilities meant that even an aircraft with only minimal damage often had to be returned to the factory where it was built for repair work to be carried out, whereas forward repair depots were a key feature of the RAF. The Luftwaffe had invested in twin-engine medium bombers as opposed to a long-range four-engine heavy bomber. Aircraft such as the Messerschmitt Bf 110 became a severe liability during the battle, as a fighter that required a fighter escort was a totally pointless resource.

The Luftwaffe also failed to understand the basic importance of the cooperative efforts of the Royal Observer Corps in combination with radar during the battle. Luftwaffe bomber formations were often picked up by the Home Chain radar stations while a hundred miles away from the English coast. Generaloberst Ernst Udet, although a brilliant First World War German fighter pilot with sixty-two victories to his credit, rejected the proposed use of radar for the Luftwaffe in 1938 purely because it failed to fit his personal ideas of air combat. Outdated thinking such Udet's, a man effectively in charge of the Luftwaffe during this period, was endemic in some areas of the Luftwaffe high command. Britain utilized radar detection to maximum effect throughout the battle and had twenty-nine RDF stations along its southern and eastern coastlines. What is largely forgotten is that information relayed back to Britain from spies in occupied France also proved invaluable in anticipating Luftwaffe planning and strategy. This, along with the breaking of the Enigma code, greatly aided the package of intelligence at Fighter Command's disposal. Even the types of fuel used by the RAF Spitfires and Hurricanes became a factor in thwarting defeat. At the outbreak of war both the RAF and the Luftwaffe were using the same 87 octane aviation fuel. In May 1940 Britain obtained supplies of 100 octane fuel from the US, which boosted performance of the Rolls-Royce Merlin engines from 1,000hp to around 1,300hp. The RAF also had the advantage of fighting over home soil. If a Luftwaffe pilot was shot down over England and survived, he would automatically become a prisoner of war, unable to rejoin the fight, unlike the RAF pilots who would be picked up and returned to their units within hours. There has also been much debate as to the use of drugs such as pervitin (crystal meth) among the Luftwaffe hierarchy which may have obscured individual command judgements. I found no evidence of the use of drugs in any of the interviews I have conducted with former Luftwaffe airmen, so I would hesitate to say the use of drugs was a factor during the battle.

The real heroes of the battle were those factory workers building the Spitfires and Hurricanes. British production, far from being curtailed, actually increased and soon overtook Germany.

# Chapter 9

# Blitz on England

Saturday, 7 September 1940 dawned as a pleasantly mild day with clear blue skies and not a cloud in sight. Few could have ever imagined the terror yet to arrive in the afternoon of an otherwise very pleasant day. Across the English Channel a force of 348 Luftwaffe bombers plus some 617 Messerschmitt Bf 109 fighters were taking off from their airfields in northern France and assembling in the skies above. This was to be the first major assault known as *Unternehmen Loge* or Operation *London*. Göring had arrived the day before to take personal command of the operation; he watched from the cliffs of Cap Gris Nez as the impressive aerial armada formed up before heading to their target, England. The first bombs that fell on London did so during a raid on the night of the 24 August 1940. In that incident bombs fell in six different boroughs of the city, making it extremely unlikely to have been the work of a single raider. As Göring observed the mass of aircraft above, he was in an ebullient mood and confident of the operation's success. One observer remarked, 'Yes, he stood there gloating and giggling like some school bully. Yet, the man was an embarrassment and disliked by those under his command. In fact, they nicknamed him "Fatty" behind his back in barrack-room scorn.' This time it was not the RAF who were to be the main target but the people of London. By 4.14pm in the afternoon, it soon became apparent to Londoners that they were in for a drubbing. Mark Simmons, who had been out playing with his friends near the Thames Estuary, recalled:

> We saw them coming before we could even hear the engines. They were like a mass of bees; that's what they looked like as they streamed in across the Channel and approached the estuary which they used as a navigational point. It was pretty obvious they were Germans; as they came closer you

> could hear that distinctive drone of their engines. At that point we thought, 'Bollocks, lets run.' We ran home and each lad scattered down a different street to get home as quickly as possible. I ran in through the door and said to my mum, 'The Germans are coming.' She said, 'What the hell are you talking about? No, they're not.' So, I told her to look outside; she went out had a look then dashed back inside. Funny thing was she locked the door behind her, I remember thinking, *What are you doing that for?* [he laughs].

As reported by men of the Royal Observer Corps, this large German force did not disperse to attack the RAF airfields, sector stations and fuel storage sites; instead, they flew onward towards London. It was an impressive sight were it not for the carnage that was to be unleashed by this force which formed a block some twenty miles wide. As they passed over Kent witnesses recalled wave upon wave flying at high altitude, the metal of the planes gleaming in the afternoon sun. Just thirty minutes later the bombs were dropping on London. Many took to their Anderson shelters in their gardens, yet curious children and adults peered out through the doorways to see what was happening. Schoolgirl Judy Finch recalled:

> The bombs were falling for around two hours. What I remember most is that dreadful drone of engines, the whistling noise that the bombs made as they fell and then the explosions which shook the ground. Even though bombs fell some distance away, the shockwaves from them could be felt. They fell in sticks one, two, three, four, bang, bang, bang, bang – it was a horrible and very frightening experience for both the children and adults of London. There was only me and my mum at the time as dad was away in the Royal Navy. One of the Germans crashed into a street not far from our house I think it was on the Ranelagh Road in the East End. It killed two old women who had been sheltering in their house, but they were frightened by all the noise and felt they would be safer out in their shelter in their garden. This Messerschmitt 109 came down directly on the shelter, killing them both. The 109 had apparently been

> abandoned by its pilot some distance away, yet it flew on, eventually coming down in the East End; it was horrible that such a thing could happen, but this was just the start for us.

This particular raid on London ended around 6.10pm, yet two hours later another wave of bombers came, 300 strong, for a second bombing attack which lasted until 4.30am the following morning. Dogfights raged as the RAF engaged the German fighters who again used hit-and-run tactics before, low on fuel, they were forced to leave the bombers. The London docks were the worst hit along with the working-class neighbourhoods which were in close proximity. The Germans were using a mixture of incendiary and high-explosive bombs. The skies above the city glowed red as if burning coals. For seventy-six of the seventy-seven nights that followed, London was subjected to the Luftwaffe bombers.

The worst raid of the London Blitz would come on 10 May 1941 which, ironically, would be the last. That day 1,400 people were killed and some 700 acres of London set ablaze, with the Houses of Parliament being among those buildings damaged. One of the great terrors of the Blitz was the Luftwaffe's use of parachute mines. Londoners feared these large high-explosive devices the most, as Judy Finch recalled:

> The mines were the worst thing of all. As they were dropped from the enemy plane carrying them, you would hear a shriek as it fell but then it would go quiet in an instant. This was due to the fact that the mine had a parachute which deployed as soon as it was clear from the plane dropping it, so you couldn't hear it and you couldn't see it at night or where it was going to fall. The Germans put these time-delay fuzes in them, so once they had come down, they could sit there for anything from forty seconds or longer before exploding. I remember mum talking about a group of firemen tackling a blaze near some crossroads. They heard the sound of a parachute mine as it fell from the German plane, so they all dropped down flat on the ground. They waited and nothing happened, so they assumed it was safe to get up. As they were in the process of getting up and walking forward to get their equipment, the mine exploded.

> It had a time-delay fuze which explains why it did not go off straightaway. Mum said they couldn't find anything of those firemen apart from small bits: they'd been blown to smithereens.

The parachute mines were an adaptation of the German air-dropped sea mines. The 1,000kg (2,204lb) SB1000 high-explosive mine was approximately six feet in length (the actual body of the mine being five feet five inches), with a diameter of two feet seven inches. The body of the mine consisted of two welded sections of steel plate, the thickness of which was .06 to .125 inches. The parachute was constructed from a coarse weave vegetable fibre, either red, green or blue in colour and held in place by sixteen parachute shroud lines. The main filling for the weapon consisted of 48 per cent dinitro benzine, 15 per cent RDX and 37 per cent ammonium nitrate. The *Stuckfullung*, or 'biscuit filling', consisted of 51 per cent ammonium nitrate, 31 per cent calcium nitrate and 16 per cent RDX. The charge-to-weight ratio of the weapon was 80 per cent. The modus operandi of the weapon was fairly simple. On release from the aircraft, the fuze, which was the type E1. A.Z. (55) A/M, was charged and the quick-release pin securing the parachute assembly was withdrawn by means of a static cord. The spring-loaded parachute platform forced the parachute outwards, the opening spring forcing the canopy to open immediately. The parachute assembly retarded the dropping speed of the bomb whilst ensuring the nose of the bomb remained vertically downward. The weapon was prevented from penetrating the target on impact or making too hard an impact which would have caused the weapon to break up. On impact, the impact switch of the (55) A/M fuze would close, initiating the igniter in the fuze, and initiating the detonation of the main charge in the weapon. The colour of these weapons was field grey with the following markings stencilled in black along the body: SB1000/410 52 A+ 52A+. At the time, Air Intelligence summaries on the weapon concluded that the reference number 410 which appeared in the markings on the casing referred to the type of aircraft carrying and deploying the weapon, namely the Messerschmitt Me 410. Yet during the early phases of the Blitz, the Messerschmitt Me 410 (which did not appear in the skies over England until June 1943) had neither the internal nor external capacity to carry the weapon.

*Right*: General Hans von Seeckt. (Wikimedia Commons)

*Below left*: Hugo Sperrle. (Wikimedia Commons)

*Below right*: Professor Willy Messerschmitt. (Profile Publications)

*Above*: A Bf 109 undergoes wind-tunnel testing at the Messerschmitt works.

*Left*: Chief of the Luftwaffe, Hermann Göring. (Wikimedia Commons)

An artist's impression of the prototype Bf 109. (Profile Publications)

Eleven-year-olds Wendy Anderton and Cathie Jones pose beside a wrecked Heinkel He 111 of KG 27. (Luftwaffe Archive)

Armament configuration of the Messerschmitt Bf 109E: a 20mm Oerlikon MG FF cannon in each wing and two synchronized 7.92mm MG17 machine guns above the engine. (Profile Publications)

The Junkers Jumo 210D. (Luftwaffe Archive)

Daimler Benz 601. (Luftwaffe Archive)

*Above left*: Bramo Fafnir radial. (Luftwaffe Archive)

*Above right*: BMW 801 radial. (Luftwaffe Archive)

*Above*: A Messerschmitt Bf 109D in the Spanish Civil War bearing the Nationalist insignia. (Luftwaffe Archive)

*Left*: A painting depicting Heinkel He 51 biplane fighters on the attack at Cadenas in 1938, during the Spanish Civil War.

*Right*: Johannes Trautloft. (Luftwaffe Archive)

*Below*: Ten-year-old Polish girl Kazimiera Mika weeps over the body of her sister after she and a group of other females were attacked by Stuka dive-bombers while digging potatoes in a field. (Julien Bryan)

A shocked Julien Bryan comforts the young Kazimiera Mika after the attack involving Ju 87 Stukas.

Gefreiter Ernst Heinrich Husse standing beside a Bf 109.
(E. H. Husse family)

Major Werner Mölders.
(Luftwaffe Archive)

Junkers Ju 88 pilot Lieutnant Horst von Riesen of 1/KG 30 who almost fell victim to RAF Spitfires on 16 October 1939. (H. von Riesen)

Major Adolf Galland.
(Luftwaffe Archive)

Judy Finch (left) relaxes with her mother Violet and aunt Gracie, July 1939. (J. Thompson)

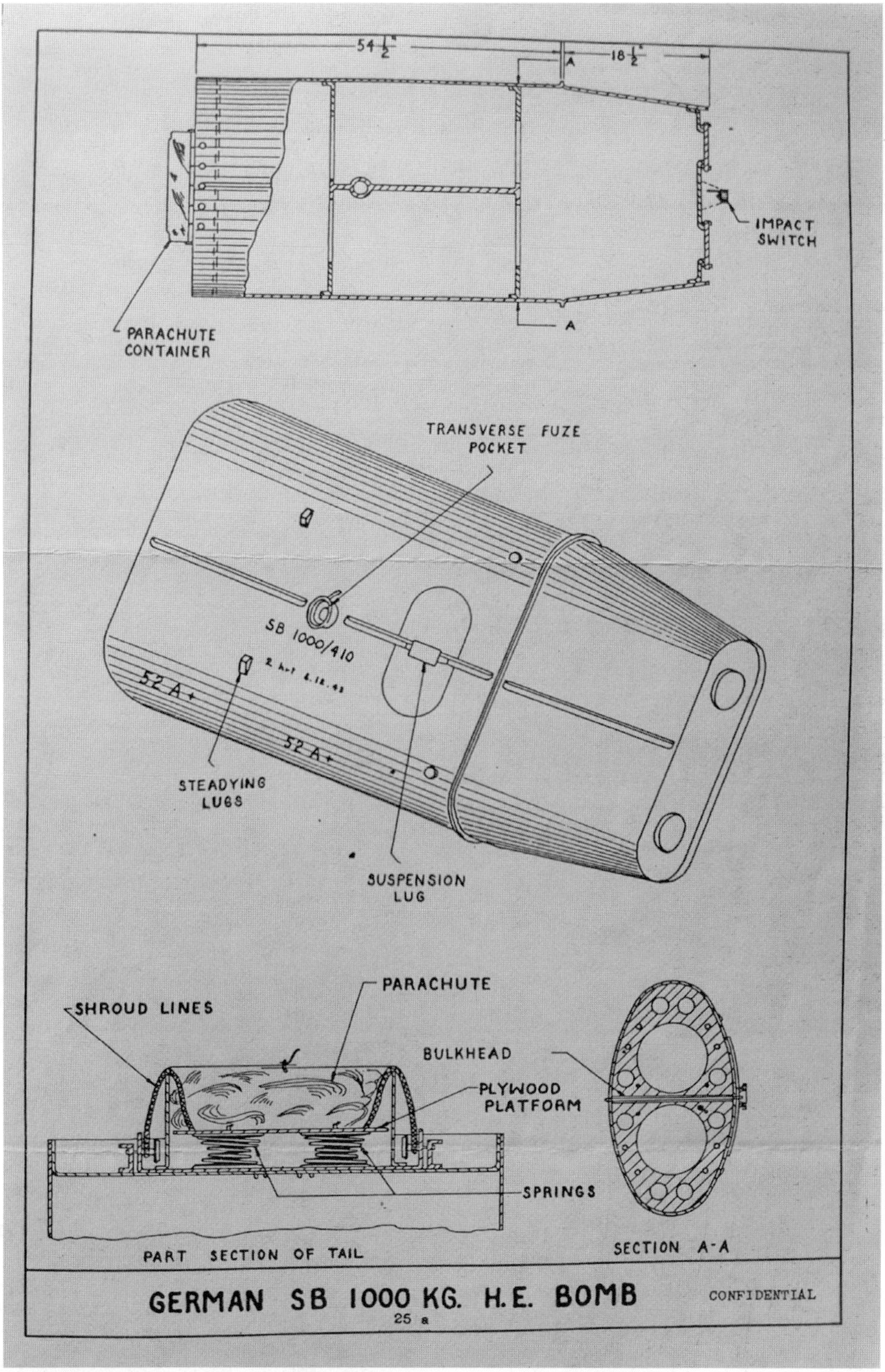


British Air Intelligence document on the German SB1000 parachute mine dropped by Luftwaffe bombers during the Blitz. (Air Historical Branch)

Major Helmut Wick, killed on 28 November 1940. (Luftwaffe Archive)

Gefreiter Richard Riedel at flying training school (*Fliegerschule*). (Author's collection via the Riedel family)

Twenty-one-year-old Gefreiter Richard Riedel in uniform at home in Röblingen am See. (Author's collection via the Riedel family)

A studio portrait of Gefreiter Richard Riedel. (Author's collection via the Riedel family)

One of the last photographs of 21-year-old Gefreiter Richard Riedel taken shortly before his death in November 1940. (Author's collection via the Riedel family)

Gefreiter Werner Messner who flew with the Luftwaffe fighter group JG 3. (W. M. Messner)

Hans Ulrich Rudel of Stukageschwader 2 (Stg 2).

Gottfried Urquhart of fighter group JG 54. (G. Urquhart)

Gefreiter Willi Schäfer of bomber group 7/Kampfgeschwader 2 (7/KG 2) smiles for the camera. (Ingeborg Stiefel)

From left: Gefreiter Willi Schäfer, Gefreiter Erich Raab, Unteroffizier Joachim Schnabel and Unteroffizier Richard Hartenberger. All four were killed on a night bombing operation over England in January 1943. (Ingeborg Stiefel)

*Above*: From left: Gefreiter Erich Raab, Unteroffizier Joachim Schnabel, Unteroffizier Richard Hartenberger and Gefreiter Willi Schäfer step out. (Ingeborg Stiefel)

*Right*: Elizabeth Schäfer, Willi Schäfer's wife, with baby daughter Ingeborg who was born the morning her father was killed. (Holger Stiefel)

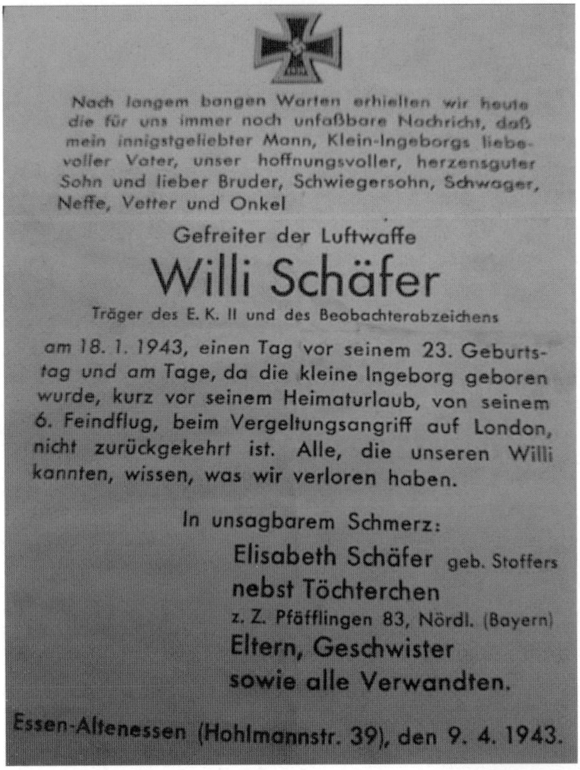

Nach langem bangen Warten erhielten wir heute die für uns immer noch unfaßbare Nachricht, daß mein innigstgeliebter Mann, Klein-Ingeborgs liebevoller Vater, unser hoffnungsvoller, herzensguter Sohn und lieber Bruder, Schwiegersohn, Schwager, Neffe, Vetter und Onkel

Gefreiter der Luftwaffe

**Willi Schäfer**

Träger des E. K. II und des Beobachterabzeichens

am 18. 1. 1943, einen Tag vor seinem 23. Geburtstag und am Tage, da die kleine Ingeborg geboren wurde, kurz vor seinem Heimaturlaub, von seinem 6. Feindflug, beim Vergeltungsangriff auf London, nicht zurückgekehrt ist. Alle, die unseren Willi kannten, wissen, was wir verloren haben.

In unsagbarem Schmerz:

Elisabeth Schäfer geb. Stoffers
nebst Töchterchen
z. Z. Pfäfflingen 83, Nördl. (Bayern)
Eltern, Geschwister
sowie alle Verwandten.

Essen-Altenessen (Hohlmannstr. 39), den 9. 4. 1943.

Gefreiter Willi Schäfer's obituary. Willi was posthumously awarded the Iron Cross 2nd Class. (Holger Stiefel)

The author with Willi Schäfer's daughter, Ingeborg Stiefel, at the German Military Cemetery at Cannock, Staffordshire, 20 June 1999. (Jon & Mary Lynn Jones)

*Right*: Aviation historian Peter Halliday during his meeting with the author, Westerham, Kent, 10 August 1998. (Tim Heath)

*Below*: Pilgrim House, Westerham, Kent, where Dornier 217E-4 U5+MR W. no. 5591 of 7/KG 2 crashed. (Tim Heath)

*Above*: A Dornier Do 217E-4 medium bomber. (Luftwaffe Archive)

*Left*: Feldwebel Joachim von Bitter relaxes between sorties, summer 1942. (Dr Christian Meyl)

*Above*: Feldwebel Joachim von Bitter in the cockpit of his Focke Wolf Fw190. (Dr Christian Meyl)

*Right*: Flight Lieutenant John Small of 266 (Rhodesia) Squadron RAF based at Exeter. (Ernest Pettiford RN retd.)

Two trawlermen pose with one of the two 20mm Oerlikon MG FF cannons from Feldwebel Joachim von Bitter's Fw190. The relic got caught up in their fishing nets one day in 1969. (Andrew Cruse)

Antiques restoration expert Andrew Cruse with the 20mm Oerlikon MG FF cannon he purchased and fully restored before being ordered by the court to throw the gun back into the sea off Teignmouth. (Andrew Cruse)

*Above*: The collected wreckage of female ferry pilot Monica Vanessa Kieler Dorsche's Focke-Wolf Fw190 after it developed engine trouble, forcing her to bale out over farmland. (M. V. K. Dorsche family)

*Right*: Luftwaffe fighter ace Heinz Knoke with his wife Lilo. Knoke finished the war with thirty-three confirmed victories, all claimed in the Western theatre of operations. (H. Knoke)

An artist's impression of Messerschmitt Me 262 jet fighters attacking US B-17 bombers during the final weeks of the air war over Germany.

What made the parachute mines more effective than say the standard SC250 (*Sprengbombe Cylindrisch*) was the fact that surrounding buildings could have a cushioning effect upon the blast of the smaller bomb types, thus lessening their effect. The parachute mines on the other hand, especially if they detonated against the rooftops of houses, could flatten an entire street, such was the power of the blast wave that covered a radius of some 330 feet and was capable of causing peripheral damage for a distance of up to a mile from the point of detonation.

On 9 September, the Oberkommando der Luftwaffe (OKL), the Luftwaffe high command, appeared to be attempting to use two strategies. A round-the-clock bombing campaign against London was a concerted attempt to force the British government into capitulation, yet it was also targeting Britain's vital sea communications. In effect, the Luftwaffe was using the age-old siege method of warfare. In spite of the poor weather conditions on 9 September, the Luftwaffe carried out heavy raids and bombs fell on the suburbs of London and the RAF airfield at Farnborough. The day's fighting cost Luftflotte 2 twenty-four bombers and thirteen Messerschmitt Bf 109 fighters. Undeterred, the Luftwaffe returned again on 15 September, mounting two large daylight attacks on London along the Thames Estuary. The targets were the docks and railway communications centres in the city. The reasoning behind this was to destroy the intended targets and draw the RAF fighters up where they too could be eliminated by the Bf 109s flying at high altitude. The air battles that ensued raged throughout the whole day, yet the damage inflicted by the Germans was minimal in comparison to the scale of their efforts. The Luftwaffe lost 18 per cent of its bomber aircraft on this day and Fighter Command, far from being eliminated, was relatively unmolested.

Göring continued to brag that with more time his Luftwaffe could achieve its objective against England. Hitler did not share either his enthusiasm or optimism. On 17 September, Operation *Sea Lion* was postponed indefinitely. Although the Luftwaffe continued to mount raids against London, they were by this time merely bait for the higher-flying Messerschmitt Bf 109s. With the worsening weather conditions and irreplaceable losses suffered by the Luftwaffe in their daylight attacks, the OKL ordered their bomber fleets to switch to night attacks.

Unteroffizier Helmut von Schieff served as the bomb aimer aboard a Heinkel He 111 in Luftflotte 3 Some 380 aircraft took off for London during the night of 14 October 1940. It was to be the heaviest attack to date. He recalled:

> We slept for most of the day but trying to sleep knowing we had an operation that evening was not conducive to relaxation. We were nervous as we had not carried out many nighttime operations or over the kind of distance this raid would be. So, we were worried about whether we would perform properly and whether we would get back safely, all the kinds of things that went through your mind before an operation, especially at night.
>
> When we took off for the operation, it was pitch black; you couldn't see anything and it was unnerving for a young crew fresh out of training school. Unlike the fighters, we bomber crews were more professional by the way we could fly in total darkness on instruments; the fighter pilots were never trained to fly on instruments; not many know that. We navigated our way to the target by means of the X-Gerät system. This was simply a method whereby you navigated your way through the darkness listening out for signals on a radio set. This task fell to the navigator of course, probably the most important task in the aeroplane on a night operation. Our technicians came up with what was known as the Knickebein system. *Knickebein* is crooked leg in German but it was also the name of a magic crow in German mythology. How it worked was very simple: the beam from a single transmitter would guide bombers towards the target area; a second transmitter was set up so when the two beams crossed, the bombs should be released. If you were one of the late arrivals over the target area, you would see the fires burning from miles away in advance and you had a visual guidance. What was it like, many have asked me over the years? On the 14th, our only real worries were the searchlights and defensive Flak or anti-aircraft guns in and around London. There was no threat from night fighters at this early stage so our only real enemy, apart

from any human errors, were these searchlights and Flak batteries. As we approached London there was a red glow in the night sky. We looked out through the glazed nose of our aircraft in amazement. The sky glowed a kind of red, yellow and orange colour. As we flew in the fires below lit up the inside of our aircraft and searchlights clawed the sky in an effort to guide the Flak guns onto us. I recall the Flak not being that heavy or accurate but it weas pretty frightening. Near misses in the form of exploding shell fragments – which we called *splitters* [splinters] – struck the outer skin of the aircraft, yet these razor-sharp pieces of steel were at the end of their trajectory and lucky for us they lacked the velocity to penetrate the aluminium. The sound these metal fragments made as they hit the aircraft was alarming though. When a Flak shell exploded nearby, the shockwave would also bounce off the aircraft. You could feel it being buffeted by the blast. If you took a direct hit or one exploded close by, you were finished. I remember we had a real scare when, for a moment, we were 'coned' by two searchlight beams. They blinded us momentarily until our pilot, Unteroffizier Schenkmann, yanked his control column from left to right; the aircraft lurched violently and lost altitude but the searchlight beams were shaken off. I recall Schenkmann saying over the radio, 'Boys, that was fucking close!' We prepared to drop our load of SC250 explosives onto the city and although we could see the target area due to the fires below, we still waited on the beams before I pressed the bomb release and shouted, 'Gone.' As soon as the last bomb fell away, the bomb bay doors were closed and Unteroffizer Schenkmann immediately put the aircraft into a shallow climb to get well above the Flak and set a course for home.

I remember looking down at the city below as it burned. I remember how it reminded me of years before, as a child, how I would watch the large open fire as it burned in our home, the coals glowing hot. That is how that city below looked to us on that night. We would return many times and experience this over and over. After a while it just became normal, part of the job.

Luftflotte 3's losses were minimal on this operation. The British anti-aircraft defences, which ranged from the 3.5-inch to 4.5-inch heavy guns, under the command of General Frederick Alfred-Pile (Royal Artillery), fired a total of 8,326 rounds of high-explosive shells yet accounted for only two raiders.

On 15 October, London was raided again and on this night 900 fires were started by a mix of 415 tons of high explosive and eleven short tons of incendiary bombs. Five major railway lines were severed plus rolling stock damaged. Judy Finch recalled the raid as it was her ninth birthday:

> This was a pretty big attack and very frightening. The incendiaries caused fires everywhere and two struck the rooftop of our terraced house and we heard them tumbling down and landing in the backyard. My mother had a scoop and bucket of sand ready as we were all taught how to tackle these incendiary bombs. My mother told us to stay behind as she went into the backyard. On the concrete floor by our dining room window, I remember seeing this bright white thing burning fiercely on the ground. The other bomb had landed further away on the small piece of ground where we kept two rabbits. The two rabbits had been killed which really upset me and my mother just kept telling me not to look and go back inside. Mum tackled the two bombs with the sand and scooped them into a metal bucket. Once the bombs were snuffed out, the bucket was placed away from the house up the end of the small garden area. The next morning these were taken away by a member of the local Home Guard. Before he left, he gave me the tailfin as a souvenir from one of the bombs. It was only small and appeared to be made from alloy material. These were quite prized, especially by the boys, and I soon swapped it for something but can't remember what it was. After that raid my mother became concerned for my safety and wanted me to go and stay with some relatives in High Wycombe. I wasn't happy about it at first as I didn't want to leave my mother, but many friends were being sent out into the countryside where it was safer. I left London on 19 October and stayed with my aunt for the remainder of the war.

As the Blitz continued, cities including Liverpool, Bristol, Cardiff, Portsmouth, Plymouth, Southampton, Swansea, Belfast, Glasgow, Birmingham, Coventry, Manchester and Sheffield all received attention from the night raiders. Coventry was hit particularly hard, experiencing a total of seventeen smaller raids between August and October of 1940, during which 198 tons of bombs were dropped. Some 176 people were killed and around 680 were wounded. One remarkable story to come out of this terrible time was that of Second Lieutenant Sandy Campbell of the Royal Engineers Bomb Disposal Company. Campbell was called to deal with an unexploded bomb that had fallen at the Triumph Engineering Company works at Canley. It was soon ascertained that the bomb he was attempting to defuse was fitted with a delayed-action fuze which was impossible to remove from the bomb. Rather than leaving the bomb in situ, he had it transported to a safer location. This was done by loading the live bomb onto the back of a lorry, where he lay next to the bomb so that he could hear if it began ticking and could warn the lorry driver to stop and run for cover. Having transported the bomb to a safe distance he was able to dispose of it with no loss of life or injury to anyone. Sadly, this brave man was killed the next night while attempting to defuse another bomb. Sandy Campbell was posthumously awarded the George Cross for his actions of 17 October 1940.

Whilst the Luftwaffe bomber crews continued their night attacks with varying degrees of ferocity, November was to witness the fall of one of the Luftwaffe's leading fighter aces. On 28 November 1940, Major Helmut Wick of JG 2 returned from a sortie to Cherbourg-Querqueville, He immediately instructed that his Messerschmitt Bf 109E-4 be refuelled and rearmed. Along with his wingman, Major Wick took off at 4.10pm and headed out to the vicinity of the Isle of Wight. He spotted a flight of RAF Spitfires and began to climb to initiate a favourable position from where to attack. Climbing to altitude above the unsuspecting Spitfires and, selecting one of the enemy machines, he made the classic high-speed dive attack. As he closed in on his prey, he opened fire with his two 20mm cannons and two 7.92mm machine guns and shot down Free French pilot Pilot Officer Paul A. Baillon of No. 609 Squadron RAF, in Spitfire R6631. Just a matter of minutes later Wick himself ended up in the gunsight of twelve-victory ace Flight Lieutenant John Dundas, also of 609 Squadron. It is also possible that Pilot Officer Eric Marrs and Polish pilot Zygmunt Klein of No. 234 Squadron contributed to Wick's shooting down. In the melee that followed, fellow JG 2 fighter pilot Rudolf Pflanz witnessed a Bf 109 being shot down by one of the Spitfires. Pflanz recalled seeing the pilot baling out then seeing the Bf 109 hit the water and vanish, leaving an oily slick on the surface. Pflanz then shot down the Spitfire that followed the Bf 109 into the sea. The Spitfire pilot was Flight Lieutenant John Dundas who was shot down with the shout of victory still on his lips. The Spitfire sank below the waves with no sign of Dundas having exited the aircraft. Pflanz then circled and noted that the Bf 109 pilot was bobbing around like a cork in the water but had managed to inflate his emergency dingy; he then watched him clamber into it out of the freezing-cold Channel water. As the sky began to darken that late afternoon the Bf 109s turned for home, leaving their comrade behind in his dingy. It was only after arriving back at the airfield in France that Rudolf Pflanz discovered that the Bf 109 pilot in the water was his comrade, Helmut Wick. What became of Wick after climbing into his dingy is a mystery as he was never seen again. With the onset of a frost, the weather that late afternoon of 28 November 1940 was very windy. The icy waters of the English Channel where Wick found himself would have been choppy and far from ideal for a dingy for any protracted length of time. It is possible that despite having been able to inflate his dingy, Wick, having been immersed in the cold water and exposed to the elements, might have perished from hypothermia. It is also possible that had Wick survived into the night, his dingy might well have got waterlogged due to the choppy seas and he could have capsized and drowned.

The loss of Major Wick hit the Luftwaffe fighter arm very hard indeed. Wick was an experienced fighter pilot who fully understood fighter tactics, with an impressive tally of fifty-six aerial victories. Adolf Galland said of Wick:

> Helmut was a good man and cared about those under his command. He was also an honourable fighter pilot who believed that despite the fact that we were fighting a war, honour should still be observed in the air. He met the fighter pilot's death, and this had a sobering effect on all those who knew him and also those just coming into the fighter groups to gain experience. I heard them grumble, 'If someone like

Wick can be shot down, what are our chances of getting out of this?' All you could do was learn from it and I think he just got carried away with the moment and failed to watch his back and got caught. It was just luck. His wingman shot down his assailant, but we lost a very good pilot and very good leader. That is never a good thing for any fighter unit. If a leader is lost, morale can suffer as a result. I always warned the pilots under my personal command to never take your eyes of your arse, no matter what the situation; it takes just a second for an enemy to get on your tail and shoot you out of the sky – that is what air combat is like. It was always better to break off an attack and live to fight another day than to end up dead.

# Chapter 10

# Death Awaits the Unwary

Aside from the threat of being shot down by the enemy in air-to-air combat, there were other less-understood dangers that were ever-present threats particularly to the less-experienced airmen of the Luftwaffe. Perhaps one such example is the death of 21-year-old Gefreiter Richard Riedel, a fighter pilot serving with 2/JG 3 in November 1940. Riedel had only received his posting earlier in the month and his sister Ingrid recalled how excited he was about joining this fighter unit but was also very nervous. Richard had trained at the Jagdfliegerschule 1 (No. 1 Flying School) based at Meersburg in south-western Germany and had learned his trade on the Heinkel He 72B, one of four training aircraft he had qualified in before going on to the Messerschmitt Bf 109E-4. From what information I was able to glean from Ingrid, Richard had by all intents made a smooth and trouble-free transition to flying the Bf 109 and had achieved good reports for both his basic handling of the type and of course the all-important aerial gunnery. Having received his posting to 2/JG 3, Richard, like many of the new pilots, was anxious to experience some action.

He didn't have to wait long and on 17 November 1940 Gefreiter Riedel, *Erkennungsmarke* (service number) 55569/20, took off in Messerschmitt Bf 109E-4 *Werke* no. 4898 coded 'Black 8' with twenty other Bf 109s on a high-altitude fighter sweep across the Channel and over the south of England. They were ranging free and looking for any targets that might present themselves. RAF Spitfires had been vectored towards an area of possible enemy air activity and were soon visible to the German fighters flying at much higher altitude. The formation Richard was flying with immediately initiated their attack and dived down upon the Spitfires who were in the process of attempting to climb up around the rear of the German fighters. Richard pushed the control stick forward and dived towards the Spitfires. Gefreiter Werner Messner of 1/JG 3 had made it his task to take the young Riedel under his wing and look out for him and recalled of the following events:

> I was in Riedel's section and as he dived, I followed. I noticed the enemy had begun to break away hard to the right in an effort to thwart our attack. I was not in any position to fire and so I pulled up, hoping to regain some altitude and select a target where I had the advantage of height and surprise. I noticed Riedel had continued his dive, so I called out over the radio for him to pull up now. I knew if he failed to do so he was going to crash. The response to my warning was garbled and filled with static as if the radio was breaking up. I could hear the sounds of erratic breathing one might suffer due to either fear or exertion. Before I could even shout out another warning, I saw the faint impact of his aircraft hitting the ground; this occurred at approximately 3:30pm. Despite experiencing problems with icing up, I dived down and flew a couple of circuits to see if I could spot a parachute, any sign that Riedel had got out of that Messerschmitt, but I could see no parachutes in the sky at all. After a few more minutes we turned for home. On return to the airfield, a report was made regarding Richard Riedel and what I and several other pilots had witnessed and so he was listed as missing and not killed in action as we were not certain until news was relayed back from the Red Cross. In my heart I knew he was dead; I never saw him bale out and I never saw any parachute. Yes, I was sad about it as he was a very likeable young man; he was good mannered, well spoken and had obviously been raised well by his parents. I felt desperately sorry for the terrible news they were going to receive in the coming days. He was soon replaced as other young men filtered out of flying schools and soon he was forgotten as just another casualty of the air war, but yes, I remember him well and I never forgot him even though I only knew him for a short period of time before he was killed.

This account by Werner Messner is unique and it is with thanks to Richard Riedel's sister, Ingrid, who put me in touch with Messner that this small, yet significant piece of information has finally been published after the passing of many decades.

This leads to the question of what happened to Richard Riedel that fateful day in November. From an examination of the wreckage retrieved during the excavation of the crash site at Melon Farm, Ivychurch, Kent, by Tony Graves and John Tickner of the London Air Museum in 1974, it was concluded that Riedel was not lost as a result of being shot down as no projectile holes were found in any of the remaining wreckage.

What has to be taken into consideration if all other factors such as enemy action, engine and instrument failure are ruled out, are factors such as weather conditions on the day and of course the aircraft's flight profile shortly before it crashed. On 17 November 1940, the weather was freezing cold at ground level and would have been significantly colder at altitude. Yet as none of the other Bf 109s experienced any serious problems with ice forming on their control surfaces, this has to be ruled out as a possible cause of the crash. This doesn't imply that there weren't problems associated with freezing temperatures and icing up at high altitude as some of the pilots did complain about their guns freezing up and failing to fire at the critical moment.

When one examines aircraft design of the 1940s, it soon becomes apparent that despite the technological advances made in aviation, these were still very much pioneering years where piston-engine fighter designs were concerned. As a result, much of the actual physics of flight were still not fully understood. It was not until much later when experiments were conducted into high-speed aircraft research that the invisible and sometimes dangerous forces exerted upon an aircraft in certain flight profiles became evident. The most dangerous phenomena occurred when high-speed monoplane aircraft were put into high-speed vertical dive profiles from high altitude. The high speeds attained in a dive caused air pressure to build along the leading edges of the wings, leading to total failure of the aircraft's controls. This high-speed phenomenon became known as 'Lock Up'. As the aircraft's dive speed increased, it would become almost inverted to the point where recovery was impossible. A pilot finding himself in this potentially fatal situation could not just bale out. Attempting to bale out of an aircraft into an airflow of 400–500mph would almost certainly be fatal even if it were possible to get out. The Messerschmitt Bf 109 E-4 could easily exceed the indicated 700kph (434.96mph) of its airspeed indicator in a dive and it is very likely that Riedel fought desperately with the control stick of his Bf 109 as it hurtled earthward to oblivion. Werner Messner agreed:

> Yes, I think our comrade Richard Riedel simply dived down too fast; the pressures acting upon the control surfaces of his Bf 109 would have been immense. Of course, today we understand all of these things but back then we had no idea of the dangers we faced, things such as Lock Up and the Sonic Wall as they called it. Looking back, our training was not as good as people think it was. For example, I did not receive any instruction on blind flying where you flew using your flying instruments only. If you flew into a cloud bank it was all too easy to become disorientated; there were no instruction cards in the aircraft for you to refer to either – nothing. So yes, each time we took off on a sortie, we faced deadly dangers even if we saw no combat.

# Chapter 11

# Developments in Luftwaffe Armament, 1941

It was in 1941 when the results of extensive research, testing and development came to fruition in the arena of Luftwaffe barrelled armament, with the arrival of a new weapon designed specifically for aircraft use. The weapon in question was designed and developed by Waffenfabrik Mauser AG of Oberndorf, Germany. Mauser, which had supplied the Kaiser's army with its standard infantry rifle in the First World War, had itself fallen victim to the political and infrastructural chaos that had blighted Germany over the years following the Great War when it barely existed as a manufacturer of weaponry. Upon Hitler's rise to power and the Nazi government's financing of weapons development and production, Mauser was among the first German weapon producers to undergo expansion. The company was most notable for the design and manufacture of infantry rifles and semi-automatic small arms which, in terms of quality, reliability, accuracy and build, were considered among the very best in the world.

Mauser's venture into the field of automatic weapons specifically for aircraft use was in 1935 when Mauser was awarded the requisition for the design and development of an aircraft gun around a new 15mmx96 high-velocity cartridge. The cartridge in question consisted of a grey, lacquered steel case 96mm in length with a rim diameter of 25.2mm and body diameter of 25.1mm. The idea behind lacquering steel ammunition cases with a clear lacquer solution during the final production process served two purposes: (a) as an aid against corrosion of the steel ammunition casing while in storage and (b) the lacquer aided the extraction process of the fired casing from the gun breech. The case contained 24 grams of propellant charge. Three main types of 15mm cartridge were developed: (a) an APT/72 (armour-piercing tracer) fitted with a tungsten-cored projectile with a tracer element in its base; the APT projectile was painted black with a red band, (b) an HET/57 (high-explosive tracer) which was painted yellow with a screw-in-type impact fuze in a threaded nose cavity and an APCR/52 (armour-piercing composite rigid) round. The APCR rigid, like the APT projectile, contained a core of tungsten alloy that was enclosed in a light alloy body which remained enclosed in the projectile body until impact. All three projectile types were approximately two and a half inches (63.5mm) in length. The complete 15mm round was 145mm in length; its correct designation was 15x96 Mauser. The muzzle velocity and kinetic energy achieved at the target attained with the three types of 15x96 cartridge were:

- APT/72 850 metres per second producing a muzzle energy of 26,000 joules
- HET/57 960 metres per second producing a muzzle energy of 26,300 joules
- APCR/52 1,030 metres per second producing a muzzle energy of 27,600 joules

Electrical priming of the ammunition was also incorporated into the design of the 15mm gun, though initial versions utilized percussion priming. Electrical priming was a requirement of the specification due in part to the fact that the new weapon would almost certainly be selected as a forward-firing armament possibly required to fire through the propeller arc of an aircraft. Electrical priming still required a pin to initiate the propellant charge of the cartridge, yet detonation was achieved not so much from the striking force of the firing pin but from the electrical current passing through the pin itself. The action chosen for the new 15mm gun was identical to an infantry light machine gun that Mauser had been working on. Operating on the short recoil principle, with a rotating bolt head for locking, the gun was belt-fed ammunition via a metal disintegrating push-out-type linked belt relying on the in-flight airflow of the aircraft for cooling during firing. The rifling arrangement in the gun barrel consisted of eight grooves in a right-hand twist with one turn in sixteen inches. The 15mm gun was a compact and relatively lightweight weapon at 42.8 kilograms yet in its 15mm guise would see limited service as a fighter gun despite its reliability and impressive muzzle velocity of up to 1,006 metres per second (3,300ft/s), which was quite considerable for a weapon of its day, and rate of fire of 650 to 700 rounds per minute. The weapon discharged a 93lb (42kg) weight of shot, much higher than an MG 17 or MG 131 and was more effective overall than the old 20mm Oerlikon MG FF cannon which fired a projectile of greater mass. The 15mm MG 151 had an effective range of 1,000 metres, offering a useful stand-off range over the 20mm Oerlikon MG-FF which would however continue in service until the war's end in 1945. The 15mm Mauser gun was given the service designation 15mm MG 151. The MG 151 denotes *Maschinengewehr* (machine gun) 15mm calibre and the '1' at the end the first model of the weapon.

The 15mm Mauser MG 151 has often wrongly been referred to as a cannon. With no disrespect intended, the 15mm MG 151 was nothing more than a heavy machine gun conceived to perhaps find a compromise between the high rate of fire of the machine gun and the destructive power of the 20mm cannon. If this was the case, then the 15mm gun achieved what its designers had set out to accomplish. Static firing tests on the ground proved very satisfactory and as a result the new 15mm MG 151 gun was proposed as the main gun armament for the Messerschmitt Bf 109F-2 fighter which was just entering service in 1941. The new 15mm weapon itself was, however, only ever intended as an intermediary in response to Rheinmetall Borsig's work on their new 13mm MG 131 heavy machine gun. There were initial concerns among Luftwaffe fighter pilots over the proposed choice of calibre for the Mauser MG 151. There was universal consensus that any weapon below the calibre of 20mm was wholly insufficient for air-to-air combat. Despite these concerns development of the new gun went ahead. As the Messerschmitt Bf 109F was unveiled to a select group of fighter pilots, which included Adolf Galland, it was met with a mixed response. Galland recalled:

> I was very impressed with the cleaner, sleeker lines of the Bf 109F, and one knew instinctively that it was a progression from the E model we had grown so accustomed to. It had a better engine and, overall, the specification was met with my personal approval until I noticed the lack of any wing guns. I asked, 'Where are the wings guns? Are there no wing guns?' The Messerschmitt representative seemed momentarily embarrassed and he quickly pointed out that

> there were the two cowling-mounted MG 17 machine guns above the engine as with the E model and a new 15mm 'cannon' firing through the centre of the engine. At that point I felt disappointed, I knew that the excluded wing guns would limit the combat effectiveness of some pilots.

Walter Rath was another fighter pilot attending the unveiling of the new Messerschmitt fighter and recalled:

> I liked the look of the new 109F and although there were little improvements in the cockpit of the aircraft, which was still too small in my opinion, it was a good improvement performance-wise over the older E-series Messerschmitt fighters. It was only when I examined the small muzzle aperture at the centre of the propeller that I felt my heart sink. I politely informed the smartly dressed, proud-looking man from Messerschmitt, 'This is not a cannon; this is a machine gun!' It did not take an aeronautical genius to work out that the small muzzle opening was not that of a 20mm cannon. When you observe the muzzle opening of a 20mm cannon for example, you stand there in amazement and think to yourself, *You could fire an egg through that hole.* I questioned the type of weapon, its ammunition, range and muzzle velocity and despite the Messerschmitt man giving me glowing reports of its usefulness, I was not convinced at all and I thought of it as a backward step. I was hoping that as with the E model there would also be the two 20mm wing cannons. I thought, *How am I going to fight effectively in this aircraft with such a light armament?* No, I had my reservations about the Bf 109F right at that moment, but I had little choice but to test it out in combat and see how I and the other pilots fared with the type. My only dislike of this early F type was its lightweight armament. The F was very effective, especially against the Spitfires and Hurricanes of the RAF and the calibre of the 15mm gun was soon increased to 20mm. However, I must say that this work was not carried out as a result of complaints from the pilots but due to a more worrying technical issue.

The technical issue which Rath refers to was of course the excessive wear and subsequent reduced life of the 15mm gun barrels due to its very high muzzle velocity. After a relatively short period of use, the 15mm gun barrels got worn out and required replacement. This technical issue proved expensive and was not cost effective, forcing Mauser to reconsider their MG 151 design.

Erich Boerschelle, another Luftwaffe fighter pilot who had flown the Bf 109E in the Battle of Britain, remarked of the F model's 15mm gun:

> The new 15mm gun had exceptional muzzle velocity and I was greatly impressed by this as I was not the best of shots and the more muzzle velocity you have at your disposal the easier it is to aim shots at your target. I liked the fact that the gun was centrally placed, firing through the engine, though the breech of the gun intruded into the cockpit but it was not a huge issue for me at all. In combat the 15mm MG 151 proved itself an excellent weapon. The Soviet aircraft I encountered during the early phases of Operation *Barbarossa* in 1941 were easily destroyed with the two MG 17s and the 15mm gun. I would fire all three guns despite the slight difference in ballistics of the different calibre weapons. My first victim was a Polikarpov fighter; I shot his propeller clean off from behind. The Russian attempted to glide in and land so I shot again into his wing root; the wing came off and he crashed to the ground in a spiral motion. The 15mm projectiles were small compared to those of the 20mm Oerlikon, but the high muzzle velocity greatly compensated for this and both the armour-piercing and explosive rounds were effective in my view.

Günther Rall, the third highest-scoring Luftwaffe fighter ace of the war with 275 aerial victories, recalled of the 15mm Mauser:

> It was an excellent 15mm gun and mounted centrally within the engine of the Bf 109F. I preferred the centrally mounted armament as opposed to wing guns and, of course, those extra wing gun packs they bolted on beneath the wings of the later Messerschmitt fighters in an attempt to increase

> the firepower primarily against Allied bomber aircraft. The only problem with the 15mm MG 151 was the barrels soon became 'shot out'. It fired at such a high velocity that the rifling inside the barrels was soon worn down, effectively turning them into smooth-bore weapons. This was an expensive flaw, yet we were confident that those in charge of weapons procurement would sort out the problems and come back with a solution, which of course they did. They simply retained the 15mm MG 151 design and increased its calibre to 20mm. This meant the 20mm version of the MG 151 would fire a larger-capacity shell as opposed to a 'bullet' but at a reduced muzzle velocity of 710, 720 and 800 metres per second respectively, depending on the type of shell. The 15mm cartridge was longer whereas the 20mm version used a shorter cartridge casing of 82mm in length (minus projectile) yet both 15mm and 20mm MG 151 rounds were of the same overall length. We used to say about these guns that 'less is sometimes more'. We had a lot of debates in the mess about this issue. What hurts the most – the smaller, yet faster, flying pebble or the slower, larger, flying brick? It was the job of our armaments people to find that compromise for us and I feel they did a good job.

In a cannon shell used in air-to-air combat there are two main types of energy which come into play: kinetic and chemical. Kinetic energy is the term applied to the force created by the projectile upon impact with the target whereas chemical energy is normally associated with the rounds filled with high explosive that on bursting release a secondary energy onto the target.

From experience in the air battles of 1940, German tactical doctrine was leaning more to a preference for explosive power in aircraft guns as opposed to high velocity and armour penetration. Yet, as time would reveal, even explosive power was not always a guarantor of success in aerial warfare.

Increasing the calibre of the 15mm Mauser MG 151 gun was not an overly difficult task for the technicians at Mauser. They simply redesigned the gun barrel and chamber to allow for the new 20mmx82 cartridge and its steel link. The 20x82 cartridge itself was created simply by expanding the neck of the cartridge to hold the larger explosive shell used in the MG FF series of ammunition and shortening the length of the cartridge casing. The projectile being longer than the cartridge case itself then matched the same dimensions of the original 15mm-calibre cartridge. The gun barrel of the 20mm weapon was also shortened in an attempt to help reduce the overall weight of the weapon. The 20mm MG 151/20 cannon tipped the scales at 42.7kg, possessed a rate of fire of 750 rounds per minute, a muzzle velocity of 792.48 metres per second (2,600ft/s) and delivered a weight of shot of some 86kg (190lb) per minute. The 20x82 cartridge came with a brown lacquered steel case and, as noted by Günther Rall, it was the same overall length as the original 15mm round. Incidentally, if you took the British 20mm Hispano 20x110 cartridge as used by the RAF and reduced the case length to 82mm, you would have the 20x82 round.

20x82 ammunition came in the following four main types: AP (armour piercing), HEI (high-explosive incendiary), HEIT (high-explosive incendiary tracer) and API (armour-piercing incendiary). The API round developed for the 20mm MG 151 cannon was fitted with an armour-piercing shell designed to penetrate the armoured structure of an enemy aircraft and ignite upon penetration. It contained a phosphorus filling which had the appearance of paraffin and which was ignited by friction and not solely by contact with oxygen. As with all 20x82 MG 151/20 rounds, the API round proved more than adequate for the task it was designed for. As with the 15x96 rounds, the 20x82 rounds were produced with both electrical and percussion primers so they could be utilized in synchronized and non-synchronized applications. The tracer elements in the ammunition were produced for both day and night fighting.

The muzzle velocity and kinetic energy achieved with the 20x82 ammunition were:

- AP: 720 metres per second (2,362.2 feet per second)
- HET: 720 metres per second (2,362.2 feet per second)
- HEIT: 800 metres per second (2,740 feet per second)
- API: 800 metres per second (2,740 feet per second)
- The muzzle energies of the above 20mm MG 151 rounds ranged from 28,800 joules (21,241.79 foot-pounds) to 29,400 joules (21,684.33 foot-pounds)
- Fuzes used with these rounds, with exception of the AP round, were non-self-destruct screw-in-type nose fuzes

When the new 20mm MG 151/20 cannon became available, Luftwaffe armourers were able to remove the 15mm guns from the Bf 109Fs in the field and install the 20mm weapons. There were many fighter pilots who believed the Bf 109F was still too lightly armed, yet the single central-firing 20mm cannon was an improvement as combat with the upgraded armament proved. The 20mm MG 151/20 rounds required far fewer hits to destroy a target. Their explosive and fragmentation effects were also far superior to the 15mm weapon. However, the 20mm AP projectile could only pierce 10–12mm of armour plate at 300 metres and 60° angle, not entirely favourable compared to the 15mm AP projectile's 18mm of armour penetration in the same conditions. The HE round could only manage to pierce 6mm of armour plate at 200 metres, yet these issues were not viewed as any significant disadvantage. The 20mm MG 151/20 had an effective range of 800 metres, 200 metres less than the 15mm gun, thus reducing the stand-off range, but this was viewed as an acceptable trade-off for more destructive power.

When I asked Günther Rall his opinion on the 20mm MG 151/20 cannon, he remarked:

> As I mentioned the 15mm Mauser gun was in many respects an excellent weapon for air-to-air fighting. It was inevitable that the calibre at some point would require some attention and an increase needed. The 15mm guns would have not been adequate against the heavy bombers of the Royal Air Force and the US Air Force. The 15mm gun performed well against the early marks of Allied and Russian fighter aircraft which we encountered and indeed some of the RAF light bomber aircraft such as the Blenheim. It was inevitable also that armour protection would increase along with the size of bomber aircraft, therefore ever-increasing calibres of aircraft cannon would be needed in order to effectively shoot them down. The 20mm MG 151/20 was not outstanding by any means and its muzzle velocity not particularly high, but it was robust and reliable, and it got the job done which is all that matters. Allied fighter aircraft were easily shot down with the 20mm MG 151/20 because, for one thing, they were smaller.
>
> The larger four-engine heavy bombers were completely different. Tackling these heavy bombers was no easy

prospect as they had good defensive weapons on board and getting in close was both difficult and dangerous. As an example, take the American Boeing B-17 Flying Fortress heavy bomber. To shoot one of these down often required twenty hits on target. In order to attain that figure, much ammunition would have to be expended and close approach to the target necessary. The effective ranges of the guns were something you understood yet in reality were of little use to us. Most air combat took place well within the effective ranges of the guns, sometimes just 100 to 200 metres, or even closer than that. We would often fly in so close to the bombers that we could clearly see the faces of the crews inside. We did not carry huge amounts of ammunition, so you can see it was by no means easy. 20mm cannon were most effective against the engines and fuel tanks of the enemy bombers and these were the areas you would fire at. Where the Boeings were concerned, you were best directing your stream of fire at or between the two engines in the wings. The idea was to put the engines out of action and the target would lose speed and altitude, making it easier for you or other aircraft of your flight to shoot them down. Our 20mm explosive shells were also very effective against the defensive gunners of the bomber aircraft. If a 20mm shell exploded in the crew compartment, the resulting steel splinters would kill or injure anyone in close proximity. The MG 151/20 also had a phosphorus-filled incendiary shell which was very effective. The explosive shells would also ignite anything flammable in these areas including fuel, oil and ammunition.

To summarize things, yes, the 20mm Mauser MG 151/20 cannon was a good basic weapon, but I think the 20mm Hispano which the RAF began to use was actually a better cannon than the MG 151/20. You might ask if the MG 151/20 cannon was not so good, how did I personally achieve so many victories? The answer is simple: success in air combat is as much down to your personal tactical thinking as it is reliance on effective weaponry. Tactics, experience and of course a target-rich environment were all

> factors in success. In my view the large batteries of guns we were later forced to take off with were unnecessary. Some Focke-Wulf aircraft were fitted with underwing blisters containing up to two more MG 151 guns per wing; that's eight in total with the four fixed-wing guns. The increase in weight and effect upon the performance of the aircraft put a pilot at an immediate disadvantage. I refused to fly with the extra guns; for me three were enough – one cannon and two machine guns. You didn't need large batteries of guns to get the job done and that has always been my personal view.

With the introduction of the 20mm Mauser MG 151/20 cannon into full production and service, the 15mm gun was almost totally withdrawn from service. It was used in limited quantity and fitted in some marks of the Dornier Do 217E-series medium bombers (usually in a flexible nose mount) and some marks of the Junkers Ju 88 night fighter. Supporters of the 15mm Mauser gun suggested the weapon could be used as a replacement for the old cowling-mounted MG 17 machine guns in the Bf 109. It was even suggested it be used rather than the 13mm heavy machine gun being developed by Rheinmetal Borsig. The two main issues with this idea were (a) there was no way the 15mm Mauser guns would have fitted beneath the tight confines of the Bf 109's nose cowling without modifications being made to the aircraft, particularly the engine cowlings, and (b) the issues regarding excessive barrel wear could not be resolved by the technicians at Mauser. Thus, the 13mm Rheinmetal Borsig MG 131 machine gun was selected as the primary heavy machine gun for Luftwaffe use. It was remarkably compact and light for a heavy machine gun. Though it is not the weight or size of a heavy machine gun that defines it as a heavy machine gun, this factor is entirely down to the calibre of the weapon. Generally, anything below 13mm is considered 'rifle calibre', anything between 13mm and 15mm 'heavy machine gun' and anything between 20mm to 50mm 'cannon'. As cannons fire projectiles with a greater mass than that of a bullet from either a rifle or heavy machine gun, often with a useful payload of explosive filling, it seems only right to point out these basic distinctions.

Another development soon to enter the Luftwaffe's airborne gun inventory was the 13mm Rheinmetal Borsig MG 131 (*Maschinengewehr* MG 131) machine gun. Design work began on the 13mm MG 131 machine gun back in 1938 (alongside Mauser with their 15mm MG 151), as it was clear that the 7.92mm rifle-calibre MG 17 machine guns would soon need replacing in service by a heavy machine gun with greater punch.

At first glance the appearance of the 13mm MG 131 is somewhat misleading. The MG 131 was small, lightweight and very compact for a weapon of its calibre and compared to say a US-manufactured .50 calibre (13mm) Browning heavy machine gun, you can be forgiven for taking this line of thought. Design and development work on the MG 131 quickly gathered momentum and two types of the machine gun were developed and underwent static firing tests. The first was a fixed-mount version designed exclusively for installation in fighter aircraft, while the second was a flexible-mount version intended for use as a defensive armament for bombers. The flexible version of the MG 131 had a pistol grip and trigger arrangement while other refinements were made for turreted installations, both remote and manned. The MG 131 utilized the recoil operation for its action, weighing in at 16.6kg (37lb) and measuring 1.17 metres in length. The cartridge designed for the MG 131 was a new 13mmx64B type manufactured in both brass and steel, utilizing electrical priming. Again, electrical priming was chosen as the weapon was to become the standard synchronized heavy machine gun for German fighter aircraft. The 'B' in the designation for the cartridge refers to the fact that the case was belted, this belt appearing just above the extractor groove of the cartridge base. The muzzle velocity attained was 750 metres per second (2,460 feet per second) with an effective range of 1,800 metres (2,200 yards). The three main 13x64B cartridge types developed for the MG 131, their muzzle velocities, mass and kinetic energy are as follows.

- APT (armour-piercing tracer) projectile mass 38.5 grams, muzzle velocity 710 metres per second, muzzle energy 9,700 joules (7,154.35 foot-pounds)
- API (armour-piercing incendiary) projectile mass 38 grams, muzzle velocity 710 metres per second, muzzle energy 9,580 joules (7,065.85 foot-pounds)
- HEIT (high-explosive incendiary tracer) containing 1.4 grams of PETN (pentaerythritol tetranitrate) and 0.3 grams of thermite, projectile mass 34 grams, muzzle velocity 750 metres per second, muzzle energy 9,560 joules (7,051.09 foot-pounds)

As noted in the table the use of PETN and thermite constituted the explosive/incendiary mix for the 13mm HEIT cartridge. Although limited damage to armour plate was observed during the static firing tests, the damage inflicted on more vulnerable areas of the target aircraft such as wings, fuselage and tail control surfaces was quite impressive for such a compact and lightweight weapon of 13mm calibre. The 13mm explosive bullets easily blew off large areas of sheet alloy skinning, severing internal structure and damaging internal components. Fragmentation from the 13mm explosive bullets was also significant enough to kill or injure anyone in close proximity. The 13x64B rounds were also fitted with intricate screw-in-type nose fuzes, something noticeably absent in all heavy machine-gun ammunition in Allied use in the war.

Despite the introduction of the new 20mm Mauser MG 151/20 cannon and the 13mm Rheinemtal Borsig MG 131 machine gun, there was still considerable room for improvement in the field of airborne gunnery. Success in air-to-air combat demanded ever-increasing amounts of firepower plus a tactically efficient means of delivering it in a rapid and accurate package. Whilst German armaments designers such as Mauser and Rheinmetal Borsig continued working on new designs, utilizing ever-increasing calibres of ammunition and degrees of technical complexity, the progress in the development of the airborne cannon was painfully slow. No more does this issue become so glaringly apparent than in the immediate postwar and early Cold War years.

# Chapter 12

# Our Führer's Folly

Shortly after 0300 hours on Sunday, 22 June1941, 117 German infantry and armoured divisions supported by fourteen divisions of the 3rd and 4th Rumanian Armies and the Hungarian Army Corps, swept into the Soviet Union along a 1,200-mile-wide front. It was an event that would herald the greatest clash of arms in the history of mankind. Operation *Barbarossa*, the invasion of the Soviet Union, was an endeavour fraught with risk and even Hermann Göring had made attempts to dissuade Hitler from going ahead with it. Many of Hitler's senior staff officers and commanders on the ground were also horrified at the prospect of having to fight a war on two fronts. Hitler was of the view that while Britain was not beaten, she was sufficiently subdued and that a massive campaign against a demoralized Bolshevist Russia would lead to its collapse within six weeks, and well in advance of the paralyzing cold of winter. The Führer needed *Lebensraum*, or living space, for his people and although a non-aggression pact had been signed with the Soviets, these, just like other pacts that Hitler had entered into, were not worth the paper they were written on. Hitler, despite 'jumping into bed' with Stalin, viewed the Soviets as an ideological enemy, *Untermensch* or sub-human were terms which would become commonplace in the savagery that would ensue in Russia. The German onslaught would unleash unimaginable barbarity, terror and misery upon the population of Russia; it became a war where no quarter was asked or given.

The Luftwaffe had been preparing for the invasion of Russia since October 1940. The *Ostbausprogramm* (Eastern Construction Programme) had already been instituted by the end of 1940 as Luftwaffe works units and construction material were steadily moved into the occupied Polish territories in readiness for the invasion. By the early spring of 1941 the establishment of aerodromes, fuel supply depots and Flak units were well under way, yet it would not be until April/

May 1941 that preparations to receive combat units began. By mid-June 1941 the Luftwaffe had moved 2,770 frontline combat aircraft to the Eastern Front, from France, Germany and the Mediterranean, including 775 bomber aircraft, 310 Ju 87 Stukas, 830 Bf 109s, 90 Bf 110s and 765 reconnaissance and maritime aircraft, out of a frontline inventory of some 4,300 aircraft.

At the opening of *Barbarossa*, the resources of four *Luftflotten* were committed as follows: Luftflotte 1 under command of Generaloberst Alfred Keller, Luftflotte 2 under command of General Fieldmarschall Albert Kesselring, Luftflotte 4 under command of Generaloberst Alois Lohr and Luftflotte 5 under command of Generaloberst Hans-Jurgen Stumpff. In addition to the powerful reconnaissance force of the Luftwaffe, were the long-range bomber units of KG1, KG3, KG4, 6/KG 30, KG 51, KG 53, KG 54, KG 55, III/KG 76 and KGr.806. Utilizing the fast and versatile Junkers Ju 88A-4 and the Heinkel He 111H-6, these units were mostly concentrated in Fliegerkorps II (Luftflotte 2) in support of the central thrust. The *Zerstörergruppen* and fighter-bombers consisted of aircraft from I and II/ZG 26 and Schnelleskampfgeschwader 210 (fast bomber squadron). A new version of the Messerschmitt Bf 109 was also to enter the fray in the form of the Messerschmitt Bf 109F, an aircraft many regard as the finest version of the Bf 109 series. Work on the new fighter had begun at the beginning of 1940, with preproduction models rolling off the assembly lines at the end of that year. The Bf 109F, or 'Friedrich', was received with great enthusiasm by fighter pilots as it was a considerable improvement on the Bf 109E-4, both faster and more manoeuvrable. In fact, the only gripe many pilots had with the Bf 109F was its lighter armament as discussed in the previous chapter. Adolf Galland admitted: 'I preferred to have the two-wing mounted cannons of the Bf 109E-4, yet here we had this new fighter aeroplane with a superior performance to the E-4 yet a lighter armament. It was something we had to get used to however much we disliked it.'

Günther Rall on the other hand liked the Bf 109F and the new 15mm Mauser MG 151 cannon:

> The 15mm Mauser cannon was not really a cannon, more a machine gun, yet its muzzle velocity was very high at 3,000 feet per second, which was a big improvement from the slower-firing 20mm Oerlikon guns of the Bf 109E-4;

> there were two machine guns fitted too, and all of this armament was positioned compact together in the nose. I liked this set-up as all a pilot had to do was point his aircraft at the target and fire. The excellent 15mm gun was more than adequate to get the job done. So, yes, the Bf 109F was a huge improvement in performance; its handling could still be tricky for a new young pilot, or 'Hare' as they were sometimes known, yet its speed and manoeuvrability were superb.

Operation *Barbarossa* saw the return of the Luftwaffe to its traditional role of supporting the German ground forces. In keeping with the Blitzkrieg principles which had served the Germans so well in the Polish campaign and indeed against France and the Low Countries, the destruction of the Soviet Air Force largely took place on the ground. Those Russian aircraft which did manage to get airborne were quickly dispatched by the superior Bf 109s. By doing so the Luftwaffe inadvertently forced the Russians into focusing on the design, manufacture and production of new aircraft, some of which would later compete admirably against the Bf 109s and Fw 190s in the skies above the Eastern Front.

Heinz Knoke, who was still flying a Bf 109E-4, recalled his eagerness for action against 'the Ivans':

> Yes, we in the fighter groups were eager to get at them [the Russians]. We knew we had the better aircraft and the better pilots and also the element of surprise. It is my belief the Russians were told of our impending plans to attack by the British, yet the Russian leader Stalin dismissed the warnings as hogwash. My first operation was a low-level fighter sweep against a Russian airfield in the opening of the battle. It was all pure textbook: we attacked at treetop height and I saw a Russian anti-aircraft crew jumping onto their gun. As I closed in, I saw the target looming in my gunsight and gave them a good burst with my 20mm cannon and two machine guns. I watched as the rounds struck the target and the gunners who had just mounted their weapon were blown off by the force of the cannon shells exploding. There was not much left of the Ivans after that. I felt satisfied.

> I came back around, firing on aircraft parked on the ground, and again I watched as my cannon fire turned them into matchwood. When we left the airfield, there were fires burning and much wreckage.

The term 'Ivan' as used by Heinz Knoke and other Germans to describe Russian military personnel is a vaguely derogatory reference to Ivan the Terrible, the Grand Prince of Moscow who ruled from 1533 to 1547. It was used in much the same vein as a British Tommy, a German Fritz or a French *poilu*.

The most notable Luftwaffe adversary in the earlier air battles of *Barbarossa* was the Lavochkin-Gorbunov-Gudkov LaGG-3 single-seat fighter. Introduced into service in July 1941, the LaGG-3 was a refinement of the earlier LaGG-1 and was one of the most modern aircraft available to the Soviet fighter arm at the time. The LaGG-3 utilized wooden construction methods, yet it was still overweight and underpowered. It was extremely unpopular with those who had to fly it in combat. The type was plagued by a rash of teething troubles including poor control response, engine prone to overheating, poor hydraulics and defective landing gear, to name a few. The build quality of each aircraft varied from factory to factory, yet it was built rapidly in large numbers in an attempt to match the excellent Bf 109 of the Luftwaffe. The LaGG-3 in some respects suffered from the same lightweight armament of the Bf 109F, being armed with a single 20mm-ShVAK cannon firing through the centre of the engine and a single 12.7mm Berezin BS machine gun mounted above the engine and synchronized to fire through the propeller blades. In combat the LaGG-3 was totally outclassed by the Bf 109E-4 and the Bf 109F. Many Soviet fighter pilots rammed German planes out of sheer frustration at the one-sided nature of the contest.

Christoph Oegen completed his training at fighter school in April 1941 and received his first operational posting with JG 54:

> I was more than ready and felt very aggressive and wanted to gain some experience and test what I had learned in combat. JG 54 was a strong fighter group where many of the top names would gain good scores; in fact, JG 54 had the honour of being the most effective Luftwaffe fighter

> group on the Eastern Front. I saw my first action on 30 June 1941, and claimed my first enemy aircraft, a twin-propeller light bomber; the bombers had been heading out over the town of Daugavpils and to our surprise had no escorting fighters with them. Over the following weeks I claimed four more victories, all single-engine LaGG-3 fighters. What surprised me most about these Russian fighters were just how easily they disintegrated under even the lightest of fire from our guns.

Heinz Knoke concurred:

> The early variants of the new Soviet fighter planes were no match even for the Bf 109E-4 which was an older aircraft. The Bf 109E-4 was far superior in every aspect to the LaGG-3. One thing I learned was that if you chased them and they tried to dive for it, they often ended up crashing into the ground. Their controls were so poor they could rarely be pulled out of a dive; it was ridiculous. The first LaGG-3 I encountered was dispatched with 20mm cannon fire at less than 200 yards range; he just shattered into pieces as my cannon shells found their mark. Those crates were made mostly out of wood and when struck by high-explosive cannon shells they just blew part and fell from the sky. It was a very one-sided battle as we had the better pilots and the better aircraft.

Help for Russia soon arrived under the Lend-Lease programme in which the United States and Britain supplied Russia with fighter aircraft. Listed here are the types and quantities of US and British aircraft sent to the USSR under Lend-Lease:

- Bell P-39 Airacobra: 5,007 supplied by the US of which 4,719 reached Russia
- Bell P-63 Kingcobra: 2,421 supplied by the US.
- Curtiss P-40 Kittyhawk/Tomahawk: 2,425 units supplied by the US.
- Hawker Hurricane: 2,952 units supplied by Britain

As the war in the East unfolded small numbers of North American P-51 Mustang fighters found their way to Russia, along with 195 Republic P-47 Thunderbolts, both supplied by the US and 1,331 British-supplied Supermarine Spitfires.

Of course, there were Soviet pilots who became aces in aircraft such as the Bell P-39 Airacobra which carried a powerful armament for a fighter of its day (one 37mm M4 cannon and four .50-cal machine guns). The British-supplied Hawker Hurricane had already proved itself a worthy opponent of the Bf 109 in the Battle of Britain where the Poles of No. 303 Squadron claimed the highest number of enemy aircraft destroyed during the battle.

The Lend-Lease aircraft, along with the production of home-built fighters such as the LaGG-3, kept Soviet Russia fighting in the air. The Soviets had learned some valuable lessons and while the Soviet Air Force would never enjoy total air superiority until later in 1943, better aircraft were the now in the pipeline.

Gottfried Urquhart was another of the new faces, or 'Hares', fresh from flying training, who joined JG 54 in June 941. He recalled his thoughts on the situation at the time:

> There was a good overall feeling and morale was high as the ground forces were giving the Ivans a good pummelling. There was this genuine feeling that the task of invading Russia would be completed far quicker than the commanders had expected. With hindsight, these celebrations were a little premature though. I had read a book about Napoleon's attempted invasion of Russia and thought, *All the Ivans have to do is wait until winter*, which will be the critical time for them to go onto the offensive, just as they did against Napoleon and the French. I won't say I felt uneasy being in Russia, but I understood enough about the Ivans to know that they would not give up easily. They dismantled whole factory units and pulled them out of reach of our bombers where they would reconstruct them and continue building aircraft, tanks and other weapons.
>
> When I arrived, we began flying patrols and it was normal for our squadron leader to let us have a crack at an enemy aircraft if we encountered any. For us 'Hares' it was merely sport, very one-sided indeed, yet it gave us time to

gain some experience and improve our gunnery. I remember going out on fighter sweeps across the vast expanse of the Soviet Union looking for victims or any ground targets that presented themselves. I would look down and see where our troops were resting up and I felt sorry for them. Our ground forces had it much harder than we did in the air; it was better to be a fighter pilot than be on the ground with the Heer, particularly as summer began to give way to the autumn and winter. At least we would have our relatively cosy huts with fires inside to sleep at night in the winter; the Heer didn't have that luxury, and to think I almost volunteered for the army before deciding to stick with the flying that I had enjoyed so much in the Hitler Youth.

My first air-to-air victims were LaGG-3 fighters. These were easy to shoot down – they never stood a chance against the Bf 109. I also claimed two bombers, one of which was destroyed while the other was a probable which flew on smoking heavily. These were claimed on 30 June in a fight that turned into a turkey shoot for JG 54. I still couldn't help that dreadful feeling, that despite our successes, we were going to have to pay for it all sometime later. I never really shared my thoughts with the other pilots apart from Christoph Oegen whom I became friends with. Christoph was more relaxed about it than me; he would say, 'Oh for God's sake, Gottfried, just be aggressive, show them no mercy at all and soon this fight will be over.' I said to Christoph, 'What do you mean be aggressive and show them no mercy?' Then he revealed to me that he had shot a number of Ivans as they parachuted to safety from their burning aircraft. He had not allowed them to rejoin the fight against us and as far as I know, nothing was mentioned about what he had done from anyone up above [commanders].

When I asked Christoph Oegen about these alleged attacks against Russian aircrews in their parachute harnesses, his response was quite explicit:

We were not sent out to Russia to piss about; shoot them down so they could jump out of their planes and return to possibly kill us later, because there's no doubt if the boot had been on the other foot, they would have done that to us. So, yes, if I saw Ivans parachuting, I would wherever possible give them a squirt into their parachute canopies; there was no way they would ever survive at those kinds of heights hundreds of feet off the ground. I didn't see it as being unfair as many did; we were there to fight and to win the war not to piss about with any false notions of honour in the air, whatever they said about it. I didn't see anything wrong with it. Do you think a Heer soldier would let an Ivan run away if he caught him without his gun in a trench? Of course not if he had any sense – he would shoot him dead, one less Ivan to worry about. I am sorry if this flies in the face of what you believe or you think. I am ranting, but this is how it was for me. I went out there to fly and to fight and win the war. You can't be sentimental and fight a war, you know.

When I asked Heinz Knoke for his thoughts on the practice of shooting enemy pilots in their parachute harnesses, I found that he held the opposite view:

> Breakdowns in discipline in the air did occur frequently. I heard that the Poles in the Battle of Britain were likely to shoot German pilots if they baled out. I personally did not and would never have condoned this practice. The problem was once a fight was underway, it was difficult to keep an eye on those pilots under my command who I knew would likely do something like that. I would be too busy trying to fight and to survive to watch what everyone else was doing. If I saw it happen then I would have severely reprimanded or even grounded any pilot I caught shooting a parachutist. My problem then was that higher command weren't interested in these things and they would probably have let the individual off the hook on the grounds of his aggressiveness and that we had a war to win, and we needed every pilot to help achieve victory. I personally never witnessed any man of my squadron doing this in Russia and if I had I would have

> beaten him when we were back on the ground, for sure. It probably did happen but I did not personally ever witness such an event. I did not condone those kinds of action in the air. To me, destroying the aircraft was the objective, never the individual pilot flying it. If he managed to get out, I was happy; if I saw him crash to his death, it did not make me feel good, as it could have easily been me. That's how I felt about it.

Karl Voght was somewhat relieved to find himself back in what he termed 'familiar military territory' from June 1941. StG 77 found itself operating in support of Army Group Centre and Army Group South carrying out bombing attacks on Soviet positions as part of a close air support package for the Heer. Voght recalled of this time:

> After the operations against England, the invasion of Russia seemed like a break, to me anyway. The operations were not unduly taxing, and we at least had mostly unlimited protection from our fighters, not that the threat in the air was that great. The greatest threat we faced was primarily from ground fire. The Soviets employed masses of Flak, especially to defend high-value targets such as supply dumps. These were defended by 12.7mm machine guns which were effective at low level, then there were sometimes cannons which ranged in calibre from 25-, 37-, 45-, 76- to 85mm. Our Stuka was a strong, sturdy aircraft but if you took too many hits from explosive shells then you could easily be brought down. My last operation was due to a lucky high-explosive round which took my port undercarriage clean off. Other than that, we had suffered no engine damage or injury to ourselves and had destroyed our target. My problem then was getting the bird down in one piece with one missing wheel. My gunner and I had considered getting some height then baling out of the bird, but we decided to try and make a crash-landing at the airfield. I guess this was my biggest mistake, but I felt I should at least try to rescue the bird. As I approached the airfield, I dropped the throttle and let the airspeed drop right down and guessed I could go in and the

worst that would happen was we'd get spun around a bit. As we neared the ground the starboard wheel touched down and my port wingtip began scraping the ground; we were almost at a stop in this position when the wingtip must have struck a rock or something in the ground. This turned the Stuka right over onto its back and in the resulting impact with the ground, I suffered a back injury. My gunner was fine and did not have a mark on him. As I was removed from the bird and placed on a stretcher, I said to him, 'Not a scratch on you, you lucky, lucky bastard!' He said, 'I will see you after your holiday and give my love to all those frauleins back home.'

I smiled but soon felt that searing pain in the middle of my back and knew I had done some damage there, but never thought for one moment that it would be serious enough to ground me and end my career as a flyer. In the event, I was assessed by the doctors and, sure enough, they told me I would not be fit enough to fly again due to probable damaged discs in my spine. I was laid up in a hospital bed behind the front where some of the boys from my unit visited me. After two days I was flown out to a hospital in Germany on a Junkers Ju 52 with other wounded airmen and soldiers. On the flight back the wounded army lads kept giving me cigarettes and asking me if I was comfortable and things like that. They really appreciated us Stuka boys and it was heart-warming. At the hospital in Berlin, I underwent an operation on my back. They did the repair work on my damaged bones then stitched me back up and I had to lie down for several weeks in a bed before I could even consider any therapy to get me up and about again properly.

It was while at the hospital I met a girl, a young nurse who introduced herself as Klara, and she told me she would be caring for me. I was very pleased about it as she was as pretty as a picture, a real German maiden in every sense. It was during this time that I told her all about my air service; usually, she would sit in the chair next to my bed at night and listen to me talk, then she would tell me about her family and where she had grown up – just normal chit-chat really. I then plucked up the courage to ask her if she was romantically linked to anyone, to which she replied, 'You mean, do I have a boyfriend or am I married? Well, of course I have had boyfriends, but I am not married, and I don't have a boyfriend at this time as I have been far too busy for that, what with all you boys coming back from the war.' I left it there as did not want her to think I was being nosy or anything, but as the weeks went by, I became braver with this lovely young lady and eventually I plucked up the courage to ask her out for dinner when I was fit again. When I asked her, she just smiled and told me, 'I will have a think about it.' My recuperation period seemed to go on forever but after what seemed an age I was up and about and walking with the aid of two sticks. I still had to take things very slowly and not put any strain on my back.

While recuperating, I had time to contemplate what I was going to do. I would never be able to fly again and thought maybe about becoming an instructor as I had plenty of experience to teach young men entering flying schools. I discussed this with an officer friend of mine during one of his visits to the hospital and he thought it would be a better prospect than being a desk soldier and said he would forward my request. With glowing reports from my commanding officer, I was given a recommendation to teach bombing tactics at the nearest training unit and my application was accepted. I still had a little way to go with my recovery, but this gave me a renewed sense of purpose. I didn't want to be a cripple sitting around at home doing nothing and staring out the window day in day out.

It was a great moment leaving the hospital where it seemed I had been living for an age. I was allotted a ground-floor apartment as I did not wish to go to my parents; I preferred being independent despite my parents' protests. Besides, I had desires on taking Klara out for dinner and although my intentions were entirely honourable, I preferred to take the young lady back to my own space following dinner, if she so wished. I could not have done that at home with my parents as they would have fussed like a couple of old hens.

My first dinner date with Klara was wonderful; we went into Berlin and enjoyed a lovely meal with some drinks. At that time Berlin was not subject to the violent air raids that were to come, and our outing was undisturbed. At the end of the night Klara accompanied me back home to make sure I got there safely, her nursing instincts still very much apparent. It was on the doorstep of my little apartment that we shared a first kiss before she left. I saw her whenever possible after that and we usually went out and had dinner or just went out for drinks.

It was not until nearly three months after I had begun seeing her that she stayed the night with me in my apartment. When I began working as an instructor our time together was very valuable as we couldn't always get together as our work schedules sometimes clashed. I remember Klara saying that more and more wounded boys were coming back from the fighting in Russia. Many had lost arms and legs, and some would be wheelchair-bound for the rest of their lives. It was also some months after my recovery I learned that my gunner who had teamed up with another pilot of our unit had been posted as missing. It hit me hard as he was a fine fellow, but he and his pilot were never seen again; what happened to them no one knew. All I was told was that they had vanished in poor weather whilst on an operation in early September of '41.

The *Stukageschwader* continued to be a thorn in the Soviet side as the war in the east developed. Perhaps one of the most remarkable moments in *Stukageschwader* history took place on 16 September 1941. This was the day that the quiet, unassuming master of the Ju 87 Stuka, Hans Ulrich Rudel of StG 2 (the 'Immelmann' wing), sank the Soviet battleship *Marat*. On that day, Rudel's aircraft was one of thirty Ju 87s, an entire Stuka wing, that was ordered to attack the *Marat* following aerial reconnaissance reports of the ship being spotted in open water. The weather that day was far from favourable for any air activity, but the attack was considered such a high priority that the order to go in was given despite the bad weather. When the wing arrived over the target area, the Flak coming up from the ground was reported as heavy, one pilot recalling that 'the anti-aircraft shells were bursting like the clap of doomsday'. The *Marat* appeared through a gap in the clouds and Hauptmann Ernst Steen was first to dive into the attack. Rudel followed, rolling his Stuka over into a steep dive as he followed Steen in. Rudel watched as Steen's bomb scored a near miss, then released his bomb and scored a direct hit. The 1000lb high-explosive bomb hit the deck of the battleship which erupted into flames. Anti-aircraft fire was intense, following Rudel up into the cloud cover. Rudel was elated in the belief that he had sunk the Russian battleship, yet his mood turned to anger and disbelief when later informed that the *Marat* had survived his bomb and was now awaiting repairs at Kronstadt harbour.

Not content with defeat, on 22 September, Rudel followed Steen into a second attack on the *Marat*. The anti-aircraft fire this time was some of the worst Rudel and Steen had ever encountered in Russia. Rudel was determined that his quarry would not escape this time and he dived to within 900 feet of the ship before releasing his new 2,000lb high-explosive bomb. So engrossed in the task of hitting his target he completely forgot that the 2,000lb bomb he had just released had a fragmentation radius of over 3,000 feet. He recalled what happened next:

> The enemy ship was plumb in the centre of my sights. My Ju 87 kept perfectly steady as I dived and she didn't swerve an inch. I had the feeling that to miss at this point was impossible. Then I saw the *Marat* as large as life in front of me. I could see the sailors running across her deck carrying ammunition. I pressed the bomb-release button on my control stick and pulled with all my strength. I blacked out momentarily and when I regained consciousness, it was to the sound of my gunner Scharnovski excitedly saying, 'She is blowing up, sir.'

November 1941 was a miserable time, particularly for the German ground forces in Russia. With the onset of the winter, temperatures plummeted and the winds increased. In some areas the temperature dropped to as low as –40°C. In such brutal conditions, the worst Russian winter in a century, the German war machine ground to a halt. A corporal on the ground remarked:

> At first, we had the torrential rains to contend with; these rains were so heavy that everything turned to a strength-sapping mud. Tanks sank in six feet or more of mud in some places, mules attempting to pull artillery wagons sank and were buried alive along with many unfortunate soldiers. Then came the winter – we had been told the fighting in Russia would be over by this time – but here we were still fighting and without adequate cover or protection from the elements. Everything froze up, the guns, the tanks and those men who had no proper clothing for the weather; they endured a slow, agonizing death in these conditions. Then the Russians went on the offensive. I knew at that point we were in a lot of trouble and in for a lot of pain.

Then came the untimely death by suicide on 17 November 1941 of the remarkable yet troubled Ernst Udet who had been a colonel-general of the Luftwaffe up until his demise. Udet had been instrumental in the development of dive-bombing techniques. However, it was Udet who impeded the Luftwaffe when at his recommendation all new fighters and bombers should be built with the capability to dive-bomb ground targets. It was this recommendation of Udet's that not only slowed down German aircraft production but also added unnecessary weight to the many new types then entering Luftwaffe service, by removing any speed and manoeuvrability advantages the original specification might have possessed. So, not everyone in the Luftwaffe was saddened by his sudden death. Udet had made enemies with individuals such as Generalfeldmarschall Erhard Milch who was in charge of aircraft production. Both Milch and Udet made no secret of the bad blood that existed between them, but it is believed the pressures of the war was the main factor in Udet taking his own life with a pistol bullet to the head.

Another more serious blow to the Luftwaffe came on 22 November 1941 with the death of the fighter ace Oberst Werner Mölders. Following the suicide of Udet, Mölders was ordered to attend Udet's state funeral in Berlin. During the flight to Berlin in a Junkers Ju 52 transport, the aircraft experienced engine problems and was forced to crash-land, at Breslau, in the Free State of Prussia. Mölders was killed along with two other passengers. He was 28 years old and had a total of 101 aerial victories to his credit. Although Mölders had effectively been grounded prior to his death for propaganda reasons and had taken up the post of Inspector of Fighters of the Luftwaffe, it is feasible that in the latter stages of the war Molders might have seen a return to operational flying had he lived.

It seemed 1941 was turning out to be a year of folly for the Wehrmacht.

Following the attack of Germany's Axis ally Japan on the US Navy at Pearl Harbor on 7 December 1941, the United States declared war against Japan. On 11 December, Germany and its other Axis ally Italy declared war against the United States who reciprocated. Many Germans saw this as a bad omen; not only had Germany failed to subdue the British, but they were also now facing the might of Soviet Russia *and* the industrial power of the US. Gottfried Urquhart recalled his thoughts at the news of the US declaration of war:

> It didn't take a genius to work out that perhaps we had bitten off a lot more than we could chew. I recall thinking, *Fucking hell, not only are we at war with the English and Russians, but now America is also joining the war against us*. The odds were steadily stacking up in the Allies' favour even this early on in the war. The invasion of Russia had not gone to plan at all; serious tactical cock-ups were made at the expense of the objectives set for the fighting men. Far too much interference from Hitler cost thousands of lives. I hadn't totally dismissed our chances of winning the war but looking at the situation in a realistic fashion, one couldn't help but have some serious doubts. Other fighter pilots shared my concerns; we spoke about them privately, never in earshot of the officers. 1941 was a year that I will always remember as being our Führer's folly.

# Chapter 13

# Ducks in a Barrel

A balmy summer's evening in 1942 turned out to be a lively one for some residents of the Derbyshire and Peak District areas when their peace was shattered by the roar of the engines of a pair of low-flying Junkers Ju 88s which had taken off from their airfield in France en route to bomb the de Havilland propeller factory at Horwich near Bolton. The Ju 88s made their way north up the Irish Sea specifically to avoid any anti-aircraft defences in the Merseyside area. Crossing the coast near Southport, the two aircraft set course for Bolton, having missed their original target. Both were flying at high speed at treetop height to avoid detection by British radar. The aircraft then entered the airspace of Lancashire and Cheshire, arriving over Woodford airfield where Lancaster bombers were being assembled. The two planes circled the airfield but neither made any attempt to drop their bombs on the hangars or workshops and rather mysteriously turned away on a course for the Pennines. As the two planes roared towards New Mills in Derbyshire, a group of young lads were out on the village cricket field when they saw the silhouettes of two low-flying planes coming directly towards them. At first there was no alarm as the group thought they were RAF planes on a low-flying exercise. The lad standing at the crease showed more concern, raising his bat in the air to stop the bowler who was just about to bowl. As the German planes roared overhead the machine-gunner of the one, 20-year-old Unteroffizier Theo Frank, fired at them and a stream of 7.92mm bullets tore up a long line of the turf all the way from cover point to fine leg. The boys threw themselves to the ground, covering their heads and thankfully none was hurt. However, seconds later, an explosion could be heard and smoke was seen rising into the air just beyond the village church. The boys abandoned their game and ran to see what was happening. One of the enemy planes had released a bomb which fell onto a couple of houses, killing two people, and more explosions followed before the two German planes flew on. The villages of New Mills and Hayfield would have been the last clusters of dwellings that the enemy planes would encounter on their course prior to reaching the higher moorland. The one rogue Junkers then fired again on a gas holder and a railway signal box. The bomb aimer, Obergefreiter Horst Wyborny, then released bombs that fell into the River Goyt plus others that demolished two groups of cottages which claimed the lives of eight people. The two planes then climbed over the Peak District hills, and turned south-east on a heading back to their airfield in France. As the planes flew on, the one gunner fired at the windows of Chatsworth House which was being used as a girls' school at the time, before speeding over the open farmland of Nottinghamshire and Lincolnshire.

However, this mini-rampage had not gone unnoticed and soon telephones were ringing both at local police stations and the nearby RAF base. Unluckily for the two enemy planes, four pilots of the Polish 303 Squadron flying Spitfires took off from their airfield at Kirton-in-Lindsay near Scunthorpe at 8.05pm on an interception course. The Poles soon spotted the two German planes and closed in for the attack. Flight Sergeant Mieczyslaw Popek was able to get a good long burst of his eight .303 Browning machine guns before breaking off his attack just twenty yards from the right-hand German plane which happened to be coded M2+BK, the one in which gunner Frank had opened fire on the boys on the cricket pitch. The method of attack utilized by the Polish fighter pilots was typical of their sheer aggression and determination. Unteroffizier Frank fired his machine gun at the attacking Spitfire, scoring hits on its propeller, yet both engines of the Junkers were now ablaze. Within seconds the machine was sent crashing in flames into farm buildings near the village of Wragby and was totally destroyed, the four crewmen killed instantly. The other enemy plane, which had also taken hits, crash-landed in a nearby field. The crew attempted to escape, running away from the aircraft but were soon rounded up by the local Home Guard.

The one Junkers Ju 88 was identified as M2+BK; its crew were Feldwebel Heinz Majer (born 8/9/1914), Obergefreiter Horst Wyborny (born 24/9/1921), Unteroffizier Karl Schachtschneider (born 8/7/1920) and Unteroffizier Theobald Frank (born 3/4/1922). All four are buried in Block 3 at the German Military Cemetery at Cannock Chase, Staffordshire, their grave numbers being 294, 295, 296 and 297.

Why this particular group of young German aircrew was so hellbent on creating so much unnecessary carnage remains unknown. Their indiscriminate use of machine-gun fire along with the death and destruction caused by their bombs only served to further infuriate an already virulently anti-German population.

Another interesting account is that given by Beryl Weller from Birmingham, who recalls a particularly frightening brush with the Luftwaffe. In an interview given in September 1999, Beryl recalled:

> I was 12 at the time and my younger sister was three. Our grandmother lived in Sandy Lane, Aston, Birmingham, and it was not unusual for me, my sister and mother to visit her twice weekly. On this one particular visit to our grandmother's house, we went to The House That Jack Built and Blacks in Newtown Row to buy some summer dresses. We were just leaving Newtown Row when the sirens began to howl; there didn't seem to be any enemy aircraft around so my mother decided we should continue on our way and the all-clear would soon be sounded. It was as we were walking down Park Lane, Aston, towards Aston Cross on the right-hand side of the road, that we saw this German bomber which was flying parallel with Park Lane from Aston Cross direction with all of its guns blazing away. The German bomber was so low that the tips of its wings could not be seen as they were obscured by the rooftops of the houses on either side. The machine-gun bullets went up the left-hand side of the road striking the cobblestones. I can vividly remember this bomber being so low that I could clearly see the faces of two of the crew as they peered down at us. I recall the leather flying helmets they were wearing. The shock was so great that we just froze with fear as the machine-gun bullets passed by us about three yards away. Suddenly a hand grabbed hold of me and my mother and my sister who was in the pram was also grabbed and the three of us were rather unceremoniously bundled down into someone's cellar. As we ended up in the cellar my mother was suddenly face to face with a very enraged air raid warden, the man who had helped us by shoving us down

> into the cellar. My mother apologized, swearing it would never happen again and that she was so sorry. I was sworn to secrecy about this incident by my mother on the pain of death almost, so I kept quiet about it. Back in those times if you were told to keep something quiet by your mother or father then woe betide you if you didn't, so this is the first time I have ever mentioned this incident. My younger sister was too young to have any recollections of that day and our mother has since passed away, so I no longer worry about keeping it secret anymore.

Whether or not civilians in the street were the intended target of the German bomber's machine-gunners is not entirely clear. Similar incidents which had taken place in Poland and the East showed that certain elements of the Luftwaffe were capable of such deeds. In many cases I believe it was down to the individual or individuals to make that moral decision, that there were those Luftwaffe airmen who adopted a code of moral conduct in the execution of their duties whilst others had no such scruples about shooting anything that moved in the air or on the ground. There were of course anti-aircraft gun emplacements situated in and around the city of Birmingham and it is possible the crew of the bomber were aiming at one of these anti-aircraft sites which may not have been visible to those on the ground. One has to consider every possible theory, but the truth is only known to those airmen who were flying that aircraft that day.

Another former resident of Aston, Birmingham, Phillip J. Hale, recalled:

> The German planes, if they got chance, would try to shoot out the searchlights during night air raids by machine-gunning them to extinguish the light, but I don't think this was common, to be fair. I heard of one or two German aircraft shooting at searchlights, one missed and the other scored a hit and put out the one light, injuring some of the searchlight crew. My dad told me all about it after he had finished his nightshift at a local former car factory where war production was being carried out. I can remember throughout the war hearing all these different stories about

the Germans being the devils of the air and things. I was more concerned with collecting shrapnel after the raids than anything else though [he laughs].

As a 10-year-old schoolboy, Keith Warren recalled in late August 1940 his first close-up glimpse of the enemy while out walking in a stubble field near his home in Margate, Kent:

> I was just doing what most young lads did back then and was wandering around the fields poking sticks into cowpats, searching around in the hedges and climbing up trees. On this day I was on my own. I remember hearing the drone of engines which by their sound were approaching at speed and at low level. I turned around and looked up as several 109s roared overhead. Maybe they had been on the return leg of a fighter sweep over Biggin Hill or something, I don't know. As the first group of 109s went over I thought that was it: show over, so carried on walking out into the stubble field as there was no sign I would be in any danger. It was at this point I heard the approach of another aircraft; this one was also very low and was heading straight towards me. I was so excited by the moment that I started waving. The 109 passed overhead but then banked around sharply, and he came in at an angle and I could clearly see the pilot with his helmet and goggles on and a black gloved hand which waved back at me. I watched enthralled as he turned then disappeared into the horizon.
>
> The next thing I knew I felt an almighty smack across the left side of my face. It was so hard that it spun me around and I fell to the ground; for a few seconds I sat there on my backside, seeing nothing but tiny silvery specks and stars. I shook my head, gathering my senses and, as they returned, standing there before me was this big, middle-aged farm labourer with a very angry expression on his face. He grabbed me by my arm and yanked me up onto my feet, shouting, 'What the hell do you think you're doing? Whose bloody side are you on? Now, go on, piss off home before I tell your parents about this.' Funny thing was I'd

never seen this man before and very much doubt if he knew who my parents were. I didn't tell my parents about it for fear of getting another thick ear.

In a war with large numbers of civilians still living and working in the cities, attempting to go about their daily lives as normally as possible in defiance of Hitler, there were bound to be times when their activities were blurred with the military and the Home Guard. For them there would most certainly have been occasions when they felt they were merely ducks in a barrel.

# Chapter 14

# Duel in the Stratosphere

On 12 September 1942, one of the most remarkable dogfights of the Second World War took place over the south of England between an RAF Spitfire Mk IX and a Junkers Ju 86P high-altitude reconnaissance bomber of the Luftwaffe. On paper one might be forgiven for thinking that a Spitfire versus a Junkers Ju 86 bomber would have been a totally uneven match, but not so in this particular instance.

The Junkers Ju 86P was a unique aircraft in more than just one respect. Like many of the Luftwaffe's Second World War bomber aircraft, the Ju 86 had been designed and developed in the 1930s, the 'P' version for high-altitude reconnaissance and bombing. It was was first flown in January 1940. The type had a longer wingspan than earlier versions, a pressurized cabin for the two-man crew of pilot and observer and, perhaps even more uniquely, the type was powered by two Junkers Jumo 207A-1 turbocharged two-stroke opposed-piston diesel engines. The main advantage of the Ju 86P was its altitude: it could fly at heights of 39,000 to 44,000 feet, way beyond the reach of any enemy fighter then in service. Prior to12 September 1942, efforts at intercepting the high-flying Ju 86s over British territory were in vain. The RAF took steps to counter this menace by creating the Special Service (High Altitude) Flight based at Northolt. Specialist training had to be carried out for the pilots selected for the role and the Supermarine Spitfire Mk IX had to undergo technical modifications in order for it to be up to the task. The Spitfire Mk IX, which would be the first RAF fighter to engage an enemy aircraft above 40,000 feet, was flown by a Russian prince by the name of Emanuel Galitzine.

The dogfight began the moment British radar detected an enemy aircraft flying at very high altitude. The aircraft in question was a Junkers Ju 86P of the high-altitude bomber squadron based at Beauvais in northern France. The aircraft was flown by Feldwebel (Senior Sergeant)

Horst Goetz and his observer Leutnant Erich Sommer. It was heading for Portsmouth on the south coast of England. Flying Officer Galitzine was scrambled to intercept the intruder and made a visual contact on passing 40,000 feet. The enemy aircraft was confirmed as being a Ju 86P, above and still some distance ahead of Galitzine's Spitfire. Goetz and his observer were aware of the Spitfire's presence yet were unconcerned until reaching 42,000 feet when they noticed the Spitfire was still in pursuit and gaining on them. It was at this point Goetz decided to jettison his bombs and activate the emergency nitrous oxide injection system in his diesel engines to boost his power and attempt to outclimb his pursuer. At the same time Goetz took the safety measure of depressurizing the cockpit cabin. This was a wise precautionary measure in case any enemy bullets were to pierce the cabin. Just one bullet entering the pressurized cabin would lead to a catastrophic explosion and instant death. Galitzine was aware of what the German intruder was doing and jettisoned his thirty-gallon external fuel tank, then began to climb above the Ju 86 to press home his attack from astern at 200 yards. Galitzine managed to let loose a burst from his two 20mm Hispano cannons before the port cannon jammed. He now had only one 20mm cannon with which to attack, not an ideal situation as firing a single cannon had an asymmetrical effect on a Spitfire's flight, making firing inaccurate. As Galitzine closed in on the Ju 86 again he was further frustrated by the vapour trail of the Junkers' two engines which not only caused turbulence, further hindering the aim of his single 20mm cannon, but also began to form ice over his cockpit. The game of cat and mouse lasted for forty-five minutes in total, peaking at 44,000 feet, the highest recorded altitude for an air-to-air engagement of the war. Galitzine, low on fuel, was forced to break off his attack and return to Northolt. Just before he turned back towards his airfield, he felt immense frustration as he watched his opponent disappear across the English Channel.

Horst Goetz, having landed safely back at Beauvais, inspected his Junkers and discovered a single 20mm cannon shell hole in his port wing. He also had the unenviable task of alerting his superiors to the fact that the British now had a version of the Spitfire that was capable of operating at the same altitude as the Ju 86P. Subsequently, the Ju 86P never returned to British skies again. It was a remarkable encounter and even more so that no one was killed in the engagement. At the end of the war Emanuel Galitzine and Horst Goetz had a meeting where they reminisced on their epic encounter, the two men remaining good friends thereafter. Horst Goetz was interviewed in the 1970s for a notable aviation magazine on his memorable battle with Flying Officer Galitzine where he recalled:

> It was the one and only time I ever felt slightly afraid. I saw him [Galitzine] continue to climb towards us and knew we were in for a bit of trouble. I was still confident that our aircraft would get us out of trouble and back to Beauvais safely. I operated the nitrous oxide system which gave my engines a power boost twice the maximum output and this allowed us to climb a little higher and faster. As Emanuel will tell you the vapour trails from my engine exhausts were blinding him and he only had a single cannon to fire at us as the other had seized. Maybe that was lucky for us. The vapour trails caused ice to form on his canopy; he couldn't see clearly to get a clean shot at us and with only one gun it was harder. We saw him turn away as we were over the Channel waters. Leutnant Sommer kept looking back and saying, 'He's gone, there's no sign of him.' Back at Bauvais we noticed we hadn't got away completely unscathed, as there was a hole in my port wing made by a 20mm cannon shell. It must have been a solid slug as there was no explosion on impact. Yes, both Sommer and I smiled at each other, as we knew we had been lucky. Later on, several senior officers came to visit us at Beauvais to discuss our exciting encounter. Some of them even expressed doubts that we could have possibly been attacked by a British fighter at such high altitude. Well, I told them, we did not make that hole in the wing of our aircraft ourselves.

# Chapter 15

# *Flammenvogel!*

Apart from the Focke-Wulf Fw 200 Condor, there was a very noticeable absence of a four-engine aircraft in the Luftwaffe's aerial inventory. Why Nazi Germany failed to exploit the asset of a heavy strategic bombing capability lies with the arrogance and complacency of the Nazi leadership itself. As early as 1936, Göring was presented with proposals for the development and production of heavy strategic bombers, yet he stated during one such conversation on the issue that 'the Fuhrer does not ask me how big the bombers are, but how many there are'. So, it would appear if the above statement was indeed made by Göring, that he was of the personal view that it was the numbers of bombers produced and not the size that counted. It is also worthy of note that Germany had to be far more frugal with its resources in comparison to Britain, for example, which could rely on America for material support. The Luftwaffe's adherence to the fast-moving Blitzkrieg principle extended even into its aviation industry. Hitler felt that his large fleet of light and medium bombers would be adequate to accomplish his goals in Europe and bomb Britain into submission, therefore there was no need to waste valuable resources on heavy bomber aircraft. If Germany had been ignorant of the destructive power of a force of four-engine heavy bombers, then I am sure that they would have learned very rapidly from the nightly visits by RAF Bomber Command. When a heavy bomber aircraft was finally given consideration, the aircraft that emerged from the design board was not a heavy bomber in the truest sense of the word, and at least during the initial stages of its development would prove far more lethal to its own crew than the enemy. The aircraft in question was the Heinkel He 177 Greif (Griffin), which has the distinction of being the only long-range heavy bomber to have seen service with the Luftwaffe in the war.

Although the Heinkel He 177 Greif first flew on 9 November 1939, it was an aircraft beset with technical problems and arguments as to its intended role, all of which caused considerable delays to its entry into service.

Designed to carry a crew of six, the He 177 was 22 metres (72 feet) in length, with a wingspan of 33.3 metres (103 feet), height of 6.4 metres (21 feet) and a gross weight of 32,000kg (70,548lb), with a useful top speed of 690kph (430mph) at 19,685 feet. The defensive armament consisted of a 7.92mm MG 81 machine gun in the forward glazed nose, a 20mm MG 151 cannon in a ventral blister beneath the nose, a 20mm MG 151 cannon in the tail, two 13mm MG 131 machine guns in an FDL 131Z remotely operated forward dorsal turret, one 13mm MG 131 in the rear of the ventral blister and one manned 13mm MG 131 machine gun in an aft dorsal turret. The He 177 could carry 15,000lb (6,800kg) of bombs in an internal bomb bay and up to 5,500lb (2,495kg) on externally mounted underwing racks.

The first flight of the prototype was memorable for all of the wrong reasons. The aircraft took off with Leutnant Carl Francke at the controls. Francke was at that time chief of the Rechlin central flight test centre. Some twelve minutes into the flight Francke was alarmed to see his temperature gauges rising rapidly into the red and was forced to return to the airfield. He was happy with the basic handling and landing characteristics but noted vibration in the airscrew shafts, the inadequacy of the tail surface controls under certain flight profiles and flutter which occurred when vigorous movement of the elevators was applied. The problems noted were not acted upon.

With a different test pilot at the controls, the He 177 V2 took off on a flight to evaluate its capabilities in dive trials, as some lunatic – shades of Udet – had suggested the He 177 Greif should be able to perform in the role of a dive-bomber as an adjustment to the original specification. It was no surprise that during these dive trials the He 177 V2 began to experience severe control flutter; the aircraft subsequently broke up in the air, killing the pilot. Modifications were carried out to the V3, V4 and V5 prototypes, the V3 being used as an engine development airframe equipped with two counter-clockwise-rotating Daimler-Benz 606A powerplants. The V4 at Heinkel's test airfield at Rostock-Schmarl also underwent dive trials. Whilst over the Baltic Sea, the V4 was put into what was termed a moderate dive profile from which it failed to recover and it crashed into the sea near Ribnitz. It was discovered that the crash had been caused by the malfunction of an airscrew pitch control mechanism. As the test flying of the He 177 continued, engine fires in particular became a common occurrence. The main reason after some study was revealed: the twin crankcase 1.5-metric-ton (apiece) Daimler-Benz 606 engines had extremely tight and confined engine cowlings. The central exhaust manifold which served twelve cylinders on the two inner cylinder banks of the twinned Daimler-Benz 601 component engines which made up a DB 606 engine were prone to getting excessively hot. This in turn caused the accumulation of oil and grease which collected in the bottom of the engine cowling to ignite. Another problem which surfaced was when the pilot throttled back the engines, the mechanical fuel injection pump on each engine 'lagged' in response, delivering more fuel than was required by the engine. The fuel injection pump connections were also prone to leaking. In order to minimize weight of the aircraft, no firewall had been provided to counter these problems; the aft end of each DB 606 was fitted so snug to the aircraft's main spar, with the rear two-thirds of the component powerplant's engine blocks being placed behind the wing's leading edge, that there was insufficient space for the accommodation of the fuel, oil, fluid lines and electrical harnesses. The DB 606 engines surfaces were often saturated with fuel and oil from leaking connections. At high altitude it was discovered that the oil had a tendency to foam due to badly designed oil pumps, which in turned reduced the lubrication of vital components. Insufficient lubrication led to disintegration of the connecting rod bearings, which sometimes led to the conrods bursting through either one of the component engine crankcases and puncturing the oil tanks. The oil would then spill out onto the often-overheated central exhaust pipe collector. A lack of routine maintenance compounded the problems with the He 177 powerplants and it became one of those aircraft that many Luftwaffe airmen dreaded having to fly.

Göring was getting severely irritated by the lack of progress with the He 177 and after reading a report by Oberst Edgar Petersen with reference to the engine problems, Göring responded: 'Why has this silly engine suddenly turned up, which is so idiotically welded together? They told me then, there would be two engines connected behind each other, and suddenly there appears this misbegotten monster of welded-together engines one cannot get at.'

Eventually, after much redesign work, the problems with the DB 606 engines catching fire were resolved and the aircraft performed satisfactorily; but despite improvements, the stigma of the early He 177 Greif flight programme stuck. Luftwaffe aircrews still referred to the He 177 as the '*Reichsfeuerzeug*' ('Reich's Lighter'), '*Luftwaffenfeuerzeug*' ('Air Force Lighter') and '*Flammenvogel*' ('Flaming Bird'). Ironically, throughout the execution of Operation *Steinbock*, the Luftwaffe's bombing campaign against England that ran from January to May 1944, on one operation fourteen He 177s took off on the sortie. Of the fourteen aircraft, one burst a tyre on take-off and did not get into the air, eight were forced to return to their airfield due to engine problems, leaving only four He 177s to complete the mission. However, during *Steinbock*, Luftwaffe bomber aircraft suffered an average loss rate of 60 per cent; however, the He 177 loss rate was below 10 per cent, making this aircraft the most survivable bomber in the campaign. Luftwaffe pilots made good use of the He 177's top speed of up to 430mph and good defensive armament. However, constant changes in altitude to thwart interception by Allied fighters proved detrimental to accurate bombing. Most pilots flying the He 177 would climb to 23.000 feet (7,000 metres) altitude while still in German airspace. Putting the aircraft into a shallow dive, the pilot could then glide into the target area with his throttles shut. After reaching the designated target area, the bombs would be released and the pilot would open his throttles again and descend back into German territory. By the time the pilot was re-entering German airspace he would be at an altitude of 2,500 feet (750 metres). This method ensured a 90 per cent survival rate. Unfortunately, the technical issues and constant modifications which had hindered the He 177 throughout its development phase meant that it came too late in the war to have any effect on the outcome. From the summer of 1944 the He 177 Greif, along with many other Luftwaffe bomber aircraft, was grounded due to the implementation of the Emergency Fighter Programme coupled with the Allied bombing of fuel and oil production facilities. To close this chapter, testimony provided by 5/KG 100 veteran Gerhard Wilsche is illuminating:

> The basic He 177 concept was not too bad an idea. When they began tinkering around, insisting it had to be able to dive-bomb, the designers had to go back to the drawing board to reconfigure things, taking into account extra weight parameters and adjustments to the design – all sorts

of things. This constant meddling meant that the He 177 was never going to enter into service at a time when it could have been most effective. It had tremendous potential but all that meddling and the accidents due to the insistence that the type possess a dive-bombing capability, plus the amount of time it took to solve engine fire problems, meant that many Luftwaffe crews feared flying in the aircraft. I only flew as part of a crew in the He 177 on three operations as a replacement machine-gunner. My girlfriend was utterly convinced she would never see me again; that's how far the reputation of the He 177 went as far as being a dangerous type to fly in. You know it's bad if your girlfriend hears about it as normally the women didn't get to hear that kind of bad press. Even Göring felt it had all been a criminal waste of time, money and materials.

# Chapter 16

# North Africa and the Mediterranean

In North Africa the Luftwaffe again focused most of its resources in support of the ground forces. For almost eighteen months of the North African and the Mediterranean campaign (1941–4), JG 27 was the only Luftwaffe fighter group in North Africa, although many others had taken part in the Mediterranean. Nevertheless, JG 27 gave a good account of itself in the air battles that took place. In one particular action 274 Squadron RAF lost six Hurricanes in an engagement with a flight of Bf 109s led by Major Gerhard Homuth, an ace who ended the war with sixty-three victories to his credit. Also on this flight was the most successful fighter ace of the North African campaign, Hauptmann Hans-Joachim Marseille, who had claimed an impressive tally of 158 aerial victories prior to his death on 30 September 1942 at the age of twenty-two. Marseille met his untimely demise when forced to abandon his Bf 109G due to an engine fire; he climbed out of the smoke-filled cockpit, pushing himself free but was then struck by the vertical stabilizer, a blow that either killed him instantly or rendered him incapable of opening his parachute. Marseille's loss was not mourned by the Allied Desert Air Force as one RAF veteran, Norman Best, remarked:

> I didn't mourn any of the German pilots; things were alright at first when it was largely the Italians that we found ourselves up against in the air. We would be sent on these stupid leaflet-dropping sorties in Bristol Blenheims like a bunch of idiots out on a Sunday afternoon walk. The moment the Krauts arrived, the whole atmosphere of the fighting in the air changed. Up until that point, I had heard of no RAF airmen being shot up in their parachutes, yet when the Krauts came, it happened regularly. I myself was shot down in one of the RAF Blenheim light bombers. We

> had absolutely no defence against the German Bf 109s at all; they just came right up behind us and opened fire into us – we were sitting ducks on these operations which were a waste of time. I heard the leaflets we dropped weren't even read as the fucking native tribespeople used them to wipe their arses – yes, used them for toilet paper. The good thing was we stuck with it and with Monty (General Bernard Montgomery) on the ground we eventually beat them. The Italians didn't want to be in the war in the first place; I don't think they had much choice, and as soon as they could, they got out of it, but I liked the Italians.

As with Operation *Barbarossa*, the Luftwaffe's campaign in the Mediterranean theatre was initially a great success despite the inherent technical challenges of operating aircraft in tropical/desert climates. Most of the Luftwaffe aircraft adapted well to the conditions, performing satisfactorily following modifications made in an attempt to aid serviceability. The only type that appeared problematic, particularly in North Africa, was the otherwise superb Junkers Ju 88, which did not like the heat, sand and dust prevalent in the Mediterranean, as mechanic Walter Boerle recalled:

> The Junkers was an excellent all-round aircraft and a vital utility in our offensive operations. Of course, in Africa sand is an ever-present nuisance to anything mechanical with moving parts; it gets inside everything and the engines of our aircraft were fitted with filters to help counter sand ingestion. I don't know, the Junkers 88 just didn't seem to perform as well as it did in Europe. I was one mechanic of a group of technicians assigned to one aircraft and whenever the crew landed following an operational flight, I would be the first to ask the crew, 'Were there any problems?' and most of the time they would have a mechanical problem of some sort, just silly things that we didn't seem to encounter with the other aircraft we had in-theatre. We had the Italians out there with us and their aircraft performed very well in the conditions, but they lacked both the firepower and quality of ours. I didn't think that we would have too many problems

> confronting the British there; they had many of the same problems as us, so we were equal in some respects, but yes, we went into it very optimistic of achieving success.

For the Mediterranean/African campaign, the Luftwaffe fielded its Fliegerkorps II that comprised the following:

**Stab JG 53**
- 1/JG 53
- 11/JG 53 all based at Comiso and operating the Bf 109F-4 with a total of 60 serviceable aircraft available
- 1/NJG 2
- 4/NJG 2 based at Catania operating the Ju 88C-4 with a total of 17 serviceable aircraft
- KGr.606
- KGr.806 based at Catania operating the Ju 88A-4 with 37 serviceable aircraft

**Stab KG54**
- 1/KG 54 based at Gerbini operating the Ju 88A-4 with 13 serviceable aircraft
- II/KG 77
- 111/KG 77 based at Catania operating the Ju 88A-4 with 36 serviceable aircraft

By 10 May 1942 the disposition of Luftflotte 2 under the command of Generalfeldmarschall Albert Kesselring was as follows (under the headings unit, aircraft type, location and serviceable strength):

**Fliegerkorps 11**

| | | | |
|---|---|---|---|
| 1(F)/122 | Bf 109F-5/Ju 88D-5 | Catania | 14 |
| 2(F)/122 | Ju 88D-5 | Trapani | 12 |
| Stab JG 53 | Bf 109F-4 | Comiso | 5 |
| 11/JG 53 | Bf 109F-4 | Comiso | 42 |
| 111/JG 53 | Bf 109F-4 | Comiso | 39 |
| 1/NJG 2 | Ju 88C-6 | Catania | 12 |
| Stab III/ZG 26 | Bf 110D-3 | Trapani | 16 |
| 10/ZG 26 | Do 17 Z-10 | Trapani | 8 |

| | | | |
|---|---|---|---|
| KGr.606 | Ju 88A-4 | Catania | 23 |
| KGr.806 | Ju 88A-4 | Catania | 28 |
| Stab KG 54 | Ju 88A-4 | Gerbini | 3 |
| 1/KG 54 | Ju 88A-4 | Comiso | 23 |
| 111/StG 3 | Ju 87D-1 | San Pietro | 23 |
| **Fliegerkorps X** | | | |
| 2(F)/123 | Ju 88D-5 | Kastelli1 | 3 |
| Stab LG 1 | Ju 88A-14 | Eleusis | 1 |
| 1/LG 1 | Ju 88A-4 | Heraklion | 29 |
| II/LG 1 | Ju 88A-4 | Eleusis | 31 |
| II/KG 100 | He 111H-16 | Kalamaki | 25 |
| 2 SAGr.125 | Ar 196A-3 | Skaramanka | 8 |
| Gr.Stab 125 | Bv 138C-1 | Skaramanka | 1 |
| 1/SAGr.126 | He 60C/Fokker T.VIII | Skaramanka | 15 |
| 2/SAGr.126 | Ar 196A-3/He 60C | Kavalla | 13 |
| 3.SAGr.126 | Ar 196A-3 | Skaramanka | 16 |
| **Fliegerführer Africa** | | | |
| 4(H)/12 | Bf 109/Bf 110/Hs 126 | Martuba | 17 |
| 1(F)/121 | Ju 88D-5/Bf 109F-5 | Derna | 10 |
| Stab JG 27 | Bf 109F-4 Trop** | Martuba | 5 |
| 1/JG 27 | Bf 109F-4 Trop | Martuba | 30 |
| II/JG 27 | Bf 109F-4 Trop | Martuba | 33 |
| 111/JG 27 | Bf 109F-4 Trop | Martuba | 29 |
| Jabo JG 27 | Bf 109F-4/B | Martuba | 8 |
| 2/NJG 2 | Ju 88C-6 | Derna | 9 |
| 7/ZG 26 | Bf 110D-3 | Derna | 12 |
| 9/ZG 26 | Bf 110D-3 | Maleme | 11 |
| 12/LG 1 | Ju 88A-4 Trop | Berca | 11 |
| Stab StG 3 | Ju 87D-1 Trop | Derna-South | 2 |
| 1/StG 3 | Ju 87D-1 Trop | Derna-South | 41 |

Total aircraft available 636 on strength of which 374 were serviceable and ready for operations.

---

* Aircraft with the designation 'Trop' were aircraft with modifications to optimize their performance in tropical/desert conditions.

While Germany may have entered into the Mediterranean and Africa with high hopes of defeating the British Eighth Army, it would be a hard-fought campaign that would ultimately see the fall of Italy as an Axis power and bring a swift end to Benito Mussolini's personal obsession with the creation of a new Roman Empire. It was clear early on in the campaign that Italy would soon become a liability. In truth, the Italians didn't want war in the first place, and many Italian soldiers surrendered to their enemy at the first opportunity. This proved a considerable headache for Hitler who was having to commit more and more resources in order to bolster the failing Italians. One of the main problems facing the Axis forces in North Africa and the Mediterranean was that the omnipresent Royal Navy posed a constant threat to Axis supply routes from Europe. The British were faced with a similar dilemma as the Axis forces. The key objectives of both sides were keeping supply lines open whilst neutralizing the enemy's ability to wage war at sea.

Perhaps the most significant action of the war in the Mediterranean was the siege of Malta. This British Crown Colony was of great strategic importance, not only to Britain who had air and naval assets based there but also the Germans. Malta was viewed as a priority target for the Axis in the Mediterranean as it allowed Germany's enemies to disrupt Axis logistics routes to Libya. If the Germans could capture Malta, it would have a devastating effect on Britain's ability to supply its forces in the Western Desert. The Germans particularly understood the importance of Malta as an enemy stronghold being so close as it was to Italy.

As a result, the island became the focus of one of the most intensive Luftwaffe bombing campaigns of the war. General Erwin Rommel, the enigmatic commander of the Axis ground forces in Africa, warned of the consequences of failure when he remarked, 'If we fail to capture Malta, we will lose control of Africa.' The Luftwaffe plan for offensive operations against Malta was simple: Malta would be bombed and starved into submission through a concentrated bombing campaign. Fliegerkorps X under the command of Hans Ferdinand Geisler duly arrived in Sicily in January 1941, tasked with offensive operations against British naval forces in an around the island as well as against RAF bases and infrastructure on the island itself. Again, the RAF would be faced with a war of attrition, outnumbered as they were in the air and inadequately equipped with Hawker Hurricane and Gloster Gladiator fighters. The following month, February 1941, Messerchmitt Bf 109E-7 fighters of 7 Staffel, Jagdgeschwader 26 arrived; led by Oberleutnant Joachim Müncheberg, it was given the task of escorting the Stukas on their bombing attacks against Malta and the surrounding waters. The Bf 109E-7 gave the Luftwaffe a huge tactical advantage over the RAF; besides its technical superiority, the Luftwaffe pilots were very experienced, confident, tactically astute, better equipped and very well trained. By way of comparison, the RAF aircrews on Malta had little actual combat experience and their Hawker Hurricane fighters were all but worn-out examples, with RAF mechanics cannibalizing spare parts in order to keep aircraft serviceable.

Major Fritz Helmut Goeth, who flew a 7 Staffel Messerschmitt Bf 109E-7, recorded in his diary a typical operation against Malta:

> The whole Malta operation was what many would call a 'walk in the park' for us. It was obvious after the first few operations and sweeps over the RAF airfields on the island that they could not compete with us on terms of quality. We had the better aeroplane and the better-trained pilots, so we had the advantage over them. It became almost tedious: the *Stukageschwader* would take off and we would follow, taking off several minutes later. We would soon catch them up and escort them to ensure they reached the island in safety.
>
> Once over Malta, it was a free for all; the Stukas would dive to hit their assigned targets of the RAF infrastructure and aircraft on the ground while we would fly higher, watching out for any enemy aircraft attempting to intercept our Stukas. Yes, Hurricanes attempted to intercept us, but we had height, speed and firepower advantages and the Hurricanes were either shot down or driven off. I chased one out to sea and he was jinking wildly from side to side in a futile attempt to throw off my aim, but it was useless. I closed in and fired my two 20mm cannons into him. I saw my shells go right through the entire length of the fuselage, tearing a gaping wound in the enemy's side. I watched as my prey rolled over onto its back and, trailing flames, it headed down into the sea. There was no malice about it; in fact, I was saying under my breath, 'Come on man, get out of the crate, get out now,' but the pilot was probably dead in

his harness and did not bale out of the aircraft. He was my fourth victory, yet it didn't feel like a victory as it was all too damn easy, almost an unfair fight.

When I turned around, I could see columns of thick smoke rising from the island where the Stukas' bombs had fallen. I opened the throttle; some of our Stukas were on their way home, passing below me. I dived down to the RAF runways, where I could see a few vehicles and bowsers dotted around and a few aircraft on the ground burning. In fact, there was so much smoke it almost concealed the target area. I flew along the runway and fired at some very dispersed Hurricanes. I used up the last of my cannon shells and turned for home. As I flew home, I was overtaken by two of our Messerschmitts. My comrades waved to me as if to say 'a good job done'. When we arrived back in Sicily there were celebrations all round. We drank a lot of wine and got quite drunk and smoked cigars. We were having a whale of a time there and Sicily was just beautiful, a paradise in many ways. Yes, I knew that the people of Malta were taking a real battering, but they had the option of surrender – our task was to assist in making that happen.

The Luftwaffe remained active in the Mediterranean theatre until the end of the war. While the Luftwaffe had achieved many successes, mainly in its ground-support role, their last victory in this theatre would come with the Battle of Leros in the Dodecanese campaign.

On the subject of aces in the Mediterranean and North African theatres, much of the credit must go to Hans-Joachim Marseille. The reason for this is that many of Marseille's JG 27 comrades were content to let 'their expert leader' rack up the kills on their behalf. Subsequently, his loss was a huge blow to the unit and had a serious effect on morale. Marseille was arguably one of the greatest Luftwaffe fighter pilots of the war; his 158-victory tally was unique as the majority of his victims were high-quality Western opponents unlike those encountered over the Eastern Front. Marseille was the typical fighter pilot of legend: he lived life in the fast lane, he liked a drink and he liked his women, perhaps too much at times, yet this remarkable and highly respected maverick was a master of his profession.

# Chapter 17

# Death of a Dornier

Sunday, 17 January 1943 saw the return of Luftwaffe bombers in force over London since the raids of July 1941. At Kampfgeschwader 2's aerodrome at Deelen in the Netherlands the bomber crews wearily stirred from their bunks where they had spent most of the day resting, reading and writing letters prior to their night foray into enemy territory.

The crews filed into the large briefing hut and took their seats. The air inside was as chilled as the frosty air outside, yet it soon became foggy with cigarette smoke as the crews anxiously awaited the arrival of the commanding officer. The men chatted amongst themselves in anticipation of what the target would be. With the sound of chairs scraping the wooden floor, the men simultaneously stood to attention and saluted as the CO came in. The briefing began: the target would be London, though many already suspected as much. Hitler had personally ordered the operation, relaying a message of encouragement from Berlin stating that he expected those flying on the operation to make every single bomb count. The targets indicated were the docks and railway infrastructures on the Thames Estuary in East London. Being relatively close to Deelen, the aircrews were to fly two missions that night.

Gefreiter Willi Schäfer aged 22, Gefreiter Erich Raab aged 18, Unteroffizier Richard Hartenberger aged 25 and Unteroffizier Joachim Schnabel aged 23 were the four-man crew of Dornier 217E-4 *Werke* No. 5591 coded U5+MR. Unteroffizier Schnabel would be flying the aircraft while Gefreiter Raab was radio operator/gunner, Unteroffizier Hartenberger would be in charge of ensuring the bombs hit their targets and Gefreiter Schäfer would take up position in the ventral machine-gun gondola.

It was a freezing-cold day and by the time the crews began to board their aircraft, a hard frost had developed. In the light of the moon the bombers appeared to be coated in a silvery sheen of ice. The aircrews had flasks of hot soup with them to keep them warm throughout the flight. The four crew of U5+MR then boarded their aircraft and took up their positions, ready for take-off. Gefreiter Willi Schäfer was particularly keen to get the night over with as his pregnant wife Elisabeth back in Essen was showing signs of going into labour with their first child, and he had hoped to take some leave to be with his wife and the baby. First, there was a job to do, as the engines were started and the two 1,970hp BMW 801s roared into life. There was a brief wait as other aircraft taxied out onto the grass strip ready to take off into the night sky. Soon the bomber force was airborne and setting course for London.

Dornier U5+MR had been fitted with an extra piece of equipment, a rather primitive radar-jamming device that the Luftwaffe hoped would help prevent detection of the incoming bomber force, especially by any RAF night fighters that might be prowling the skies over the target area.

Following the X-Gerat transmission Gefreiter Raab observed the intersection of the guiding radio beams to the target, the so-called 'blind bombing system'. Arriving over the capital for their first bombing run, the anti-aircraft defences appeared to have been caught off guard and little Flak was encountered. U5+MR dropped its bombs over the docklands of the East End before setting course back to Deelen to rearm and refuel for the second phase of the operation. The crew were in good spirits on the return flight and while over the North Sea, the hot soup was passed around in an almost ritual fashion.

Back at Deelen the crew filed their sortie report before grabbing sandwiches, refilling their flasks with more hot soup from the canteen and having a pee, usually on the grass behind the aircraft. Fresh bombs were loaded into the bomb bay as the crew anxiously waited to board the aircraft for the second trip to London. They were briefed to be wary of night fighters and anti-aircraft fire as the British defences were by now aware that a major bombing operation was under way. There was some apprehension at the possibility of experiencing some heavy searchlight and Flak activity over the target. With a fresh bomb load, they were then ordered to take off. The ground crew and armourers waved them off and watched as they climbed once again into the moonlit sky. Unteroffizier Schnabel set course for Abbeville and for a landfall just west of Hastings to central London. Fires from the previous raid would have been immediately visible along with the searchlights and anti-aircraft fire which was reported as being 'lively'. Schnabel was aware of the threats as he approached Kent. Although RAF night fighters were now airborne, they were extremely difficult for the Luftwaffe bomber crews to detect in the darkness.

Wing Commander Michael Cathcart Wight-Boycott and his AI/WO (Air Interception Radar/ Wireless Operator) Flying Officer Tony Sanders were airborne with orders to orbit Beacon 'K'. At approximately 0430 hours, Sanders picked up a contact on the cathode ray screen of his AI radar set. In his seat well aft of the pilot's cockpit of the twin-engine Bristol Beaufighter, Sanders guided his pilot into visual contact with Dornier U5+MR. It was possible at this point that the crew of U5+MR were aware of the presence of the night fighter now stalking them, as the aircraft was seen to go into a spiral climb, turning left and right, yet with no violent evasive action nor machine-gun fire. Wing Commander Wight-Boycott, having established that the aircraft before him in the night sky was indeed an enemy Dornier 217, approached his target from astern, switching on the light of his optical gunsight and, closing in to a range of 300 to 400 yards, he depressed the gun button, firing his four 20mm Hispano cannons and six .303-inch Browning machine guns for a two-second burst at 5° to the starboard side of the Dornier which immediately burst into flames and dived earthward. At the approximate altitude of 11,000 to 12,000 feet the crew would have had very little time to get out of the aircraft that was engulfed in flames as it fell. U5+MR crashed into the ground 300 yards north of Pilgrim House in Westerham, Kent. The bombs on board exploded and as a result, the aircraft was totally destroyed, disintegrating in the resulting inferno. All four of the crew of U5+MR perished. It was a cruel irony that Gefreiter Willi Schäfer's wife back in Essen was giving birth to a baby girl named Ingeborg around the time he lost his life, a day before his twenty-third birthday.

U5+MR was one of four raiders to fall to the guns of Wing Commander Wight-Boycott and Flying Officer Sanders that fateful night. While Wight-Boycott and Sanders were duly credited with the destruction of four enemy aircraft that night, research conducted by aviation historian Simon Parry disagreed. Parry examined the incident carefully, accessing the relevant wartime documents and it would appear that the most that Wight-Boycott and Sanders could claim that night was three of the raiders and not the originally reported four. This does not imply that Wight-Boycott and Sanders were fiddling their kills, merely that confusion existed in the heat and disorienting conditions of night combat and it was all too easy to make errors, which frequently occurred on both sides

Peter Halliday spent his childhood in Westerham, Kent, and recalls the crash of Dornier U5+MR. I arranged a meeting with Peter, who had since moved to High Wycombe, Buckinghamshire, to interview him in early 1998, as he recalled:

> We were young lads back then and word soon got around when anything happened, like a German plane coming down or anything. It was my friend Bob who suggested we go up to the crash site and take a look, and it was on a Saturday around a week after the crash had occurred. Bob lived near Gray's Farm and the Dornier had gone into the ground just below the farm up behind this house called Pilgrim House. There was a small wood behind the house and the Dornier had gone in there. It made one hell of a hole in the ground, like a small quarry. Most of the big pieces of wreckage had been taken away by this time, but there were lots of smaller bits lying around and lots of twisted pieces of shrapnel, as the plane had gone in with a full bomb load. To the right of the crash site under some bushes we noticed there were four wooden crosses marking four graves. As the plane blew up on impact there was very little left of the crew, so they buried them there at first which was common at the time. One thing I recall was the terrible smell at the site – it was a mixture of burnt aluminium, aviation fuel and oil – and it was quite overpowering. I was scratting around the site when I found this cylinder-like container. It was blue painted with a white stripe around the top and a tap at the one end. As we left the site due to the awful smell and headed back up the hill towards Gray's Farm, I was fiddling with the tap on the cylinder which suddenly broke off in my hand. There was a loud hiss as the tap came off in my hand and I dropped the thing in some bushes and we all ran. We stopped around fifty yards or so away and stood listening to the loud hissing noise, but there was no explosion or anything. At the time we thought it could be dangerous, gas or something, so we

> felt it was better to leave it there. We went home for tea, leaving that cylinder where it was, and as far as I know it could still be there to this day.

The mystery cylindrical object Peter found was nothing more dangerous than one of the oxygen bottles from the Dornier. At the time I owned two such oxygen bottles found at the crash site of U5+MR and either one could have been one of those thrown into the bushes by Peter on that day back in 1943. I took one of the bottles along with me to our meeting and took a photograph of Peter holding it.

I later visited the library at Sevenoaks in Kent, hoping to perhaps find some more information about the incident. I had gathered what information was available in the public domain, including any records held by the Imperial War Museum, Public Record Office and Air Historical Branch. The staff at Sevenoaks library handed me a book titled *Westerham at War* and inside were six references to Dornier U5+MR. Having read through them carefully, I dismissed all of them as being spurious. No names were given as to the identity of the contributors and what information they gave I knew to be wrong in two of the listed accounts.

After conducting intensive research into this particular crash and the Luftwaffe airmen who lost their lives that morning of 18 January 1943, I finally made contact with Willi Schäfer's daughter, Ingeborg Stiefel, who was still living in Essen at the time in 1998. We exchanged letters and I was able to give her more information on her father's loss, including many things the family had never previously known. Ingeborg also sent me some photographs of her father and the three crew who lost their lives that day. The following year, in June 1999, I met Ingeborg at the German Military Cemetery at Cannock Chase. She had come to England with a party organized by the German War Graves Commission at Kassel in Germany. Thankfully, there was an interpreter present as Ingeborg could speak no English. After exchanging greetings which, despite the language barrier, were very emotional, I then took Ingeborg to see her father's grave for the first time. I recall how she took a deep breath before accompanying me out into the cemetery and to her fathers' grave. Again, this was an extremely emotional moment for her and for a moment I thought that maybe it hadn't been such a good idea. For some time, I felt a terrible sense of guilt, yet, later upon Ingeborg's return to

Essen, she was able to telephone me and with the aid of my German-speaking friend, Tanya Rivers-Boyce, who spoke to her on my behalf, she explained that her visit to England had been beautiful and she was very happy to see what a beautiful place her father's place of rest was and that she would definitely be visiting again. The one piece of information Ingeborg recalled that troubled her mother greatly was the narrative of a Red Cross letter her mother received after it was confirmed that Willi had lost his life. The letter insinuated that the dead airmen had been buried in an unmarked grave. I explained to Ingeborg that this referred to the burials at the crash site which was commonplace at the time with all the action going on. I explained that the crew remains were then exhumed and reburied at Greatness Park Cemetery in Sevenoaks, Kent, before being finally laid to rest in the German Military Cemetery at Cannock where most of the Luftwaffe airmen killed over the UK are buried.

Ingeborg recalled during our meeting that while she was too young to have any memories of the last two years of the war, she recalled how her mother told her how incredibly hard life had been after the loss of her husband. It was this one piece of research that vividly brought to me the whole tragedy and sheer wastefulness of the war.

I felt that including the following information on the four crew of U5+MR might be useful for those wishing to research further:

| | | |
|---|---|---|
| Gefr. Willi Schäfer | Service No. 58214/197 | Born 19/1/1920 (22) Essen |
| Gefr. Erich Raab | Service No. 58214/194 | Born 3/2/1923 (18) München |
| Uffz. Joachim Schnabel | Service No. 58214/198 | Born 5/6/1919 (23) Lauta |
| Uffz. Richard Hartenberger | Service No. 58214/191 | Born 7/3/1917 (25) Jagerndorf |
| The location of the grave for this crew at the German Military Cemetery at Cannock Chase is Block 9, Row 9, Grave 57 | | |

# Chapter 18

# Tip-and-Run Terror

On Sunday, 10 January 1943, 10-year-old James Barnet was walking happily along the seafront at Teignmouth, Devon with his mother Tilly. James's father was away serving in the Royal Navy at the time. He and his mother would visit his grandparents every Sunday afternoon where they would usually stay until teatime, talking, playing cards or listening to the wireless. It was around 2.20pm and both James and his mother were about to witness a particularly indiscriminate form of Luftwaffe bombing attack first-hand and at very close quarters.

James recalled what happened next on that otherwise peaceful Sunday afternoon:

> Me and mum hadn't long set out for my grandparents' house; this was my father's mum and dad who we used to go and see every Sunday come rain, sun or snow. It was something we enjoyed and looked forward to. I remember we had left our house at around ten past two and were soon walking along the seafront.
>
> Suddenly, there was the sound of engines; they were very distant and at first, we took no notice as we thought the engines were those of the regular RAF fighter patrols over the area, so we continued on walking. I said to mum, 'Those engines are getting closer now,' so we both stopped and looked out to sea and could just about make out six to eight little specks coming in very fast and heading straight towards where we were standing. As the planes came closer, I felt this shiver run down by spine, the kind of sensation a kid that is terrified of dogs experiences when he comes face to face with one. I saw these great big radial engines and the black crosses on their wings and the swastikas on their tailfins

– they were Jerries! I recognized them as being Focke-Wulf Fw 190s, one of the most lethal German fighters then in service. The German planes came screaming in so low that you could see the faces of the pilots as they looked down at us. I remember the black flying helmets and the goggles they wore; I could see them very clearly as they flew over us. Then there was the clatter of cannon and machine-gun fire and you could see spits of flame coming out of the wings of the planes as they fired their guns. They were shooting at some small fishing vessels on the way in and I could see the crews scattering like ants to avoid being hit by the bullets. There were splashes as cannon shells hit the water too. My mother screamed, 'Get down Jim, get down now and don't move' My mum, bless her, literally threw me down on the ground and covered me, placing her arms over my head. I could feel her hands shaking, bless her; she must have been terrified. Naturally, being a kid, I wanted to see the action, but my mum's will was far stronger on that occasion. As the German planes roared overhead, I heard the whistle of several bombs being dropped, followed by explosions which shook the ground beneath us. There was the sound of the anti-aircraft guns opening up on the Germans; yes, there was lots of 40mm Bofors having a good old crack at them.

I could still hear the engines of the German planes as they flew over and back around the town, like a swarm of wasps, and firing their guns quite indiscriminately. I don't recall having heard any warning of this attack and a lot of people were caught by surprise. All I can recall seeing was smoke billowing up from behind the seafront houses, and there was a lot of screaming and shouting either from those who had been wounded or people who were just terrified. One voice I do remember – it was the very distinctive voice of a Northerner gentleman: 'The RAF are coming!' My mother still had me very much pinned down on the ground, but I managed to catch a glimpse of two RAF planes – I first thought they were Hawker Hurricanes – that came sweeping in over the rooftops and were chasing the German raiders out to sea. Two of the Germans were heading towards the pier. More explosions went off in the town beyond the seafront as the other raiders either dumped their bombs or tried to hit the railway tracks again, as the railways were, I think, the most likely target. I soon recognized the RAF planes as Typhoons, most likely from the 266 (Rhodesia) Squadron who were based at Exeter at the time. We heard the sound of cannon fire and as we got to our feet, we could just about make out the large splash of an aircraft or maybe a bomb hitting the sea somewhere north of the pier. It was soon apparent that the splash was one of the Germans going into the sea, not a bomb. Mum and I looked around to see if we could spot a parachute in the air but there was nothing. It hadn't really occurred to me that the German pilot had been flying far too low to have been able to bale out and he was probably dead. I know that three days later the body of a young German pilot was washed ashore at Dawlish, and we knew that this was one of the Germans being chased by the RAF planes and the one we saw going into the water by the pier.

From the moment we first heard those engines approaching across the sea to the German plane going down by the pier was a case of just minutes, though it all seemed to happen in slow motion and go on for ages. Mum and I were both frantic with worry and ran to my grandparents' house to make sure they were safe. I could still hear people screaming and crying. It didn't take long for the emergency services to arrive and they tended to the wounded. When we arrived at my grandparents', we were just so overjoyed to find that they had sought shelter in their shed in the garden. They were both a bit shaken up, more by the sound of the bombs going off; thankfully, they were unhurt, but they were quivering with fright, bless them both. We all went inside the house and first thing we all did was have a nice hot cup of good old English tea to calm ourselves down.

Later that afternoon, on the way back home, I noticed some people were out climbing up gutters and scratting around the pavements for pieces of shrapnel or bullet casings. I found a couple of cannon shell cases and a link

> myself which I picked up out of the gutter. My aunt Rachel, who also lived in the town, told me a few days later that a large piece of a German bomb had fallen into her elderly neighbours' fishpond. The shrapnel had gone clean through the bottom of the pond and emptied it. The old lady who lived there was a brawny old Scots woman and the fishpond was her pride and joy. Despite the fact there was an air raid in progress, she came out with a hand-rolled cigarette hanging off her lip and looked up at the sky, shaking her fist and shouting in her distinctive Scots accent, 'Ya fockon bastards, look what ye doon ta ma fockon pond, ya conts!' My aunt watched in amazement as the old Scots woman stood there with her hands on her hips, shaking her head at the destruction of her fishpond as chaos reigned all around. It was one of those lighter moments but the human cost of that raid on Teignmouth that Sunday afternoon in January 1943 was high for a little seaside community.

The raid had lasted for just three minutes but in those three minutes five bombs were dropped on the town and two into the sea; eighteen people lost their lives, seven were severely wounded, seventeen slightly wounded with one person recorded as missing. Twelve houses were completely demolished. The Great Western Railway line that ran through Teignmouth received some damage and there was disruption to gas and electricity supplies. One of the SC500 bombs dropped during the raid ricocheted off a railway line, smashed through a wall, crossed another set of railway tracks, went through another wall and crossed a road before crashing through the bay window of number 8 Alexandra Terrace, and exploding four feet above an Anderson shelter near the parlour. The bomb demolished the house, blowing the Anderson shelter thirty feet back into the road and killing four members of the Brooks family sheltering inside; one of the dead was a twenty-month-old baby.

During the raid naval personnel manning an onshore battery fired forty anti-aircraft rocket projectiles known as UPs (unrotated projectiles), while forty to fifty 40mm Bofors anti-aircraft rounds were fired at the raiders. One Bofors round had hit one of the German aircraft in the tail. The aircraft were indeed Focke-Wulf FW 190 fighters operating in the fast fighter-bomber or *Jaboeinsatz* role. The Fw 190 that had been shot down into the sea 300 yards north of Teignmouth Pier was believed to have been the one hit by one of the 40mm Bofors rounds shortly before being finished off by one of the RAF Typhoons.

After conducting some research into this particular incident, I discovered that the dead German pilot was 21-year-old Feldwebel Joachim von Bitter of JG 2, the Richtofen Geschwader based at Amiens at the time of this attack. His aircraft was a Focke-Wulf Fw 190A-3 *Werke* no. 5424, armed with four 20mm cannons, two 7.92mm MG 17 machine guns plus a single SC500 high-explosive bomb. Unteroffizier Otto Wilhelm Schenker was one of the Fw 190 pilots of JG 2 on the raid that day and he recalled:

> We had an early morning briefing on 10 January 1943 for a sortie across the sea which was due for the afternoon. The target was the coastal town of Teignmouth and we were ordered to destroy the railway lines in and around the target vicinity. It was straightforward enough and I personally had no sense of foreboding or anything. Take-off was to be 1.45pm and approximate arrival over the target would be 2.15 to 2.30pm. Orders were that we were expressly forbidden to engage in air-to-air combat with the enemy if they appeared; we were simply to drop our bombs and get out as fast as possible, a basic hit-and-run attack. When the order to take off came over the loudspeaker, our formation of eight Focke-Wulf fighters took off from Amiens a little after 1.55pm. We were soon airborne, heading west, directly to the target. We flew as close to the sea as possible to avoid detection by the British radar network; in fact, we flew so low our propellers created a wake on the surface of the sea. We stayed down as low as possible all the way into the target area and we only climbed to higher altitude to ensure we did not get hit by the blast from our own bombs.
>
> We came in in a line-astern formation. There were what looked like fishing boats and I selected one of these and fired my guns. I was still very low as I fired and the target got obscured by spray as my shells hit the water in front of the target, so I could not be certain I had scored any hits. We knew the railway lines lay beyond the rows of houses on

the seafront and pulled up, ready to release our bombs. The Flak gunners were not immediately aware of our presence, but once they woke up, they started firing at us, yet we had caught them by surprise.

Teignmouth was not an easy target to bomb, as the town sat in a kind of depression that required a very low-level approach, which gave the Flak gunners a very good chance to shoot at you horizontally as you approached; it was lucky for us that we caught them totally off guard, for a moment anyway. As I cleared the seafront, I pulled my Focke-Wulf into a steep climb, rolled her to port so as I could get the bearings that I had memorized from the reconnaissance maps we had studied earlier. I was right over the railway line, so I nosed her down, released my single bomb and turned hard starboard. I kicked her round, opening my throttle and I headed back out to sea at zero altitude. I noticed bursts of Flak on the way out, but it was nothing of great concern. I looked over my shoulder and saw the other pilots following me out. I noticed two big splashes – obviously bombs dropped into the sea. I heard over the radio two of our comrades were in some difficulty; enemy aircraft had appeared from astern and were now closing in on their tails. Gefreiter Hutner managed to shake off his pursuer by using his emergency boost and jinking his wings from side to side to throw off the attackers' aim. Feldwebel von Bitter had an enemy closing in rapidly on his tail, and over the radio he shouted that he had been hit by Flak and his tailplane controls were not responding. The flight leader shouted to him to, 'Use your boost; repeat, use your boost' but we never heard from Feldwebel von Bitter again.

We landed back at Amiens at around 2.40pm. Gefreiter Hutner waited around by his aircraft, hoping to see Joachim von Bitter return. After waiting for some thirty minutes Hutner joined the rest of the flight for a debrief of the operation. It was noted that Joachim von Bitter had failed to return and was thus presumed taken prisoner or dead. At the time we had no idea if our comrade had managed to get out of his aircraft alive. Hutner noted that at the time they were

> attacked by enemy cannon fire, they were still very close to the shoreline, so we had hoped that our comrade had been rescued and was now enjoying the hospitality of the British. It was not until almost a week later that our group received news via the German Red Cross that our comrade was dead. The report stated that the body of a young German airman was washed ashore at 1200 hours at Dawlish on 13 January, and that the young man was identified from a small wallet and a few personal effects as being Joachim von Bitter. It was harsh; he was just 21 years old, another boy gone. We mourned his loss in the mess by raising a glass to him. He was a likeable young man and a very good pilot; it was just a case of bad luck, really, and we all knew tomorrow we could suffer the same fate. None of us was invincible; that was the nature of war – people die in war.

The pilot who shot Feldwebel Joachim von Bitter down on that Sunday, 10 January 1943 was 32-year-old Flight Lieutenant John Small of No. 266 (Rhodesia) Squadron RAF, based at Exeter, within easy reach of the British south coast. 266 Squadron was equipped with the excellent Hawker Typhoon, a powerful, fast fighter-bomber with a heavy armament of four 20mm Hispano cannons. The Hawker Typhoon Mk IB was one of the few fighters of the RAF able to outperform the dreaded Fw 190 of the Luftwaffe which entered service in 1941 and which had given the RAF a considerable headache for some months until an improved version of the Spitfire entered service. On 10 January 1943, Small was flying Hawker Typhoon Mk IB serial number R. 8937 and gave the following combat report of his victory over Joachim von Bitter's Fw 190:

> 1415 hours we were on 'anti-rhubarb patrol' [defence against freelance enemy fighter sorties against ground targets of opportunity], Exmouth to start point. On the third leg of the patrol, flying south at zero feet when four miles off Teignmouth saw eight Fw 190s flying six in line-abreast and two line-abreast 100 yards to port. All of the enemy aircraft were flying at zero feet heading north-west for Teignmouth. Yellow section turned starboard and followed the enemy aircraft and saw bombs dropped on the waterfront as the

> enemy aircraft went in. Using 7lb of boost and 3,700 revs, I quickly closed the range and fired two short bursts of four 20mm cannons with deflection at a range of 250 yards, at one of the two outside enemy aircraft that was not carrying any bombs. I continued to close the range and as the enemy aircraft was crossing the coast going out, I fired another burst of four 20mm cannons at 100 yards range with little deflection. A bright flash occurred in the enemy aircraft that then went straight into the sea about 500 yards offshore north of Teignmouth. I had been flying so close behind the enemy aircraft that I flew through the splash created by it as it hit the water. When I looked back, I could see a slick of oil on the surface where the enemy aircraft had gone in. Both enemy aircraft had made no attempt to turn and fight.

Upon Small's return to his airfield at Exeter, an inspection of his aircraft revealed some damage to the air intake and engine cowling caused by fragments of metal from von Bitter's Fw 190 as it hit the water.

Jon Small was born the son of Robert and Jessie Small, a farming family from Scoonie, Fifeshire in Scotland, on 24 March 1911. He also had a brother named Robert. John, known to his friends as 'Johnny', emigrated to Southern Rhodesia in 1933 where he found employment as a foreman with a diamond-mining company based at Shamva but returned to England some years later. He enlisted in the RAF Volunteer Reserve on 29 November 1940. On 9 July 1941, he was granted a commission as a pilot officer on probation in the General Duties Branch of the RAF Volunteer Reserve for the duration of the war. On 9 July 1942, his appointment as flying officer was confirmed, which was his official rank until his loss on 15 August 1943. In some of the official RAF documents John's rank is given as flight lieutenant. This caused some confusion at times and led me to believe that this rank was awarded in a posthumous context, which I was later able to confirm. John Small was killed on 15 August 1943, just six weeks after he had married a local girl named Kay.

On that fateful day John was involved in the 10 Fighter Group circus attack on the Luftwaffe airfield at Brest-Guivapas, France. En route to the target and just off the French coast, the RAF fighters were bounced by Fw 190s, most likely those from Feldwebel von Bitter's unit, JG 2.

A fierce dogfight ensued, and John's aircraft was badly shot up, forcing him to bale out. One of the RAF pilots recalled: 'I saw John get hit by heavy cannon fire from one of the Fw 190s. I watched as his Typhoon went down, leaving a trail of thick black smoke. I saw John bale out but then I lost sight of him in the battle that was still raging all around, and I never saw him again.'

Mystery surrounds the death of Flight Lieutenant Small as he was seen exiting his burning aircraft, so was alive at that point. It is possible he had been mortally wounded, dying of his wounds soon after landing in his parachute. It is also possible that he was hit by shot and shell from the dogfight which was raging around him. The German authorities recovered his body and Small was buried with full military honours at Le Folgoet district cemetery, fourteen miles north-east of Brest.

Joachim von Bitter, *Erkennungsmarke* (service number) 803-40/53523, was born in the small, picturesque village of Hotensleben, Germany, on 5 August 1922. Jagdgeschwader 2 was, according to his nephew Dr Christian Meyl, his second posting since joining the Luftwaffe fighter arm. In a letter I received from Dr Meyl in March 2004, he thanked me for my interest in his uncle's fate and enclosed two photographs of Joachim as requested.

Another twist to the von Bitter story surfaced in 1969 from perhaps one of the most unlikely of sources. Two Devon fisherman had been offshore at Teignmouth when they caught some unusual objects in their nets. The fishermen hauled the unidentified objects aboard their boat and on return to port, had them examined. The mystery objects turned out to be parts of Feldwebel Joachim von Bitter's Fw 190. One of the pieces of wreckage was identified as part of a wing and the other, heavily encrusted with sea life, was identified as being one of the two 20mm Oerlikon MG FF cannons. Andrew Cruse, an antiques restoration expert from Teignmouth, bought the 20mm cannon off the two fishermen for £10 (a lot of money back in 1969). In an interview in 2005, he recalled his purchase:

> I paid the princely sum of £10 for the cannon and I bought it with the view of restoring it as a museum piece which I would display in my home. The work required removing all of the encrusted sea life from the metalwork was a very considerable, painstakingly slow task. The sea life encrusted

on the metal was just one of the problems; the second was that it had been immersed in salt water for a considerable length of time. The cannon had to firstly be placed into a tank of fresh water where it remained for several days. I then had the task of removing the loaded magazine which contained a full load of sixty 20mm cannon high-explosive and armour-piercing cannon shells. I was able to remove these and have them made safe and these were sold off soon afterwards to local collectors. With the live ammunition removed and being pretty certain that there was not a live cannon shell in the chamber, the cannon was then treated in water with an electrical current. This gradually removed all of the rust and encrustation from the weapon to a point where I could begin cleaning and refurbishing it for display.

I spent a few years gradually working on the cannon until it looked as good as it did the day it was made. In 1973, I then applied to the Home Office to keep the cannon even though it was incapable of firing and the 20mm ammunition that the gun required was now classed as an obsolete calibre. As a result of my application, a lengthy legal battle ensued between myself and the Home Office regarding the lawful ownership of the gun. The Home Office was not happy about me owning the gun and this even made the local press headlines. Several suggestions were made to me which reflected the attitude at the time towards such relics of war. One of the most absurd suggestions was that the gun be cut up into pieces, while the more rational ideas included it being offered to a museum. Official deactivation was never made available as one of the considerations either. I contacted all of the major aviation museums, but none of them was interested in having the gun. In the end the Home Office referred the case to the courts to decide the fate of the gun. The sad outcome of this case was that the courts decided that the gun was to be disposed of, that it was be taken three miles out to sea by local police and members of the British Army and thrown overboard back into the sea where it was found in 1969. It is most likely still there to this day.

In a sense Teignmouth lost a piece of what would have been today a highly desirable piece of its wartime history in what was an utterly senseless bureaucratic exercise.

The idea of having single-engine fighters operating in the fast fighter-bomber role was nothing new at the time. Attacks carried out by groups of single-engine fighters had been conducted as early as 1942, targets normally being coastal towns, waterfront rail networks and shipping. The Focke-Wulf Fw 190 was designed as an air superiority fighter. Although never intended specifically as a fighter-bomber, it was an aircraft well suited to this task, being of sturdy construction, heavily armed and fast. The Fw 190 was without doubt one of the best German fighters of the war. Of course, these tip-and-run raids achieved little in comparison to those carried out by the Luftwaffe bomber groups and served only to terrorize the British civilian population. The Luftwaffe raids of 1943 were born out of desperate times, proving costly in both the men and materiel. By 1943 the Luftwaffe could ill afford to lose experienced pilots and these bombing raids carried out by single-engine fighters only served to hasten the demise of a once formidable fighting force. The raids had little to no effect on the British war effort; the Luftwaffe high command was obviously aware of this yet continued to sacrifice experienced aircrews in futile and indiscriminate attacks. It was a sign to many, particularly in the Allied camp, that the tides of war were now steadily turning against Germany.

# Chapter 19

# Increasing the Punch

The 30mm Rheinmetal-Borsig Maschinenkanone Mk 108 was a purpose-built aircraft cannon, originally developed as a private venture by the Rheinmetal-Borsig company in 1940. The design was submitted to the Reichsluftfahrtministerium (Reich Aviation Ministry) as a result of the requisition for an aircraft cannon capable of bringing down the heavy Allied bombers that were appearing in ever-increasing numbers over the Reich, especially following the onset of the Allied strategic bombing campaign over Germany which began to gather momentum from 1943. It was clear at this stage in the air war, that despite the popularity of aircraft cannon of 20mm calibre, these weapons were proving inadequate for the task of bringing down the four-engine heavy bombers such as the Boeing B-17 Flying Fortress and Consolidated B-24 Liberator.

The 20mm Mauser MG 151/20 cannon was the primary fighter gun of the Luftwaffe and proved itself as a hard-hitting, reliable weapon, its 20mm ammunition more than adequate for the task of dispatching enemy fighters, yet against the heavy bombers its 57g high-explosive shells (of which 3 grams was explosive filling) required an average of twenty to twenty-five strikes to ensure destruction of the target. Günther Rall explained it best:

> The heavy bombers were a problem: the 20mm MG 151 was a very good gun; it could shoot down enemy fighters very easily and without expending a hug amount of ammunition, but the bombers like the B-17 were completely different. They were large, lumbering beasts that required repeated attacks at close range, which then put you in danger from their gunners. The B-17 was heavily defended with 13mm machine guns and the Bf 109G, which I was flying then, could be easily damaged by a 13mm bullet in the wrong

place. The idea was to attack, inflict damage then come around again or, if you were bounced by the enemy fighter escorts, then one of your squadron would follow up your attack. Getting enough concentrated fire into the target was a problem, as often there was not the time to get twenty-five to thirty rounds into a single target and destroy it; often we were forced to break off an attack to focus on another situation such as an enemy escort coming up on your tail. So, the first enemy you fired on and maybe damaged had suddenly gone and you had to pick out another target and so on, and by that time often you ran out of ammunition.

The younger, less-experienced pilots tended to open fire too soon at too great a distance from the target, where the rounds would either fall short or miss completely. This was a natural instinct for new pilots; they felt fear and would open fire too soon and dive away. Those of us who had won victories already knew we had to get in very close: 200 to 250 yards was the normal range I opened fire, but on occasions I opened fire much closer to the target which had a high degree of risk attached.

During the attacks we were being fired at constantly and you had to be aware of this, you couldn't ignore it. We lost many pilots from return fire from heavy bombers during attacks. So, a bigger gun was a good solution as it fired a larger shell that caused more damage which equated to less rounds being necessary to destroy the target. The only problem with the 30mm Mk 108 was its low muzzle velocity which necessitated a close approach to the target. The gun had a high rate of fire though and fired a 330-gram thin-walled high-explosive shell of which 85 grams was RDX explosive filling. If you could get in close and get just four or five shots on target, it was curtains for the bomber. That was the difference.

The 30mm cartridge developed for the Mk 108 cannon was the 30mmx90RB (rebated/reduced rim). This designation basically referred to the calibre of 30mm, the cartridge case length which was 90mm and the cartridge case having a rebated or reduced rim at the primer end of the case. The cases for these rounds were manufactured from steel and coated with a brown lacquer solution. As with the 20mm MG 151/20 rounds, the cases were coated with the brown lacquer solution during production to help prevent corrosion of the steel while in storage or under operational conditions in the field. The lacquer again also aided the extraction process of the fired case as it also acted as a lubricant. Rounds were held in place by means of a metal, disintegrating, linked belt. Several types of 30mm cartridge were developed for the Mk 108, including a target practice (TP) which was usually a solid shot of the same weight and dimensions as a high-explosive round but containing no explosive filling and used specifically for air gunnery training, being a less expensive alternative to using service rounds for practice purposes. There was also an armour-piercing (AP), a standard high-explosive (HE) and an incendiary round. The two main types of 30mm round were the mine shell (*Minengeschoss*) and high-explosive incendiary. The mine shell projectile was made from drawn steel instead of being forged and machined. This produced a projectile with a very thin steel casing and a substantially larger inner cavity which could contain a greater amount of explosive or incendiary filling when compared to a conventional cannon shell.

The 30mm Mk 108 was designed from the outset for ease of mass production. Some 80 per cent of the weapon's construction was stamped parts and the number of moving components in the weapon was kept to a minimum by the adoption of the advanced primer ignition blowback (APIB) principle. In brief, this is a system of operation for self-loading weapons that garners energy from the motion of the cartridge casing as it is pushed to the rear by expanding gas created by the ignition of the propellant charge of the round.

Being made of mostly pressed parts with a simple and lightweight construction, unskilled factory workers, particularly women who began to fill the roles of men, could easily be trained to assemble these weapons.

In the field the 30mm Mk 108 was an easy weapon to maintain and service. It was 41.6 (106cm) inches in length of which 23 inches (55cm) were the barrel, tipping the scales at just 128lb (58kg), it was a remarkably compact and light-weight weapon. These key features and the utilization of electrical priming made the Mk 108 an ideal weapon for application in both fighter and bomber aircraft.

During the initial development and experimentation phase of the 30mm Mk 108, it was installed to fire through the centreline of a

DB 605 engine while the engine was running to test the efficiency of the weapon under the most severe conditions. The weapon fired consistently with the muzzle velocity of 1,770 feet per second, which was low in comparison to the 20mm Mauser MG 151/20 cannon, yet the Mk 108 was specifically designed for use against the slower-flying Allied bombers so a high muzzle velocity was not a necessity. The Mk 108 fired a full magazine of ammunition with no jams or stoppages. The process was repeated several times as is common when a new weapon is undergoing testing. The process was deliberately severe as it was better for any flaws to come to light during the testing phase than when the weapon was entering production. Following a satisfactory series of ground-based testing, the weapon was then fitted in a Messerschmitt Bf 109 for final evaluation. Again, the weapon performed faultlessly, and the weapon was then accepted by the RLM and quickly entered production.

The Mk 108 was also selected for the future Messerschmitt Me 262, the first operational jet fighter. The Me 262 would be fitted with four 30mm Mk 108s, all arranged in the nose of the aircraft. In the case of the Me 262, the ammunition magazines for the armament arrangement were loaded differently, the upper pair of Mk 108s being fed via a linked belt of 100 rounds while the lower pair were fed by the same method but with just sixty rounds of ammunition. The Mk 108 was also selected as the armament for the Messerschmitt Me 163 Komet, a rocket-propelled point defence interceptor that would be armed with two Mk 108s arranged one in each wing root and both with sixty rounds of ammunition.

The Allies soon gave the Mk 108 the nickname of the 'Pneumatic Hammer' due to its monotonous firing tone. Yet, it was a fearsome bomber destroyer that many Allied aircrews came to dread.

Aircraft designated to receive the new 30mm Mk 108 were the Messerschmitt Bf 109G, Messerschmitt Bf 110, Messerschmitt Me 163 Komet rocket fighter, Messerschmitt Me 262, Focke-Wulf Fw 190, Focke-Wulf Ta 152, Focke-Wulf Ta 154, Heinkel He 162 Salamander jet fighter, Heinkel He 219, Horten Ho 229 jet-powered flying wing and the Junkers Ju 388. Of these, the Focke-Wulf Ta 152, Focke-Wulf Ta 154 and Junkers Ju 388 saw little combat service and the Horten Ho 229 jet fighter only reached the prototype phase by the war's end.

In air-to-air combat, fitted in the Bf 109G6 and Bf 110G-2 *Zerstörer*, it was noted that the drop of the shell was 41 metres (135 feet) at a range of 1,000 metres (3,300 feet). Luftwaffe pilots, whose Bf 109Gs were kitted out with the new Mk108 cannons, advised that a close approach to the target was necessary due to the low muzzle velocity and subsequent reduced range of the weapon, indicating that one should open fire at 200 metres (656 feet) to 300 metres (984 feet) range for maximum effect, yet the realities of air warfare often meant that many air-to-air contests with Allied bombers (and fighters) took place at much closer ranges, sometimes less than 60 metres (200 feet). It took much nerve and a good degree of skill to get a Messerschmitt Bf 109 to within 200 feet of a Boeing B-17 Flying Fortress bomber of the US Eight Air Force. The B-17s bristled with defensive .50-calibre heavy machine guns and flew in specially arranged combat boxes in which each aircraft of the formation could effectively cover the other against German fighter attack. The results, however, were devastating when the Bf 109s, armed with the new 30mm Mk 108 cannon, did register hits, as Heinz Knoke recalled:

> I flew a Bf 109G equipped with the new 3cm motor cannon; its effects in combat were deadly – just two or three shells in the right place was often all it took to bring a heavy bomber down. The only problem was its muzzle velocity was not great, and it was imperative to get in close to the target. If you fired from 200 metres, it was much like throwing eggs at a school bus; the rounds would experience drop and they would miss the target. I followed my usual rule and closed to within 182 metres which is around 600 feet; with the closing speed you had just split seconds to fire, but the results were spectacular. I observed bright flashes and debris flying up from the B-17 I had attacked, half expecting to have to attack again, this time from the front. I turned and climbed to gain the advantage, ready for my second attack but when I had come around, I could see the B-17 was now falling from the sky. I watched as parachutes came out of the stricken monster's belly and wished them a safe passage to the ground.

Other Luftwaffe fighter pilots recalled their successes thanks to the 30mm Mk 108's firepower. One young Luftwaffe pilot who had served with JG 26, Theodore Hoff, remembered:

> I was used to the excellent velocity and reach [range] of the 2cm machine-gun 151 cannons, so, finding myself in a Bf 109G, armed with just a single 3cm cannon, I was dubious about it. We knew getting close to the target was essential; they told us all this during the briefings held before our first flight with this new equipment. One of our pilots remarked, 'If we get any closer, we will be taking a lift home with them.' The beauty of the 2cm 151s was that you could open fire further away and still score hits and you had more ammunition. Excuse me if I sounded pessimistic at the time; I was, very much so [he laughs]. Anyway, we were ordered into the air to meet and greet a strong formation of B-24 heavies. On sighting the formation, we climbed above them to open fire from above. We dived down and, as we did, we each selected an enemy target which soon filled our gunsights. I opened fire and saw powerful strikes along the port engine and within seconds I had to take hard evasive action to avoid almost colliding with my target. As I dived down, I saw something very strange; there was this large, broad section of metal falling as if a leaf from a tree, then a complete propeller blade just missed my Bf 109 – it must have passed within twenty feet of me. What had happened was that the B-24 I had fired up had literally disintegrated in the air and as I dived the wreckage was falling around me. A comrade yelled over the radio, 'Hoff, you fool, get up here or you will be curtains.' I looked around as I began to climb, the air full of smoke, and when I looked down, I saw the fuselage of the B-24 spiralling down on fire. I watched it hit the ground; I don't think anyone got out of that one. Following that fight where I had claimed my ninth heavy bomber, I went on to severely damage three more, two of which reportedly went into the North Sea but could not be confirmed as mine. I warmed to the idea of the slower-firing yet harder-hitting gun.

The introduction of the Mk 108 cannon did not herald the demise of the popular 20mm MG 151/20 cannon which remained the standard Luftwaffe aircraft cannon until the end of the war. In light of the increasingly heavy strategic bombing of German cities and industrial centres, German fighters such as the Bf 109 and Fw 190 had their armament augmented with gun packs which could be bolted beneath the wings to provide more firepower against the bomber formations. Not all Luftwaffe fighters of a particular squadron would go into action with these extra guns fitted. Due to the increased weight of these gun packs, some fighter aircraft would go into action with their standard armament which in the Fw 190A-8 was four 20mm MG 151 cannons and two 13mm MG 131 machine guns, and in the Bf 109G a single 20mm MG 151/20 or 30mm Mk 108 cannon and two 13mm MG 131 machine guns. The fighters with the standard armament would take on the fighters escorting the American bombers into the Reich, while the fighters with the extra guns would concentrate on attacking the bombers. The extra gun packs came in two main types: a pod containing a single 20mm MG 151/20 cannon plus ammunition which the Bf 109 would be fitted with, a pair under each wing. The second variation was a heavier twin 20mm MG 151/20 gun pack of two MG 151/20 cannons plus ammunition. This configuration was added to the FW 190A-8s as a twin pack beneath each wing. So, the Fw 190 would be going into action with eight 20mm MG 151/20 cannons plus two 13mm MG 131 machine guns, an exceptionally heavy armament even by modern standards. The reaction of the pilots who flew these bomber destroyer fighters was mixed: Günther Rall expressed his views:

> I didn't like flying with the extra guns on the Bf 109, as they gave all kinds of problems. For one, the Bf 109 struggled to keep up with the new American fighters such as the P-51 [Mustang] and P-47 [Thunderbolt]. These extra cannons were bolted underneath the wings and the extra weight and adverse effects on performance were very noticeable. One of the biggest problems with these cannons slung under the wings was that in a dogfight where you are turning and twisting, the centrifugal forces often interfered with the metal ammunition belts in the magazine and when you pressed your button to fire, the cannons wouldn't

> work. I don't think these extra cannons were worth all the trouble. I didn't believe in having large batteries of guns in a fighter aircraft. I knew that the Focke-Wulf Fw 190A-8 was sometimes fitted with up to eight 2cm cannons; it was possibly the only single-seat, single-engine fighter aircraft we had at the time that was capable of carrying such a load. I never flew one of these but can imagine the strain this put on both the aircraft and the pilot trying to fly it and fight in it. If caught by the escorting fighters, you'd be finished as the weight and drag must have been through the roof. Yes, if you could get through to the bombers, you could blow them out of the sky with all those guns firing at once, but you would be a sitting duck for a Mustang or a Thunderbolt.

Perhaps the only development in high-velocity 30mm cannon for the Luftwaffe came in 1942 with the 30mm Rheinmetall-Borsig Mk 103 which was a refinement of its predecessor, the Mk 101. The Mk 103 was an exceptionally powerful cannon intended as dual-purpose weapon which could be used in the air-to-ground and air-to-air combat role. The cartridge developed for this formidable weapon was the 30mmx184B, this designation referring to the 30mm calibre, then the length of the cartridge case (minus projectile) at 184mm and the B referring to the fact that the cartridge had a belt just above the extractor groove. The cartridge came in two main types, an HE/M or high-explosive mine shell and an APCR or armour-piercing composite rigid. The muzzle velocity of the HE/M round was 2,800 feet per second and the APCR 3,100 feet per second, quite considerable for a 30mm, or 3cm, weapon of its day. Rounds were fed into the gun via a disintegrating, metal linked belt. The cartridges were manufactured from both steel and brass and both likely coated with lacquer in line with other Luftwaffe cannon cartridges. The weapon was far more complex in design than the Mk 108 and considerably larger at 91.9 inches (233.4cm) in length – 52.7 inches (133.8cm) of the length being the gun barrel – and weighing in at a whopping 311lb (141kg). The Mk 103 utilized a gas/recoil operation; after firing the gas pressure from the expended round served to unlock the breech of the cannon, while the recoiling barrel acted to cycle the action by way of ejecting the fired cartridge case and loading a fresh round into the chamber in a single movement. The Achilles' heel of the Mk 103 was fourfold. The fact that it was being manufactured late in the war and had to be constructed from lower-grade steel meant that the mechanism of the Mk 103 was not as strong as the original Mk 101 cannon. To resolve this issue a lower-charge cartridge was used which resulted in a 100m/s reduction in muzzle velocity compared to the Mk 101. Also, the limited ammunition capacity when used in aircraft was a tactical hinderance. The heavy weight of both the weapon and ammunition often meant only a single Mk 103 cannon could be carried even on a twin-engine aircraft, which ruled the Mk 103 out as a suitable gun for single-engine fighters such as the Bf 109. The original specification of the Mk 103 required that it be capable of being fitted to fire through the engine centreline of a single-seat fighter. However, it proved too large and heavy to fit as a centrally firing armament in the Bf 109. When first considered, it was soon dismissed as the breech of the Mk 103 would have barely left room for the pilot's legs in the cockpit. Nor could it have been fitted as a wing armament in the Bf 109 either as the asymmetric forces generated by the cannon's firing would have caused too much disturbance to its flight, and caused the nose of the aircraft to yaw to one side. In fact, the only known use of the Mk 103 in an engine-mounted configuration was in the Dornier Do 335, and this was a modified version of the Mk 103, the Mk 103M, with the profile of the barrel greatly reduced. It is also believed that experiments with the Mk 103M were conducted with the view of possible installation as the centrally firing armament of the Bf 109K, but whether this saw any active service is highly unlikely.

The one Luftwaffe aircraft which did make good use of the Mk 103 cannon was the twin-engine Henschel Hs 129B ground-attack aircraft where a single 30mm Mk 103 was fitted beneath the centreline of the fuselage. To close on the subject of the 30mm Rheinmetall-Borsig Mk 103, it was also rumoured that on the Eastern Front the Luftwaffe were using these cannons along with a small quantity of ammunition containing a crude form of uranium material in the projectiles. These rounds were specifically intended for use in the ground-attack role, primarily against Soviet tanks. In my opinion I believe this to be from the realm of fantasy, as the processes involved and the materials required to manufacture such munitions just did not exist in Germany at that time nor in the quantities that would have been required, even to produce just a few such rounds.

If the Mk 103 was construed as a heavyweight amongst barrelled German aircraft armament of the war, then the BK 3.7 (Bordkanone 3.7, or onboard cannon 3.7) set the bar where the cannon was replaced by what was effectively airborne artillery. The Germans began experimenting with ever-increasing calibres of airborne guns mainly for use against Soviet armour. The 37mm BK 3.7 was probably the most tactically useful arrangement of its kind deployed by the Luftwaffe and was introduced into service in 1942, remaining in service until the end of the war.

The BK 3.7 was designed and developed by Rheinmetall-Borsig, notably from their highly successful 3.7cm Flak 18 anti-aircraft gun. The weapon weighed in at 295kg (650lb) and was 3,630mm (11 feet 11 inches) in length. It utilized the same 37mmx263B cartridge as in the ground-based anti-aircraft version, with only two dedicated anti-armour rounds being introduced specifically for use against armour, these being the tungsten-cored 37mm APCR weighing 380 grams (13oz) and 37mm AT weighing 685 grams (24.2oz). The standard anti-personnel round was the HE which weighed 640 grams (23oz). These high-explosive rounds had a grenade-like effect and were lethal against lightly armoured targets and troops out in the open. The cartridge cases were usually made from steel, making them heavy and powerful rounds for aircraft use. The weapon functioned on the short recoil principle and fired at 160 rounds per minute at a muzzle velocity of 780 to 1,170 metres per second (3,800 to 2,600 feet per second) which is very respectable for a weapon of this calibre. The effective range of this weapon was quoted at 500 metres (550 yards/1,650 feet).

The most notable application of the weapon was as a twin wing-mounted arrangement on the Junkers Ju 87G Stuka used in the anti-tank/ground-attack role. The weapons were carried in pods slung beneath each wing just outboard of the undercarriage legs. Ammunition was fed to the guns via a twelve-round, linkless box-type magazine fitted to the left-hand side of each weapon. When the weapon was first used in action, the results were surprisingly disappointing. Accuracy was described as poor, weight was considerable and tactically it had insufficient ammunition. However, with a skilled ground-attack pilot like Hans-Ulrich Rudel at the controls, this configuration proved its worth. Rudel destroyed 519 Soviet tanks in 2,530 sorties in the Ju 87G armed with two of these 37mm cannons. It proved that with both practice and patience, high kill tallies with these large airborne weapons were feasible despite their drawbacks. One of Rudel's comrades recalled of the man:

> Rudel was a curious individual as he never drank alcohol – in fact, he preferred milk – he never smoked cigarettes or cigars, and never attempted to sow tales of womanizing. In his spare time he preferred to indulge in sporting activities. He was a decent, quietly spoken man that you'd find very hard to dislike. His combat experience prior to arrival on the Eastern Front had been somewhat limited, yet he showed what a quiet, unassuming individual could aspire to. To some he was recklessly brave in combat. For example, when he attacked, he would go in much lower than the rest of us would ever dare; as a result, he had a higher success rate. He was also the master of the Ju 87; yes, Rudel and the Ju 87 were like two lovers making love; they worked in perfect harmony with one another, a combination which made both him and his aircraft a very effective combination. I once saw Rudel dive onto a tank; he destroyed it by firing directly into the turret roof while a nearby anti-aircraft gun opened fire on him, only for him to turn his attention to this weapon and destroy it too. It was remarkable to watch him in action. Despite the danger and fury of battle, Rudel remained consummately cool and focused on the task of destroying the enemy.

In a rare interview via letter before his death on 18 December 1982, Rudel himself recalled:

> Perfection in warfare is a state of mind as is the hunter's instinct. To be sure of hitting your target and not blasting away at long range and wasting your ammunition, you had to get in close to your target. It is the same for an African lion in pursuit of the gazelle – the lion is not successful by just chasing his quarry. The techniques I used were nothing unique to me personally; many of the *Jagdflieger* [fighter pilots] applied much the same techniques in destroying enemy bombers. 'Let your target fill your gunsight,' they used to say before firing. I took that same advice, applying it to ground-attack operations. From practical experience you soon learn, and it is like anything: there will always be those who do better than others.

> You ask about the 3.7cm Bordkanone as fitted to the Ju 87G which I flew in the Russian campaign. To fit two such guns to the Ju 87 was not my original idea. We did not have a cannon capable of knocking out a tank which could be carried by conventional fighters at the time; the only way this could be done was to fit larger-calibre guns to an aircraft which was capable of bearing the extra weight where aerodynamics was not a vital necessity. The Ju 87G was ideal for this role and so it was agreed to trial pairing 3.7cm guns in an arrangement of one beneath each wing, complete with ammunition boxes for twelve shots each. These 3.7cm guns were large and powerful but only so long as the rounds you fired hit the right mark. With the Ju 87 you could climb above the Soviet tanks, select your target and dive vertically down upon him and strike him in his most vulnerable area of the topside and turret roof where the armour plating was generally at its thinnest. Yes, getting close, firing your guns and then pulling up at the last minute was physically demanding for any pilot for the obvious reasons of the g forces coming into play and how they affected you. Yet I would always tell anyone that if you're firing and find yourself just shooting dirt, you are not close enough.

Another airborne gun concept that may have appeared technically outlandish was that of the Rheinmetall Bordkanone 5, a weapon in existence from 1942/3 yet did not enter service, albeit in small numbers, until 1944. The earliest recorded use of this weapon on board an aircraft was in the Flak-suppression role on the Eastern Front, near Stalingrad, early in the winter of 1942/3. A small number of Heinkel He 177 heavy bombers were fitted with these heavy guns and tasked with carrying out this rather pointless exercise.

This weapon of 50mm calibre was an adaptation of the KwK 39 tank gun as fitted to the Panzer III tank. It utilized a 50mmx419R cartridge which offered both high muzzle velocity at around 600 metres per second (1,968 feet per second) and substantial kinetic energy at the target. The weapon could be fired at American bombers well beyond the range of the bombers' defensive machine guns, which in turn required its own unique sighting system separate from the standard Revi gunsight. Other Luftwaffe aircraft selected to be fitted with this weapon were the Messerschmitt Me 410A-1/U4 Hornisse (Hornet) bomber-destroyer (one gun fitted internally with drum-type magazine), Junkers Ju 88 (one gun fitted in ventral blister) and in a purely experimental context the Messerschmitt Me 262A-1A/U4 (single weapon fitted in the nose with the barrel protruding well forward of the aircraft's nose). In the Me 410 Hornisse the 50mm guns were installed in the type as a factory modification, or *Umrust-Bausatze*, with twenty-one rounds carried in a circular drum magazine. The weapon weighed in at 540kg (1,190lb) and was 4.348 metres (14.27 feet) in length. The primary ammunition type for destroying bombers was the HE round, which possessed considerable incendiary and fragmentation effect: just one hit was all that was required to bring down a heavy bomber. In all only some 300 of these 50mm guns were produced, clearly reflecting the limited use of the weapon in combat. Intended as a long-range, one-shot, one-kill weapon, it was fitted with a special long-range sighting telescope. Of the fifty-three Me 410s of II/ZG 26 fitted with this weapon, a total of between nine and twelve B-17 Flying Fortress and four B-24 Liberator bombers were claimed over five to six interceptions, while losing nine of their Me 410s in the process. An example of the BK 5's effectiveness against Allied bombers is perhaps the account given by the *Staffelkapitan* of 5/ZG 26, Oberleutnant Fritz Stehle:

> We had the Messerschmitt Me 410/U4 adapted for the *Zerstörer* role. Each aircraft had a 5cm-calibre cannon loaded with high-explosive incendiary ammunition. On 22 February 1944, the Allies conducted a major air offensive aimed at our fighter production facilities at Prufening, where parts for Messerschmitt fighters were produced. The fighter assembly plant at Obertraubling was also targeted. Ten of our BK 5-armed Me 410s took off from Oberpfaffenhofen where our airfield was located. By the time we were in a favourable position and altitude to attack the enemy bombers, they had already unloaded their bombs on the targets. As the enemy began to set their course for their return flight, we were ready to greet them, and we went in to attack the enemy bombers which were the

heavy Boeing-type aircraft with four engines [B-17s]. At 1310 hours, I claimed my first kill using the BK 5. I fired a single shot into the enemy aircraft at close range and was preparing to fire a second when the aircraft exploded and fell in flames, crashing in the vicinity of Dachau. My comrade, Feldwebel Baunicke, was also successful in shooting down one of the enemy. He claimed a Boeing as destroyed at 1300 hours. The BK 5 was very effective provided your aim was correct which was not always easy. The BK 5's explosive shell was lethal, requiring just a single hit from my own experience. The blast and incendiary effect of the BK 5 shell was sufficient to blow a Boeing out of the sky. However, the sighting of the weapon could be problematic: vibration from the engines, especially when at full throttle, often caused visual distortion of the optics, making aim difficult. This necessitated yet again a close approach to the target and losing a degree of standoff advantage. That aside, in all other respects, the BK 5 was very reliable, powerful and accurate for a weapon of its calibre set to a task for which it was never designed.

Another colossus born of desperate times was the even larger-calibre. fully automatic Rheinmetall BK 75 cannon of 75mm calibre. The weapon was already in existence in the form of the ground-based infantry weapon, the PaK 40 anti-tank gun. This particular weapon had already undergone modification for proposed use on the Ju 88P-1 and was further modified for use in the Henschel Hs 129. Despite its weight at 1,200kg (2,600lb), the BK 75 was actually lighter than the PaK 40. A new hydraulic, recoil-dampening system was designed along with a more aerodynamically efficient muzzle brake. An automatic loading system with twelve rounds of 75mmx714R ammunition was contained within a rotary magazine located in the empty space well aft of the pilot's seat to the rear of the cockpit. The 75mmx714R cartridge was exceptionally powerful: the charge had to be reduced in order to moderate recoil. The 75mm armour-piercing shot weighed 6.8kg (12lb) and possessed a muzzle velocity of 700 metres per second (2,296 feet per second). The weapon plus its associated recoil mechanism occupied a substantial gun blister beneath the fuselage of the aircraft. A circular duct was located to the rear of the blister where expended ammunition cases were ejected after firing. (One might imagine that an overhead Hs 129 firing this weapon might prove hazardous to troops on the ground owing to the size of the shell casings.) As effective as this large-calibre weapon might have been, it saw only limited use in the war. It proved highly unpopular with Hs 129 pilots who found that the aircraft could barely take off with this gun system fitted. Despite the efforts made to counter the recoil on firing, it still made any aircraft fitted with it unstable, sluggish and a prime target for enemy fighters.

Kurt von Brauschnig worked for the Rheinmetall company's technical department from 1942 to 1944 and recalls the work carried out on the BK 75 weapon:

> I feel it was a good weapon that could have done its job, but it would have been better to conduct more research into smaller-calibre weapons that could have been capable of doing the same job without all the additional problems that big guns incurred, not only on the aircraft to which they were fitted but also the logistics train involved. With the BK 75 we went out to the frontline airfields to oversee what amounted to a settling-in period for the pilots whose Hs 129 aircraft were fitted with the gun. There were some problems with the gun failing to fire on occasions. This was down to jamming of the feed mechanism. Pilots also reported problems with effective sighting units as those in service at the time did not lend themselves well to use from the air, due mainly to vibration experienced in flight often giving a blurred field of view. Then pilots complained that the extra weight made them sitting ducks for Soviet fighters, so escorts had to be provided to protect them which was a further headache for resources which at the time were dwindling rapidly due to the war situation. In my own personal reports to the Luftwaffe armaments offices the BK 75 performed reasonably well in a tactically favourable environment yet reliability was still questionable; more research needed to be done and the pilots' accounts taken into consideration. I could hardly go back to them with reports of, 'Oh, well, this idea is a pile of shit and it is endangering the lives of our

> pilots' as they'd have probably had me shot or something, I don't know, so I was diplomatic to say the least with what I passed on to my superiors.

Along with the introduction of ever-increasing calibres of automatic cannons for Luftwaffe use, applications where the guns fired upwards into the belly of an enemy aircraft were also in use. *Schräge Musik* – colloquially, 'music with unusual tuning' or 'slanted' music – was one such application often fitted to night-fighter aircraft such as the Bf 110G-4 and Heinkel He 219 where various combinations of 20mm and 30mm upward-firing cannons were trialled quite successfully and soon introduced into service. The most effective combination was the utilization of two 30mm Mk 108 cannons. *Schräge* refers to the slanted angle by which the guns were fitted in the aircraft. The Luftwaffe night-fighter crews were vectored in to the vicinity of the Allied bomber streams where they would seek out and attack their victims from their most vulnerable spot below. This method of attack was not without its risks as Oberleutnant Otto Wilhelm Leyke recalled of a night interception mission in late 1944:

> We took off at 0300 hours as warning of a large formation of enemy bombers had been detected assembling over East Anglia; from the moment we had received that warning, we had been at a state of readiness to take off. Once the course of the enemy was ascertained that they would be entering our sector airspace, we prepared to intercept them by following instructions from our ground-based radar network. Their job was to direct our night fighters into the enemy bomber stream where our own airborne radar detection equipment usually did the rest. Night interception was fraught with all kinds of dangers such as a mid-air collision with either friendly aircraft or the enemy you were pursuing. On several occasions I was also hit by splinters from our own Flak. It was a hostile and confusing arena to have to fight in, but you got used to it with time.
>
> We orbited our sector and the ground controller warned me that enemy bombers were passing through and I should detect them. Our own radar picked up an aircraft some

600 yards ahead of us, so I opened my throttle to catch up with him. The Heinkel He 219 was a fast aircraft and we soon caught up with whatever was ahead of us in the darkness. I could feel a vibration through the aircraft, which was unnatural, which was of course the slipstream or air disturbance caused by the propeller wash of the enemy bomber I was closing in on. I knew he was close, but I had to establish a visual contact to be sure; this was the moment of greatest risk: if he saw me first, he would get the first shots off which could prove deadly for us. Closing in carefully, I could make out against the dark blue of the night sky the silhouette of twin tails. I throttled back for a moment and, happy that he was unaware of my presence, I opened the throttle and put the aircraft into a shallow dive, levelled out and then reduced my speed again. I looked up and he was right where I needed him, directly above me. As I prepared to fire the two fuselage-mounted, upward-firing 3cm cannons, I had one hand ready to open up the throttles to maximum power. Once I depressed that cannon switch, I would need to dive away as fast as possible to avoid debris hitting my aircraft, or worse, being blown to smithereens if his bombs went off. This was always a tense moment: synchronizing speed to match that of my enemy, steadily dropping down to a safe distance before preparing to fire. I held my breath for a moment then squeezed the firing button; the two 3cm cannons fired for two seconds. I pushed the throttle open full, diving hard to the right as an orange ball of flame erupted above us. As I dived away there was crashing sound and it was clear something had hit us. It was not return fire from the enemy – I was sure of that – but what the hell was it? I told my radar operator sitting immediately behind me to be prepared to eject from the aircraft on my command. Control of the aircraft seemed fine and our engines were running as normal but with one enemy bomber claimed as destroyed, we decided under the circumstances to return to the airfield. When we landed and made an inspection of the aircraft, we found what was approximately a six-foot-long piece of an enemy bomber propeller blade embedded in the

> rear fuselage. The propeller was identified as being from a Rolls-Royce engine. Our victim was a British Lancaster that had crashed to the ground in pieces as the bombs had detonated when my cannon shells hit home. If that propeller blade had come through the cockpit, it would have taken both our heads clean off. The structural damage to our aircraft was severe enough for it to be written off and we were given a new aircraft and were in action again some four nights later.

Apart from the barrelled weapons, two rocket/mortar-launch tubes designed to be carried by both single- and twin-engine fighter aircraft were introduced into service. The 21cm (8-inch) Werfer-Granate 21 (Wfr.Gr.21) was an interesting development, specifically for use against the tightly packed formations of American bombers. In the official Luftwaffe armourer manual this weapon is referred to as the BR 21 or Bordrakete 21. This weapon was the first onboard air-to-air rocket to enter service with the Luftwaffe. Developed by the Rheinmetall-Borsig company, it was introduced into service in mid-1943 under the leadership of Dipl-Ing (Engineer) Rudolf Nebel who had pioneered the use of wing-mounted offensive rocketry systems in the First World War with the Luftstreitkrafte. Basically, the 21cm projectile was a development of the Nebelwerfer 42 infantry-barrage rocket projectile reconfigured for aerial use by the addition of spin stabilization. The rocket, referred to as a mortar, was propelled by 18.4kg (41lb) of solid diglycol fuel. The warhead weighed 40.8 kg (90lb) and the round had a muzzle velocity of 320 metres per second (350 yards per second) travelling at a speed of 1,150kph or 716mph out to a range of 1,200 metres (1,300 yards). The rocket tube was no lightweight at 112kg (247lb) and any single-engine fighter carrying two of these tubes would find its performance and manoeuvrability seriously hindered as a result. Due to the ballistic drop of the relatively low-velocity rocket, the launch tube had to be fitted at roughly a 15° angle upward of the line of flight. It was quite obvious the amount of drag this would create on the airframe carrying it. Fighters not fitted with these rocket tubes would sometimes – tactical situations permitting – act as a form of escort for those fighters who were. The launch tubes could be jettisoned after use, enabling the fighter to return to its 'clean performance' yet, until the tubes were discharged, the aircraft carrying them remained highly vulnerable to enemy fighter escorts. The rocket warhead was fitted with a time fuze which detonated the warhead at a pre-set distance of some 600 metres (2,000 feet) to 1,200 metres (3,900 feet) from the point of launch, which resulted in a lethal blast area covering 30 metres (98 feet). Fighters such as the Bf 109G carried two launch tubes, one under each wing, while the *Zerstörer* heavy twin-engine fighters such as the Bf 110 were fitted with two under each wing. Again, despite the fact that these launch tubes could be jettisoned after use, the effect on aerodynamics and general performance until they were fired was quite considerable and as a result, this weapon was unpopular with aircrews. Accurate aiming of this weapon was also particularly difficult, requiring good judgement by the pilot in order to achieve success. In many cases the rockets exploded either too far ahead of the bomber formations or too far behind them. For the bomber crews on the receiving end of even near misses, they were an alarming sight, often having the effect of dispersing the formations sufficiently for the Luftwaffe fighters to engage them with their conventional cannon and machine gun armament. Heinz Knoke recalled the use of these 21cm rocket weapons:

> We were constantly searching for ways to tackle the huge formations of American heavy bombers, particularly methods of taking multiple targets down in one pass. This could not be achieved with a standard gun armament. As you know, I trialled methods of dropping bombs from above onto the American formations and this did achieve devastating success when you got it right.
>
> The rocket projectiles then were first-generation weapons of their kind, but it would take many years for rocket armaments to be truly reliable and accurate; the launch apparatus was heavy and unwieldly and was a severe hinderance to your aircraft's performance. When used in action, delivering them accurately, even into a huge formation of heavy bombers, was no easy task. The weapons either exploded before they were in the right place or, sometimes, they were way off target. The only way success could be guaranteed was a close approach to the target which defeated the object of using them really.

> The American bombers were heavily defended and were dangerous to take liberties with, even with these rockets. My experience with the 21cm weapon was that it was not that effective, large numbers were required and some of the rockets actually passed clean through the target without exploding. Those people in charge of developing armament systems were constantly toiling to improve on these weapons and I think, with the R4M [Rakete, 4 kilogramm, Minenkopf], they were finally starting to get things right as the R4M was a very effective air-launched rocket and could be lethal against the bombers.

Fighter groups JG 1, JG 11, ZG 26 and ZG 76 all made use of the 21cm Wfr. Gr.21 throughout the spring of 1943. The FW 190s, Bf 109Gs and Bf 110s fitted with these weapons attacked the American bomber formations in groups of three to four aircraft and in *Staffel* strength of up to ten to twelve aircraft. Most attacks using this weapon were carried out from the flanks or astern of the bomber formations. The lessons learned from the combat use of the Wfr.Gr.21 were put into the vastly superior R4M.

The R4M (Rakete 4 kilogramm Minekopf, or Rocket 4-kilogram Mine-head) entered service in 1944, too late to affect the outcome of the air war. Had it entered service earlier in sufficient quantities, along with the Me 262, the first operational jet fighter, then this weapon might have proved decisive in the fierce air battles that took place over Europe. The was far superior in most respects to the Wfr.Gr.21 and came in a far more compact package. Manufactured by Heber AG of Osterode, each rocket weighed 3.2kg (7lb), was 81.2cm in length (31 inches) with a calibre of 55mm. The muzzle velocity was 525 metres per second (1,722 feet per second) equating to 1,175mph. Each rocket contained 520 grams (18oz) of brisant (shattering capability) hexogen explosive for the air-to-air role, and was provided with enough propellant fuel to be fired from a distance of 1,000 metres, which was just outside the range of the .50-calibre heavy machine guns that formed the American bombers' defensive armament. The rockets were of simple construction of a steel tube with eight base-hinged, flip-out stabilizing fins which deployed the second the rocket left its launch apparatus. A typical battery consisted of two groups of twelve; once all twenty-four were salvoed into a formation of heavy bombers, they would fill an area around 15 by 30 metres (450m$^2$) at 1,000 metres.

This density of munitions made it almost a certainty that enemy aircraft would be hit. R4Ms were also fired in four salvoes of six at intervals of 70 milliseconds from a range of 600 metres. These would fly at supersonic speed towards the target with a 60 per cent higher velocity than the Wfr. Gr21. One R4M rocket was designed for use against ground targets such as tanks and utilized a shaped-charge warhead similar in construction to that of the Panzerschreck anti-tank bazooka as used by the Heer. This remarkable and highly effective weapon proved devastating in the few air contests where it was used. The R4M was first deployed in combat on 18 March 1945. Six aircraft of 9 Staffel, each armed with twenty-four R4M rockets, attacked an Allied bomber formation over Rathenow. The Luftwaffe pilots were Leutnant Schnorrer, Oberleutnant Seeler, Oberfhanrich Windish, Fahnrich Ehrig and Oberfhanrich Ullrich. Leading the attack was Oberleutnant Wegmann. The fighters released their rockets at a range of 400 metres and the effect was devastating. Oberleutnant Wegmann recalled:

> We watched as the rockets streaked towards the enemy formation at very high speed, leaving a silvery trail behind them. As the rockets exploded among the formation of enemy aircraft, all you could see were shattered fuselages, broken-off wings and tails, ripped-out engines and debris of every kind falling like metal confetti. It looked as if somebody had taken a full box of tools and tipped them up: there was falling debris everywhere, swirling in the air around us. Had we had more aircraft armed with these rockets, say a couple of years earlier, we could have defended the skies over Germany with far greater effect than what we ever did with guns. Had we received the R4M say in 1942/3 we could have changed the outcome, that I am sure of. Of course, it is frustrating to think back on it now.

Notable aircraft fitted with this weapon were mostly the Messerschmitt Me 262 and the ground-attack version of the Focke-Wulf Fw 190 where the small boxlike launchers were mounted on wooden racks in a one launcher under each wing configuration.

Also devised for Luftwaffe use were mortar-type weapons which worked on a similar principle to the *Schräge Musik* cannon installations.

Most notable was the *Jagdfaust* (hunting fist) which comprised four 5cm launch tubes; designed primarily for use in the Me 163 rocket fighter, there were intended to fit in the wings firing upwards, each tube containing a 5cm-calibre high-explosive projectile. A unique feature was the firing mechanism. All the Me 163 pilot had to do was fly beneath his intended target and, as he passed below it, an optical photocell detected the dark shadow of the enemy aircraft which in turn automatically initiated firing. Once the tubes had discharged their projectiles, such was the force that on firing the retaining pins which were purposely designed to break would shear, and the empty metal tubes would be ejected downwards, falling away from the aircraft. This served not only to offset the recoil but also to counter any effect on aerodynamics so as not to hinder the aircraft with unnecessary weight.

The Luftwaffe had also pioneered the development and use of a new revolutionary radio-controlled bomb for anti-shipping operations. The difficulty faced by Luftwaffe bomber crews, particularly when attacking moving enemy vessels at sea were concerned, resulted in the Fritz X, the world's first truly precision-guided weapon. Fritz X was a development of the PC1400 (*Panzersprengbombe, Cylindrisch* 1,400kg), an aerial bomb designed to penetration armour. The Fritz X was guided to its target by means of a Kehl-Strasbourg radio-control link which sent guidance signals to moveable spoilers of the bomb's tail unit. As the bomb was launched and propelled towards its target by a rocket motor. the bombardier of the launch aircraft would visually steer the bomb onto its intended target. The bomber wing III/KG 100 was the only Luftwaffe bomber wing to deploy the Fritz X in combat and the results showed the weapon's potential. The Fritz X claimed its first victim in spectacular fashion on 9 September 1943 when a Dornier 217 of KG 100 deployed the weapon and sank the Italian battleship *Roma*.

As with all of the potentially war-winning weaponry produced by Nazi Germany, the R4M came too late to change the inevitable outcome of the air war. Ironically, the R4M would set the standard for postwar Allied development in air-to-air rocketry.

# Chapter 20

# Jet and Rocket Aircraft

It would be somewhat unfair at this juncture not to highlight the credit that Ernst Heinkel rightly deserves in respect of the development of jet-propelled aircraft in the Second World War. Heinkel had been conducting research into high-speed flight for some years and the end product of this research was the Heinkel He 280, which was the first turbojet-powered fighter aircraft in the world. It was developed through its predecessor, the Heinkel He 178, which was powered by a single Heinkel HeS 3 (Heinkel Strahltriebwerke 3) turbojet utilizing diesel fuel which produced 992lb of thrust and a top speed of 372mph (600kph), not bad for an aircraft which made its maiden flight on 27 August 1939, just days prior to Germany's invasion of Poland.

Much of Heinkel's work had been subject to secrecy, and even the Luftwaffe was not aware of the existence of either the testbed or prototype aircraft. On 1 November 1939, Heinkel arranged a demonstration of his new turbojet-powered aircraft. In attendance were Ernst Udet (head of the RLM's development branch) and Erhard Milch (Minister of Aircraft Production and Supply). Göring had been invited but typically chose not to attend.

The test pilot at the controls was Erich Warsitz, a man who has the honour of being the first to fly a rocket-powered aircraft, namely the Heinkel He 176, on its maiden flight in June 1939, followed up with the He 178 in August. At the demonstration, to his rather limited audience, Warsitz put the He 178 through its paces, yet on landing, both Udet and Milch were less than impressed by the new aircraft's performance. From a technical perspective the new aircraft had proved a point, so undeterred, Heinkel immediately set about work on another design which would emerge as the Heinkel He 280, a twin-engine jet-fighter design produced as a private venture utilizing research gained from both the He 176 and He 178. The design utilized elliptical wings, dihedralled tailplane, twin fins and rudders plus a tricycle undercarriage arrangement. It was soon revealed that the undercarriage, apart from possessing little in the way of ground clearance, was found to be too fragile for the grass or dirt airstrips of the time, yet the tricycle undercarriage layout soon gained acceptance. The He 280 was also unique in being the first aircraft to be equipped with a pilot ejection system. This came in the form of an ejector seat which in an emergency would eject the pilot from the aircraft by means of compressed air rather than the explosive cartridges employed later.

The first prototype He 280 was ready by the summer of 1940 yet the HeS engines which were to power the aircraft had run into technical difficulties. As work on the engines progressed, the prototype He 280 underwent glide tests with ballistic pods fitted in place of the engines. It was some six months later, on 30 March 1941, that test pilot Fritz Schäfer flew the second prototype under its own power. The new aircraft was demonstrated to Ernst Udet on 5 April but, as with the other Heinkel prototypes, they failed to impress. One factor that did impress was that the He 280's engines could burn kerosene, a fuel which required less-expensive refining than the high-octane fuel used by piston-engine aircraft; however, government funding for the He 280 was not forthcoming at this critical phase of the aircraft's development. Subsequently, further work was painfully slow mainly due to the development of new engines.

Yet, a third prototype was constructed, this aircraft being fitted with an improved engine version, HeS 8. In the demonstration the He 280 took part in a mock dogfight with a Focke-Wulf Fw 190. The He 280 displayed the merits of its vastly superior speed, completing four laps of an oval course before the Fw 190 could only complete three. Only at this point did the RLM begin to realize the possible merits of a jet-powered aircraft.

The RLM placed an order for twenty preproduction test Hs 280s, to be followed by 300 production aircraft. Due to continued technical issues with the engines, the RLM ordered Heinkel to abandon all further work on the HeS 8 and HeS 30 engines to concentrate their resources on a follow-on engine, the HeS 011. This engine was a far more advanced design that presented a whole new array of technical problems which Heinkel's technicians had to attempt to overcome.

The first prototype He 280 was re-equipped with pulsejet engines and the aircraft was towed to altitude for testing. Poor weather conditions brought the test to a swift end when test pilot Helmut Schenk began to experience control surfaces icing up and, unable to regain full control of the aircraft, he was forced to eject, becoming the first man to put an ejection seat to the test. The ejector seat functioned perfectly but the aircraft was lost and never recovered. With further delays in the engine department, Erhard Milch finally postponed the Heinkel project indefinitely. Heinkel was instead asked to focus on the development and construction of bomber aircraft, something which he remained angry and bitter about until his death. The sad fact about the cancellation of the He 280 was that Ernst Heinkel was never in as favourable a position, socially or politically, as was Willy Messerschmitt. The granting of contracts appeared very much to operate along the lines of an 'old boys' network' – who was in favour and who wasn't, a case of not what you knew but who you knew. Either way, the He 280 debacle left a nasty taste in the mouths of those who had test flown the aircraft. As news reached Heinkel of the cancellation of the project, test pilot Erich Warsitz recalled:

> For a while we had the initiative over the Allies as we were working on an aircraft that was more revolutionary and faster than anything which had previously flown. The early tests were all the proof that people like Milch and Udet needed, yet they couldn't see any further than their noses. Had we been given more time to sort out the problems with the engines, which I feel was achievable, then we could have had an operational jet fighter far earlier than what we did, and our pilots could have gained total air superiority with sufficient numbers despite the low engine-service life. As a test pilot, when you feel something is right and you are trying to convince those to listen to you and they don't, it is the worst possible feeling. I felt victory in the war slipping through my fingers like sand at that point. We didn't have time on our side, and we failed to exploit the merits of the He 280. Yes, it was bad for Heinkel whom I had worked very closely with. I had much respect for him and naturally he felt all his time had been wasted. It was bad for the outcome of the war too as we all now know.

It is sad that the potential of the Heinkel Hs 280 was not seized upon by either Udet or Milch. Had the two taken the aircraft more seriously, it could have been in frontline service as a fighter more than a year earlier than the Messerschmitt Me 262. When one considers all of the facts regarding the He 280, it is plain to see that had the powers that be in both the RLM and Luftwaffe utilized this aircraft, it may have provided a competitive interim solution between the Fw 190 and Me 262, and it may well have assisted the Luftwaffe in maintaining air superiority at a time when the Allied air forces lacked a comparable fighter.

It beggars belief that Nazi Germany's research and development into the feasibility of rocket- and jet-powered aircraft had been in existence as early as 1936, yet this new technology was never fully exploited, at least not early enough. Due mainly to political reasons it would be Messerschmitt whose name became synonymous with the honour of having provided Germany's first two operational jet- and rocket-powered fighter aircraft.

When the Messerschmitt Me 262 was first rolled out of its hangar, it heralded the dawn of a new era in aerial warfare. The Me 262 was an aestheticist's dream, its technically flawless design was like something from the twenty-first century, yet its captivating beauty belied its lethality. Even static in its hangar, the Me 262 possessed an aura of menace, yet this potentially war-winning aircraft had been dogged with problems throughout its extensive development. Although design work at Messerschmitt had started before the outbreak of war, the Me 262 was so revolutionary in concept and design that the engines took considerable time to perfect and the metallurgical requirements alone caused considerable issues during development.

The Me 262 was developed under the Projekt 1065 (P.1065) programme as a result of the RLM requisition for a jet aircraft capable of an hour's endurance and a speed of at least 530mph. For its day such a request was a tall order yet Woldemar Voight heading the design team at Messerschmitt, with Messerschmitt's chief of development Robert Lusser overseeing the daily running of the project, it fell to Ludwig Bolkow to actually design the Me 262. The original design concept by Bolkow for the Me 262 was very different from the aircraft which eventually emerged as the finished product. The revolutionary swept-wing design came about more as a result of the weight of the BMW 003 engines which necessitated that the wings were swept slightly by 18.5° to accommodate a change in the centre of gravity. As efforts to resolve the problems with the jet engines continued, a lack of funding slowed the development programme. Many high-ranking Luftwaffe officials, including Hermann Göring, were convinced, at least initially, that the Me 262 was an unnecessary diversion of valuable resources, that the war could still be won by conventional fighter aircraft. The major problem with the jet engines at that time was the lack of an alloy with a sufficiently high melting point to endure the high temperatures experienced in a jet propulsion unit. The types of alloy materials required for the Me 262's engines were rare and in very short supply.

Despite all the technical issues the Me 262 made its first flight entirely reliant on the power of two Junkers Jumo 004 jet engines, on 18 July 1942. A previous flight where the aircraft had been fitted with two BMW 003s resulted in a double flameout; basically, the engines lost power due to the extinguishing of flame in the engines' combustion chambers. The performance of the Me 262 as displayed on 18 July 1942 proved the aircraft's potential and was such that those who had previously dismissed it for whatever reason now began to take notice. However, the problems for the Me 262, despite the urgency of the situation for the Luftwaffe at the time, were far from over as Hitler insisted the new aircraft be developed more in keeping with a bomber aircraft than a fighter. This was a serious tactical blunder, typical of a man who was neither capable of understanding the problems faced by the Luftwaffe fighter arm nor able to make a coherent military decision.

Despite Hitler's continual interference in matters regarding the brilliant Me 262, on 19 April 1944 the Luftwaffe unit Erprobungskommando 262 was created as a test wing. Under the command of Hauptmann Werner Thierfelder, the unit's objective was to not only ease the Me 262 into operational combat service but to oversee the introduction of pilots to the new aircraft and aid in the flight-conversion process. Following the death of Hauptmann Thierfelder in July 1944, Major Walter Nowotny took over leadership of the unit, steadily increasing combat flying operations; by July 1944 the unit had claimed nineteen Allied aircraft shot down for the loss of six Me 262s. Nowotny himself was killed after defying orders to remain on the ground when he took off to intercept a formation of Allied bombers on 8 November 1944. He claimed a pair of P-51 Mustangs before his aircraft suffered an engine failure at high altitude. In an attempt to restart his engines, he put his Me 262 into a dive and while in the process of doing so, he was bounced by several other P-51 Mustangs and forced to bale out but was killed in the process.

The Kommando was withdrawn following this incident. The Luftwaffe high command then insisted a revision of combat tactics be undertaken to determine the best way to utilize the advantages of the Me 262.

Generalleutnant Adolf Galland, who led the all-jet-equipped Me 262 fighter wing Jagdverband 44 (JV 44) that at the time consisted of the some of the most experienced and highly decorated Luftwaffe fighter pilots, recalled of the Me 262:

> The Me 262 was a misspent resource: so much time had been wasted with tactical infighting over how the aircraft should be used. Hitler was obstinate in his belief that it should be used as a high-speed bomber, yet we fighter pilots who were seeing our comrades swept from the skies every mission we flew, understood that this was the one weapon that could turn things around for us. We all knew that but Hitler was a fool; he knew nothing of military tactics, yet no one could overrule his poor decision-making.
>
> In combat, once you had taken off and allotted sufficient time for those early jet engines to power up, there was nothing the Allied air forces had that could catch us. We had the advantage in pure speed and also in firepower as the Me 262 carried four very powerful 3cm Mk 108 cannons. Some of your historians in the UK have mentioned the Me 262 being armed with four 2cm MG 151 cannon, but this is untrue as the 3cm Mk108 was specifically developed for use in the Me 262 which was never armed with 2cm cannon. Yes, it was tremendously fast, so fast you had to judge your approach to your target very carefully and the closing speeds could be as much as up to 700mph with head-on attacks on Allied bombers. With Allied fighters it could be higher, and this took some getting used to as aiming your guns and firing them at the precise time was very difficult to master. The best way to attack in my opinion was from astern and above: sweep down from high altitude using speed as an advantage and fire your guns as you closed in – the formations were so tightly packed you could not really miss them. You'd hit one or two for sure, then you would turn and assess your first attack and repeat the tactic.

> If a Mustang or Thunderbolt tried to get too close, you just opened up the throttle and disappeared – that shook him off then you came back around. They couldn't touch us. It was like cat and mouse up there.

Unteroffizier Eduard Schallmoser of Jagdverbande 44 had a frightening near-miss in combat in the Me 262:

> I was closing in on the bombers and when sufficient range presented itself, I depressed the gun button – only nothing happened, my guns had jammed. I can't even describe the anger I felt at that moment and the frustration; I cursed very loudly. My temper had caused that momentary lack of concentration that could prove detrimental to your own wellbeing in the Me 262. I was closing in so fast that all of a sudden there was this tremendous crash followed by a banging and tearing sound; pieces of metal flew past my canopy and I thought, *Damn it, I've been hit*. It was not enemy fire that had done the damage though: I had been going so fast and with the distraction of my guns jamming, I had actually flown my aircraft through the propeller arc of my intended victim, a B-26. He managed to limp away as I had got the worst of it. I had to bale out and I watched the Me 262 fall to the ground.

Another former Luftwaffe pilot who had served as an instructor during the early years of the war, recalled of the Me 262:

> I had always been of the personal opinion that Professor Willy Messerschmitt was overrated. Yes, that's what I thought and still do to this day. Yet, when I first saw an Me 262 in the flesh, parked up with several others on an airfield outside of Berlin in early February 1945, it took my breath away. I can recall thinking to myself, *How does one create or think up something like this and how does all of this work?* Looking at it from the front, it looked like a true fighter aircraft should look: sleek and almost sharklike in appearance. Due to my expertise as an instructor, I was

> called in to replace a pilot who had been killed three days earlier in an Me 262. They expected me to be able to fly the thing after just a few days which of course even for me was impossible, but the situation demanded we had to adapt and just get on with it. There were a lot of new things to take in and understand; remember, the Me 262 was not an aircraft that tolerated a fool at its controls – if you displayed a serious lack of judgement, it was as deadly to you as it was your enemy. I flew only five operational missions before fuel and ammunition ran out [across the Reich]; we were forced to leave perfectly serviceable aircraft parked up with empty fuel tanks and empty guns. We left on foot and made it to the nearest aerodrome only to find Bf 109G crews standing around with the same problem.

The Me 262 was more than proving its worth as a war-winning weapon but like so many of Nazi Germany's wonder weapons, it came too late and in too few numbers to alter the inevitable outcome.

The Messerschmitt Me 163 Komet was another revolutionary design that entered the aerial fray in 1944. The design of the Me 163 was originally conceived in 1937 yet in its operational guise was intended from the outset as purely a point defence fighter, this concept referring to a weapon designated to a confined local area of operations. It was not quite as aesthetically pleasing as the Me 262 but what the Me 163 lacked in looks was made up for by sheer performance. Unlike the Me 262, the Me 163 was a rocket fighter powered by a Walter HWK 109-509A rocket motor of limited flight endurance. Once the fuel had been expended, the pilot would glide back to the airfield and land on a skid semi-recessed into the aircraft's fuselage. The Me 163 carried two 30mm Mk 108 cannons in a one-in-each-wing-root configuration with sixty rounds of ammunition per gun. The Me 163B and C models required a ram air turbine fitted at the extreme point of the aircraft's nose which was linked to a backup lead-acid battery inside the fuselage that in turn created electrical power for the radio, the Revi 16B-C or D reflector gunsight, direction finder, the compass, cockpit lighting and, of course, the firing circuits for the two 30mm cannons. By the time the Me 163 had undergone sufficient development and was ready for combat operations in May 1944, it had reached speeds close to 600mph, with a rate of climb of 16,400 feet per minute, a service ceiling of 54,00 feet and fuel capacity for a maximum of eight minutes of powered flight. The aircraft took off using a specially designed wheeled dolly which separated from the aircraft once it left the ground. When Allied bomber crews first saw the batlike form of the Me 163 closing in on them at astonishing speed, many would admit it was an unnerving experience. United States Eight Air Force waist-gunner Tod Welland was one of the few American veterans to experience the Me 163:

> Intelligence had warned that the Germans had been up to something; you see, they had seen the scorch marks made by propulsion units on the ground from their reconnaissance photography. In areas where these jets were known to operate, we had even greater numbers of fighter escorts with us. When they came at you, it was like you would see this white vapour trail in the distance and it would be closing on you very rapidly in a kind of arc like it was swooping down from space or something like that. By the time you got a bead on him, he was gone; the speeds they were flying at was just incredible. It was pretty scary as you just wondered what the fuck would they throw at us next.

The Me 163 may have been fast and did perform admirably throughout its relatively short career, but it had a serious Achilles' heel that was of huge concern to the pilots tasked with flying it. Apart from the fact that the Me 163 was a sitting duck once its fuel was spent, forcing it to glide back to its airfield, the very fuel that powered the fighter, a fuel consisting of two extremely volatile and corrosive elements, was extremely dangerous, posing a very significant threat to both aircraft and pilot. These two propellant mixes were T-Stoff oxidizer (hydrogen peroxide) and C-Stoff (methanol hydrazine). The whole propulsion system depended on the controlled mix of the two propellants as they came into contact with one another. This fuel mixture was so deadly a corrosive that in some accidents experienced with the Me 163, the unfortunate pilots were literally vaporized in their seats. Fuel leaks also led to mid-air explosions before the aircraft even reached its target. Landings also presented a serious threat as residual fuel was also known to spontaneously combust upon landing. In fact, more Me 163 pilots were lost due to accidents than in aerial combat. The Luftwaffe's first dedicated fighter wing was Jagdgeschwader 400 (JG 400) which was formed in the winter and spring of 1944. Yet, by the beginning of May 1945, all Me 163 operations had been cancelled and many of the pilots were sent to fly the Me 262. In its brief career the Me 163 shot down sixteen Allied aircraft, mostly bombers. Many historians would agree with the prognosis that the Me 163 in reality proved a failure, yet Captain Eric Brown, naval chief test pilot and commanding officer of 1426 (Enemy Aircraft) Flight, said of the Me 163 Komet:

> It was not an aircraft that one could just jump into and fly to its limits. One had to very much familiarize oneself with it as it was in all respects a state of the art and technologically unique aircraft. When I first experienced the power of the Komet in the climb, I describe it as being in charge of a runaway train – the aircraft reached 32,000 feet in altitude in two minutes forty-five seconds. During the flight, while practising attacking passes at an imaginary bomber, I was surprised at just how fast the Komet accelerated in the dive even with the engine shut off.

Following the flight, Captain Brown had no issues on the approach to the airfield apart from a slightly restricted view from the cockpit due to the flat angle of glide. The aircraft touched down at 120mph and safely skidded to a halt. Following this memorable flight, Brown and his ground crew celebrated with a much-needed drink. Brown's flight was the only one of its kind to have taken place in Britain due to the danger of its hypergolic propellant fuels. He looked back on the Me 163 with some fondness and when asked of the five tailless aircraft he had test-flown, including the British de Havilland DH 108 which he liked, the most he replied was, 'The Komet was the only one that possessed good flight characteristics, the other four were killers!'

Another remarkable jet-powered aircraft to enter service in the later stages of the war was the Heinkel He 162 Volksjager (People's Fighter) also known as the Salamander. This aircraft was conceived through the Emergency Fighter Programme, a specification as with others in late-war Nazi Germany born through desperate times. It was an aircraft conceived and built very quickly, primarily constructed from wood due to the scarcity of metals at the time. The aircraft was designed for production by unskilled workers and the single BMW 003 powerplant was not in demand for any other frontline jet fighter, so it would not interfere in the production of any existing aircraft types. It was also designed to be very simple to fly, so simple that it was proposed by the Nazis that thousands of young men from the Hitler Youth with limited training could be capable of flying the He 162. The performance of the aircraft was satisfactory at 470mph, and the armament proposed were either two 20mm Mauser MG 151/20 cannons with 100 rounds of ammunition each or two 30mm Mk 108 cannons with fifty rounds of ammunition each. Most He 162s that entered service were armed with the 30mm Mk 108 cannon. The He 162 did not enter full-scale production and even Ernst Heinkel said after the war that 'the unrealistic notion that this aircraft should be championed as a "people's fighter", in which the Hitler Youth, after a short training regime with clipped-wing two-seater gliders like the DFS Stummel-Habicht, could fly for the defence of Germany, displayed the unbalanced fanaticism of those days'.

The first operational unit to fly the He 162 was 1/JG 1. Due to the overwhelming effects of the Allied bombing offensive, the unit was forced to relocate to an aerodrome at Ludwigslust and just a week later the unit moved again to an aerodrome at Leck near the Danish border. The He 162 received its first taste of combat flying in mid-April 1945, yet thirteen He 163s were lost with ten pilots killed. Some of the losses were due to flameouts and structural failures in flight; only two were shot down by Allied aircraft. As with the Me 163 Komet, the He 162 was far from being a pilot-friendly aircraft, as Walter Schlecht recalled:

> The Heinkel He 162 was downright dangerous, it was lethal, and I hated it. I was just 21 when they bundled me into this thing and began to school me in the workings of the instruments and throttle controls. There was not that much to it, and yes, it all looked very simple until actual training began. I recall one student taking off in one and he did very well until his engine crapped out on him. He was clear for a deadstick landing which you could do blindfolded with a Bf 109, not a problem, but this thing was dangerous when attempting an unpowered landing. We watched as the thing rolled over to the left and ploughed into the ground and

> burned out. So yes, this was our Hitler Youth initiation into the death trap they called the *Volksjager*, the people's fighter that even a woman could fly if instructed to. It was pure madness and a reflection of the hopelessness and how the hierarchy began to gamble with people's lives to try and save themselves. If there was ever a best aircraft of the war then that aircraft was not just one but three types and these were the Focke-Wulf Fw 190, the Messerschmitt Bf 109 and the Messerschmitt Me 262. All these so-called emergency fighter jet aircraft that they were hoping to rush into service were nothing more than flying coffins.

The top-scoring jet fighter ace of the war is an honour that goes to Oberleutnant Kurt Welter who claimed a total of sixty-three enemy aircraft destroyed in ninety-three sorties, though Welter has been accused of exaggerating his claims. Either way, he was one of the most successful jet fighter pilots of the Luftwaffe. Welter's impressive scores and other notable Luftwaffe jet fighter pilots proved that had the jet technology been appreciated early enough and time and effort invested in its development, the Luftwaffe may well have had that essential resource that could have achieved victory for Nazi Germany.

The Luftwaffe also flew the world's first operational jet bomber, the Arado Ar 234, an aircraft which first flew on 15 June 1943, powered by two Junkers Jumo 0048 axial-flow, turbojet engines. This remarkable aircraft could carry a bomb load of up to 1,500kg (3,309lb) and achieved a top speed of 461mph (742kph) at 20,000 feet. There was also provision for a pair of rearward-firing 20mm Mauser MG 151/20 cannons, yet these weapons were only ever fitted in the prototype aircraft. The Arado Ar 234 was produced in limited quantity and was primarily used in the reconnaissance role. Its performance as a bomber was quite outstanding and Allied fighters attempting to intercept it found this an impossible task due to its high speed. The Ar 234 was also the last Luftwaffe aircraft to overfly UK airspace in the war, in April 1945. The Arado Ar 234 was yet another case of 'what might have been', especially when one considers the resources wasted on death traps such as the Heinkel He 177 Grief.

# Chapter 21

# Invitation to Valhalla

By 1944 the Wehrmacht was under severe pressure on all fronts. For the Luftwaffe the once-comfortable initiation into the arena of air combat that was Russia in 1941was now a much tougher proposition, especially for the less-experienced pilots filling the boots of those who had been killed. With the introduction of the Yakolev Yak-3 into service with the Soviet Air Force, there was a definitive shift in the balance of air power over the Eastern Front. The Yak-3 proved a considerable headache for the Luftwaffe. At just over two tons, the Yak-3 was one of the smallest and lightest fighter aircraft to see combat service in war. Its power-to-weight ratio meant it was fast and manoeuvrable and its armament of one 20mm ShVAK cannon and two 12.7mm Berezin UBS machine guns made it more than a match for both the Bf 109 and Fw 190. On 16 July 1944, eighteen Yak-3 fighters took off to intercept a flight of twenty-four Luftwaffe fighters. In the fierce dogfight that ensued the Russian's lost just one Yak-3 while claiming fifteen German fighters. This incident among others led Luftwaffe fighter ace Gerhard Barkhorn to recall: 'I had fought against almost every type of Soviet fighter, including those sent to Russia from Britain and America under Lend-Lease, and I thought out of all of them the Yak-3 and Yak-9 were the best.'

The Lavochkin La-7 was another superb Soviet fighter entering service – these fighters were delivered to the cream of the Guards Air Regiments. The Luftwaffe reacted by sending their finest fighter pilots to oppose the new menace over the battlefront. In fact, such was the concern caused by the presence of these new Soviet fighters that the elite German fighter wing Jagdgeschwader 54 was often redeployed to frontline zones where the La-7 fighters were most active. Despite the early losses experienced against the might of the Luftwaffe, the Soviet Air Force had made a remarkable recovery. Their new breed of fighter now surpassed their technically advanced enemy and while the Red

Army was now relentlessly driving the Heer back on the ground, the Red Air Force was regaining control of the skies over their homeland.

The western Allies' strategic bombing campaign, the combined aerial efforts of the RAF and USAAF from 1943, was finally beginning to take its toll on Nazi Germany. By November 1944 the once-mighty Luftwaffe was merely a shadow of the once-fearsome, all-conquering spearpoint of the Blitzkrieg strategy. The last ten months of aerial fighting in the western sector of German airspace witnessed some of the most ferocious and desperate air-to-air engagements of the war. The Allied landings in Normandy of June 1944 had served their purpose, and Allied ground forces were now streaming towards Germany while the Russians were advancing rapidly in the East. It was clear at this point that defeat of Nazi Germany was inevitable and just a matter of time. The most sensible option would have been for Germany to surrender to spare further unnecessary death and destruction, yet with Hitler still alive, surrender was totally out of the question. The airmen of the Luftwaffe were now faced with the unenviable task of attempting to defend the crumbling Reich against insurmountable odds.

With this chapter being almost the last, I would like to avoid the literary traditions of focusing on the already-well-documented exploits of the Luftwaffe aces and focus instead on those who fought with equal tenacity yet whose names are unknown to most. These individuals did not rack up the high kill scores of the likes of Erich Hartmann, Gerhard Barkhorn, Günther Rall and others, yet they fought with the same bravery and determination, in many circumstances against vastly superior odds, witnessing the often-fiery deaths of close comrades on a daily basis leaving many to wonder at that time when they might be receiving their 'invitation to Valhalla'.

Former Hitler Youth glider flyer Christoph Oegen was a 23-year-old joining the fighter unit JG 1 in the autumn of 1944. This was a dismal time to be a fighter pilot in the Luftwaffe; the glory days of conquest were now long gone and being a 'Hare' in the Luftwaffe was as much a fight for one's personal survival as it was against the steadily growing uneven odds over Reich territory. Oegen recalled:

> All the romantic notions one had of flying and fighting for the Fatherland were soon dispelled in the short period of taking off for your first combat operation. First, there was

a preparatory discussion with the 'Hares' who had been assigned to the unit. I remember it very well: our flight leader simply told us, 'You have to follow to the letter what you are told when we are in the air and when the enemy is sighted. I expect you to listen and to not be foolish. I have had to sit down six times this month and write letters to the mothers of young airmen just like yourselves to explain to them their sons will not be coming back home, that they died the airman's death in the service of their country. Dead pilots are of no use to me at all, so it is imperative you listen to what you are told and do as you are told. This is not glider school; this is a serious business and if you do not pay attention you will pay for it with your life. If we can work together as a team together with how we have all been trained, we will hit the enemy hard and make the them pay for their daytime visits to our country. Now do you all understand me?' Of course, we all said at once, 'Yes, sir.' He then dismissed us, informing us we would be at dawn readiness and to get some rest as the weather was looking good for the next day's hunting.

You couldn't really sleep, being in unfamiliar surroundings and the nerves prevented you from relaxing sufficiently to be able to sleep. I spent the night tossing and turning and it was in some ways a relief when we were called to readiness at daybreak. We got up, washed and dressed and drank hot coffee and prepared for the alarm we knew would come at some point. I was warned by one pilot not to drink too much coffee: 'You cannot simply flip open the lid of your crate, stand up and take a piss up there, so don't drink too many cups.' Nerves made you go to the toilet constantly, you developed that dryness of the mouth, you chain-smoked, you read newspapers, you paced around – that was the worst part of it all, waiting on the ground for things to happen, for the call to take off.

…There is some advance warning that things are happening. Enemy formations have been detected over the eastern sector of the UK, their progress carefully monitored so the fighter units can be sent in to intercept them in the shortest time possible. When the alarm call does come, it is a simple command over a loudspeaker, 'Enemy formations to the north-west. Take off all flights, repeat take off all flights.' That's when the adrenaline kicks in, your heart begins to race and your body trembles as you jump up into the seat of your aircraft, mine a Bf 109G. The relationship I have with my aeroplane is one of love and hate. Sometimes I loved her, other times I hated her, like a marriage of sorts. You have to work together in the service of destruction, and it will either be yours or the enemy's; only God can decide. All the instructions you had been taught race through your mind as the engine roars into life as you quickly check your instruments and flight controls. The groundcrew pull the blocks away from the wheels of the Messerschmitt and give a wave as if to say, 'Off you go.'

Within minutes we are all in the air; the 'Hares', myself included, are to remain in the middle of our attack formation and are instructed to stick with our assigned wingman and follow his instructions. Climbing up towards the clouds, I feel the discomfort of this crate; it is cramped, the fumes that fill the cockpit are unpleasant, making my already dry mouth feel even worse; the noise is deafening despite the headphones we wear inside our flying helmets – the reception through the headphones is not that good and when commands come through, they are static and crackly and sometimes I have a job to hear what is being said. It is freezing cold even with all the heavy clothing on, and I develop an instant throbbing pain in my head. Unteroffizier Knopf is my wingman. I doubt he is too enthralled having to perform the duty of babysitter on this occasion; he warns me to stay close when the action starts and to ensure that he is nowhere near my gunsights if and when I open fire and to not waste ammunition but make my shots count.

We come out of a bank of clouds and immediately below us is the American formation. Our flight leader calls out, 'There they are; let them have it.' At this point the attack is pressed home, other comrades are attempting to lure the fighters escorting the bombers away to give us the best chance of pressing home our attack. I focus on Knopf and his every move; as we close on the enemy Knopf is some 500 yards ahead of me. I hear a series of noises that sounds like I am being hit by enemy fire. I look around in panic for the tracers but there is nothing behind me other than other fighters of our flight. What is happening is Knopf is firing at the bombers and his discarded shell cases are bouncing around in the air and hitting my aircraft. I throttle back enough to allow myself to manoeuvre slightly above him and watch as Knopf peels away in a hard left manoeuvre, allowing me a clear field of fire. I hear him tell me in a calm yet firm tone over the radio, 'Yellow 3 and I am watching your back; let them have it!' I see the B-24 looming ever closer in the gunsight; the moment I have a bead on him, I squeeze the trigger and the 2cm 151 cannon and two cowling machine guns fire. I pull a hard right manoeuvre and climb away at full throttle, looking over both shoulders to ensure my back is clear of any enemy escorts, Knopf is circling and about to attack our target again. We have both scored hits but the B-24 lumbers on unwounded and is now alert to us and returning fire as we attempt to reposition for a second pass. Like two lions stalking a buffalo, we have to keep calm; our enemy is dangerous. Knopf initiates his attack with the sun behind us; with luck the American gunners will not see us until it is too late. If we can get some good hits, we may bag him this time. Again, I watch as Knopf fires a good three seconds worth of 2cm 151 cannon before pulling hard away to the right and climbing back around to watch my rear as I press home my attack. The Americans are firing back furiously, their tracers pass overhead and I instinctively duck down. I hear strikes and know they are scoring hits on my aircraft. I fire again and give the Americans a good long burst, but I almost misjudge my approach and nearly collide with the B-24. I pass just below the waist of the lumbering beast which is now trailing smoke from both port side engines: our cannon fire has found its mark. I look around for Knopf and call him over the radio, but I receive no reply. I look to my left and right, jinking the wings to check my position and for enemy fighters. The B-24 is losing altitude and dropping back from the main American formation. I decide to make another pass and use my remaining ammunition on him. I have a perfect field of fire yet as I squeeze the trigger, only the machine guns respond: my 2cm 151 refuses to fire. I cannot finish him off with peashooters and have to abandon him to my comrades who are now hot on his tail as I turn back for base.

When I land, I report a probable B-24 damaged and losing altitude, not bad for my first outing. Other aircraft of the flight are returning, some with holes in their wings and fuselage. My aircraft has several holes mid-fuselage and in the tail, but nothing serious and these will be patched up. Knopf has yet to land. I am told all the flight is accounted for apart from three pilots. Knopf is one of those three missing. Maybe he had problems and was forced to land elsewhere. Then I receive the news his aircraft was seen going down at high speed with a P-47 close on his tail. Our ground forces report an aircraft crashing twenty-five miles to the south of our airfield, and it is later confirmed as Knopf's Bf 109. His body or rather what was left of it was totally incinerated in the fire, with only a few charred bones.

This was the harsh reality, it was far from heroic or romantic, you are dead on your feet from the physical exhaustion that is combat flying, yet you know before the day is out that that alarm could call us into battle again, once maybe twice more before it gets dark. It is at this point you sit down as a young man and think about what you have done. Did I kill anyone today? What awaits me if the good Lord decides my time is up? Yes, I said a lot of prayers at that point. I promised God that if he allowed me to survive this then once it was all over, I would be a different man to the one who had entered into this pact with the devil. That's how it was day in day out; the more I flew the more I learned the techniques to stay alive, to not be afraid to dive for the ground and get away if things got too hot. I remember the words of the CO that first day, 'Dead pilots are of no use to me.' I count myself very lucky indeed to have survived and

> I kept my promise to God. I am not ashamed to admit that war changes you as a survivor when many just like you, some even more experienced, did not survive. Why did I live and they died? I can't answer that, but I ask myself that question over and over.
>
> After the war I visited Knopf's widow; it was one of the most upsetting experiences of my life. He had a little daughter, and she came up and sat on my lap. This little girl with her big brown eyes looked up at me and asked, 'Were you one of my daddy's friends?' It was as much as I could do to hold back my emotions as I told her, 'Yes, I was one of your daddy's friends and your daddy looked after me.' I actually helped them out as much as I could after the war and remained in contact with the daughter for many years, but yes, it is something which still haunts me today.

Despite the horrors of the brutal realities of war in the air over the Third Reich, by late 1944 there were some lighter moments as Unteroffizier Specht of the night fighter unit NJG 2 recalled:

> Both my comrade Unteroffizier Rudolph Weiss and I had had a lively evening in our Bf 110. We had scored a victory during the night, shooting down a British Lancaster which crashed into open farmland. We were relieved to hear that four of the crew got out before it hit the ground in a ball of orange flame. Having experienced some technical difficulties with our aircraft during the flight, we had radioed in and were recalled to our airfield which we didn't mind as it meant an early sleep and we were very much looking forward to our bunks as we were both stiff from the cold and very tired from the previous hours of action. We had a hot drink, smoked a cigarette and climbed into our bunks. Other crew members were either sound asleep or doing the same as us, preparing for our beds where we would sleep the daylight hours away.
>
> Our hut was blacked out completely but as dawn broke there was this one menace that we dreaded. As our airfield was situated near a farmhouse, which was not unusual,

there was this cockerel that would come strutting around our sleeping quarters as dawn broke, making this ungodly racket, crowing as you call it in England. A few of us had just settled down to sleep when this bird came scratching around against the side of the hut then crowing for all it was worth – it was quite deafening. I remember well this one occasion as we were startled awake by this pestilent bird just as we had dozed off. There were moans and groans and one of the pilots said, 'Oh, fucking hell, here we go again!' Another voice in the darkened hut called out angrily, 'Can somebody please shut that fucking chicken up?' Another voice in the darkness retorted, 'It's not a chicken, it's a cockerel.' The other voice then replied, 'Well, I don't care what it fucking well is; just shut it up as it's driving me mad,' The bird, having done its deed, then moved off to annoy someone else no doubt.

This happened on a few occasions – it was one of the hazards of having a base located so close to a farm. Some of the men found it difficult to get back to sleep, especially in the summer when it was stifling hot inside the hut, which compounded the irritation. The funny thing was, a few days after this latest rude awakening, the cockerel mysteriously disappeared. Even the farmer came up to the airfield looking for his prize bird, clearly distraught. Of course, we saw nothing – we hadn't – and one pilot suggested it might have been taken by a wild animal. Either way we never heard it or saw it again, yet some weeks later a pile of white feathers was found concealed behind one of the other huts and questions were asked if we knew anything about it. Again, we denied all knowledge and suggested if this bird's disappearance was of such importance maybe we should call in the Gestapo to unravel the mystery. We had a very good idea of who the culprit was [he laughs] as we had a little extra meat in one of our stews the one evening and we were told it was a locally caught rabbit. I have eaten rabbit on many occasions before and I knew full well this was not rabbit, that the cockerel had met its untimely demise at the hands of one of our comrades.

> Yes, we laughed about that a lot. Even the female auxiliaries were relieved that the cockerel had vanished as two of them told us how the bird would sit up on the fence near the base perimeter and proceed to attack them as they approached the gate when on foot. They told us they used to be too scared to come through that way, sometimes fearing the vicious bird would appear from nowhere and mount an attack and scratch the backs of their legs with its claws.

Michael Ott witnessed the desperate battle in the air above the Reich in September 1944 at the tender age of 22 when he joined the Focke-Wulf Fw 190-equipped II/ JG 26. JG 26 was among the Luftwaffe's premier fighter units yet found itself like many others suffering from a shortage of experienced pilots. Michael recalled his experiences:

> The training was, what shall we say, fairly basic by late 1944. Hitler just wanted to get as many fighters into the skies over Germany as possible. The problem was there was insufficient training at that stage; they gave you the minimum and it was, 'Okay, off you go boy, do your job.' The unit itself was doing its best under immense pressure. The Americans had introduced the long-range escort fighters like the P-51 Mustang, the P-38 Lightning and the P-47 Thunderbolt. Of the three I found the P-47 Thunderbolt the hardest of all to shoot down. My first four or five missions were merely scuffles; you see, if you lacked experience, it was easier to just dive to lower altitude of around 9,000–10,000 feet where the Fw 190 performed slightly better than the P-47. The advantage in a turning fight with the P-47 at this altitude was only maintained through effecting a slight climb in your turn; it wasn't much but you soon learned. If you couldn't shake him off, you used the excellent emergency power-boost system which would get you out of harm's way if nothing else. I had several fights with P-47s and they were built like tanks. I put a good burst of 2cm cannon fire into one and he still got away from me. I was quite astonished by how rugged they were. They possessed good firepower too; if one got onto your tail and you couldn't shake him off, you were finished.

It was thanks to a P-47 that I survived the war as I'm sure that had I not been shot down and quite badly hurt, my time would have soon been up. It was in December 1944, a bright, clear and freezing-cold winter's day. It had snowed during the night, but the day broke with this beautiful sunshine and clear blue skies. We were at readiness to take off from first light and it was not long before we were ordered into the air to meet yet another large American formation. We were in a favourable position to attack from above and behind but were ordered to attack from the front, head on this time. We flew around the flanks of the formation to position ourselves ahead of the enemy, when to my right I noticed some large groups of smaller aircraft which I knew were the escorts. We had set up a diversionary tactic where some aircraft of our wing, usually the more experienced fliers, would attempt to lure the escorting fighters away so we could press home our attack. For a while this seemed to work and while the melee began above and to the rear of the enemy formation, we were able to get in our first pass at the bombers. You had to remember the closing speeds with head-on attacks; if you were not mindful of these dangers, you could risk running into the target; you had to allow perfect timing in order to open fire and then pull up to avoid a collision. On my first pass I picked out a victim and made him the focus of my attack. I was committed at that point and determined to do damage. I began firing a little too far out, giving their dorsal gunner time to shoot back at me; then the nose gunner started firing too. My rounds were going just beneath the nose of the enemy but then, with precise aim, I watched as the high-explosive 2cm shells burst about the nose and cabin area. I dived hard left and disappeared beneath his starboard wing; for a moment my aircraft was thrown about quite violently – this was the propeller wash from my enemy's four engines, a powerful force in itself. I recovered and climbed and turned in for a second pass as by this time it was every man for himself. I looked over my shoulder and down and I could see my victim falling from the sky. There was no way anyone could have survived those shells directly into the pilot's compartment and the enemy fell much like a leaf from a tree.

I felt a momentary sense of elation but then felt a sharp shudder from behind which seemed to throw my aircraft forward like it was being shoved by some giant hand. I looked back to see two P-47s on my tail, blazing away with their machine guns; I could see the muzzle flashes from their wings and tracers inches above my canopy. I did as the instructors had told me and dived for the ground in a kind of spiral flight envelope to give my friends less of a chance of hitting me further.

I levelled out from the dive at just over 9,000 feet and the next thing I was being shot at from the front; my engine was hit and there was a terrible crash and smoke filled the cockpit. I could see treetops and I told myself if I could just get clear of them, I could put the 190 down in one of the pastures beyond if the P-47s didn't get me first. I looked back left and right, and my American friends were lining up behind me to shoot again. I knew I was in serious trouble. I cleared the trees and reduced my speed as low as I dared as one of the P-47s roared right over the top of my canopy and for a few seconds was right in front of me. I could have shot him down had I had the presence of mind but I was so focused on getting the 190 down without killing myself that I overlooked what may have been an opportunity. I saw bullets hitting the ground in front of me as it [the ground] came closer and closer. I knew I was in for a rough landing, but the ground looked relatively flat, and I was confident I could get the 190 down in a belly landing without too much drama.

The moment I hit the ground I felt a terrible pain shoot up my back and I was knocked unconscious. I was very lucky that a nearby Flak artillery crew risked their lives and ran across an open field to my aid. As they came to my rescue one later told me they were fired on by the American planes which were still firing into my crippled 190. I knew this was true as all I remember before passing out is the pain in my back, nothing else, yet when I came to in the hospital,

> I had machine-gun-bullet wounds to my legs and feet. The doctor who treated me said they pulled out three slugs from my legs and there were two other holes in my feet where the bullets had gone clean through; my flying boots were testimony to this as they brought them in to show me the bullet holes. I asked how long it would be before I would be fit to fly again and it was then they told me that I would not fly again. The injury to my back was pretty bad and I was still in hospital recuperating when news came that the war was over. In my brief career as a fighter pilot, I shot down four enemy heavy bombers. While I was in hospital, I was presented with the Iron Cross second class.

Unteroffizier Albert Tuga, another JG 26 pilot, recalled this extreme period of attrition:

> It was utter madness; each day experienced pilots were shot down and either badly wounded or killed, then more and more inexperienced young men were shipped in to replace them. This was no good as these young men had no idea of what it was like up there; most of them came to us trembling in their boots; they should have been at home with their mothers, not here being offered up as cannon fodder. We knew the end was coming. When you take off day after day (if weather permits) and you're meeting more and more escort fighters, you can't get close enough to the bombers to shoot them down; the escorts swarm all over you and you have to fight back or die; the bombers fly on and do their job of dropping bombs on our cities. Then the high command asks, 'Why have you not shot any bombers down? Are you losing your nerve or something?' They are basically criticizing us and insinuating a degree of cowardice. Yet, on one day alone I took off and battled the enemy four times. I went up to face their Mustangs and Thunderbolts which outnumbered us sometimes ten to one, or more. There were even Spitfires coming over with them and we were losing a lot of men.
>
> One day I landed, took on more fuel and ammunition and then took off again and did the same three more times. When

I landed after the last sortie of that day, I could barely climb out of the cockpit; I had to be helped out of it. I was dead on my feet only to be told that the damage to the American formations had been minimal, that we weren't pressing home our attacks with enough aggression, and we had lost more pilots than what we could replace. I felt physically ill, and they grounded me for a couple of days' rest in which I slept solidly. I felt better for the rest but then discovered a good friend of mine serving in another fighter wing had been shot down and killed. He was a good pilot too, a better pilot than I ever was, yet he was dead and I was still alive; it didn't make sense. When I attacked enemy bombers, I knew there was every chance I was killing someone's son, husband or even father. Even if I shot no enemy aircraft down, wounded bomber crews often died through loss of blood, shock or both on the return trip home.

As exhausted as I got, I still had a ritual where at the end of a day's fighting I would walk a little way from the base to this quiet spot. I would sit there and I would ask God to forgive me for what I had had to do that day. To me it wasn't about killing anyone, it was just about stopping the bombers. Yes, I am not ashamed to admit I wept for those enemy crews whose planes I saw falling in huge sheets of flame from the skies: were they really any different to us besides the political and ideological goals of our leaders? The funny thing is I began to realize I was on the side of evil and that there would be punishment for that at some point.

Christoph Oegen recalls a multitude of frustrations other than being outnumbered in the air by the Allied escort fighters:

Fuel deliveries were becoming sporadic near the end of the war. Sometimes it would be brought in on mule carts during the hours of darkness, but it was never enough for the whole flight. Then ammunition was a problem. The phosphorus incendiary rounds used in the 2cm Mauser MG 151/20 cannon were in short supply. These were better than high-explosive rounds in my opinion, yet they began

> to run short on these too. The young men who appeared as the replacements for dead or missing comrades had to be babysat in the air or they would be shot down within minutes, so we had the problem of trying to look out for them and give them enough experience to at least survive, but it was hopeless. Most were in a shocking state, frightened young boys, some as young as 18 or 19 years old. I knew most would be dead within days as their training was totally inadequate. The defence of the Reich was becoming more of a rout. The high command was devising all these mad tactics such as forming squadrons of Bf 109s or Fw 190s specifically for ramming operations against the American formations. Yes, I knew some pilots who carried out these ramming attacks and were lucky to have been able to bale out safely and live to do the same again.

Ramming operations as mentioned by Christoph are well documented and, in many senses, reflect the desperate situation facing the Luftwaffe by the closing stages of the war. Eugene 'Slim' Slimmer was a waist-gunner in a B-17 and witnessed such an attack in March 1945:

> At first, we thought these guys were just young pilots pressed into air service who had misjudged their attacks or something through lack of experience. It hadn't occurred to us that someone could be crazy enough to try this kind of thing; to our reasoning it was pure madness. Yes, I saw this 109 come in and I thought, *Jeez, he's going to run into that ship if he doesn't pull up* and no sooner had that thought gone through my mind, I saw him run into the tail of the aircraft. He sort of hit it and cartwheeled over to the other side and just fell out of the sky. I watched him falling until he vanished from my view. I didn't see the pilot get out of it either, so I don't know whether he lived or not. I didn't really care at that point; I just thought it was crazy and became just that little bit more extra-vigilant. If they were going to start doing this kind of thing, we'd have to try harder to blow them out of the sky before they could get close enough. The ship in question, the one that got hit,

> miraculously survived and got back home; the 109 came off worse on that occasion.

Christoph Oegen revealed to me that Allied fighter escorts provided special treatment for Luftwaffe pilots who rammed their bombers:

> Yes, I know the ramming attacks sometimes were successful and a pilot would tear off the tail or a wing from an enemy bomber which would then plummet earthwards. I did notice that some Luftwaffe pilots who carried out successful ramming attacks, if they got out into their parachutes then American escort fighters would shoot them in their harnesses. Sadly, I myself witnessed this behaviour near the end of the war; it was like we had suddenly abandoned any sense of chivalry in the air – it was kill or be killed.

Heink Knoke summed up the hopelessness of the situation even for those skilled fighter pilots when he commented: 'Each time I close the canopy of my aircraft, I feel as if I am closing the lid on my own coffin.'

Luftwaffe air dominance would finally and comprehensively die following the failure of Operation *Bodenplatte* that was launched on 1 January 1945. *Bodenplatte* was an ill-fated attempt at crippling the Allied air forces on the ground in the Low Countries. The goal was to gain air superiority over the Ardennes battlefront in Belgium so the Heer and Waffen-SS ground forces could regain the initiative and resume their advance. Bad weather had delayed the proposed original 16 December 1944 date for the attack and the Luftwaffe was forced to wait until the weather improved which was not until 1 January. Although the Luftwaffe operation achieved the element of surprise and enjoyed a degree of success, it was ultimately a failure. When German fighter ace Adolf Galland was asked about the operation, he remarked:

> *Bodenplatte* was yet another gamble that we Luftwaffe crews could ill afford to take. It was like someone entering a casino with no money in his pockets. The majority of the pilots we had available were not trained to a high-enough level to be able to execute such an ambitious plan. Worse still is that the operation had been so secret that even our own Flak

units were unaware of it and subsequently we lost aircraft as a result of being shot down by our own frontline Flak artillery. The reality was that in the wake of that operation we used up virtually our last set of resources; many pilots were lost and we could not replace them. In fact, we lost 143 pilots who were either listed as killed or missing. Some 70 pilots were captured by the enemy and some quote 21 as being wounded but I would say there were more than that. It was the darkest day of my career as that was the day, I said to myself, *This is it, this is the end, it is over.*

# Chapter 22

# V for Vengeance

The German V1 flying bomb deployed by Nazi Germany in the Second World War was a weapon in the Luftwaffe inventory and so it deserves brief analysis. The V2 weapon that followed the V1 was a Heer weapon and so falls outside the scope of this work.

The Vergeltungswaffe 1 or Vengeance Weapon 1, often known simply as the V1 flying bomb, was the product of nine years of research and development carried out by Professor Georg Hans Madelung and Paul Schmidt who submitted a design for a flying bomb for the Luftwaffe in 1935. Considering this design was conceived at a time when conventional engines or explosives were used to propel projectile weaponry, the V1 was a highly innovative proposal, yet original research carried out in 1915 by the Sperry Gyroscope company relied on propellers for propulsion. It was whilst Fritz Gosslau was employed by the Argus Motoren company in Berlin that he set about the design and development of a remote-controlled target drone, known as the FZG 43 (*Flakzielgera*t 43).

In October 1939, Argus brought forth a new proposal called *Fernfeuer*, which was a remote-controlled aircraft capable of carrying a one-ton explosive payload that could return to its base after expending its ordnance. To develop this new specification Argus cooperated with C. Lorenz AG, a German electronics firm also based in Berlin, and the aircraft company Arado Flugzeugwerke. The Luftwaffe studied the new proposal yet declined to award a development contract for the weapon. It was in 1940, a year into the war, that Schmidt and Argus began their cooperation, utilizing Schmidt's shutter system with Argus's atomized fuel injection. Initial tests were carried out in January 1941, the first flight being made on 30 April 1941 with a Gotha Go 145 biplane trainer aircraft.

It was on the 27 February 1942 that the weapon we know today as the V1 began to take on its characteristic form. Designers Gosslau and

Robert Lusser set out a design on paper of an aircraft with a pulsejet engine mounted above the tail; this design was the benchmark for future development work on what became the V1 flying bomb. In April 1942, Lusser introduced a gyroscope-guided design known as the 935 Efurt. The specification boasted a range of 186 miles, a speed of 435mph and was capable of carrying the originally proposed one-ton high-explosive warhead. What then became Project Fieseler Fi 103 received approval from the Luftwaffe on 19 June receiving its codename *Kirschkern* and cover name *Flakzielgerat* 76 (FZG 76). The flight tests for this new weapon were carried out at the Luftwaffe's coastal test centre at Karlshagen, Peenemünde-West. Erhard Milch who was in charge of aircraft production awarded the contract to produce the pulsejet engines to Argus while the airframes were to be built by Fieseler, with the Askania company tasked with the production of the guidance system.

By 30 August Fieseler had completed construction of the first fuselage and the weapon was assembled. The first flight of the Fi 103 V7 took place on 10 December 1942, where it was deployed by a four-engine Fw 200 aircraft. On Christmas Eve that year, the V1 was ground-launched and flew for 1,000 yards for approximately one minute. On 26 May 1943, Germany put the V1 weapon into production. As flight testing continued with the weapon, in July 1943, the V1 flew a distance of 152 miles, impacting its proposed target area within 1,093 yards.

It is worthy of note here that the Luftwaffe carried out experiments with the piloted version of the V1, known as *Reichenbergs*. Pilots were inevitably killed. Female test pilot Hanna Reitsch was tasked with discovering what the problems were with the piloted V1s. She discovered after simulated landing attempts at high altitude, where there was sufficient air space to effect a recovery, that the V1 possessed an extremely high stall speed. She discovered that previous test pilots with little experience of high-speed flight had attempted to land at much reduced airspeed. Her recommendation following her own successful flights in the piloted V1 were that pilots would require much higher landing speeds. Her recommendations were then passed on to the Reichenberg volunteer pilots. The Reichenberg V1s were all launched from a host aircraft and were never launched from ramps as wrongly portrayed in some film depictions. Despite the desperate situation for the Luftwaffe in the closing stages of the war, the Luftwaffe never deployed the piloted Reichenberg V1s in combat. However, the principle of using a piloted bomb such as the V1 appealed greatly to Nazi Germany's ally Japan who utilized a similar design in their Yokosuka MXY-7 Ohka which did enter combat service in the war.

The V1 flying bombs launched against London weighed 4,740 pounds (2,150kg), were 27.3 feet (8.3m) in length, 17.6 feet (5.4m) wide and 4 feet 8 inches (1.42m) in height. In the nose of the weapon was an explosive warhead weighing 1,870 pounds (848kg) that contained Amatol-39; later versions of the V1 warheads contained trialen explosive. The weapon was fitted with an electrical fuze designed to detonate the weapon the moment it made contact with the ground. A secondary impact fuze was fitted which acted as a failsafe for the main impact fuze. Lastly, there was a time fuze fitted that was designed to destroy a V1 which fell to the ground intact and failed to detonate, to prevent the enemy from gaining any technical knowledge of the weapon.

Klaus Adler had just celebrated his eighteenth birthday in July 1944 when ordered for compulsory military service in the Luftwaffe where he was immediately posted to France. Klaus had undergone training in the handling and launch preparation of the new V1 for operational use against England. The V1 was a weapon that Klaus described as being 'beautifully crude yet easy to deploy and launch'. He recalled:

> It was barely days after my eighteenth birthday when I received orders to report for duty immediately as special attack operations were about to be mounted against England from locations in and around the Pas de Calais in France. I had been in training for some weeks previous, but it seemed they had waited until I had turned 18 to call me up for duty. At the time lots of young men were being handpicked from the Hitler Youth for these special duties as they were known. We had been trained how to transport, assemble and arrange the V1s on their launching ramps; in training we used mock-up weapons, most of which were constructed from wood. We did not need to fully understand the technical aspects or aerodynamics of the weapon, just how to assist in the deployment and firing as crewmembers. It was in some ways an easy job, better than being sent to the East to the fighting there which many young men like me dreaded. Until I arrived in France for operations, I had

never seen an actual V1 launch, so it was a first for me and it was very exciting. We understood that there was not much time as the Allies had landed at Normandy and there was heavy fighting all around that area. There were daily reconnaissance reports telling us where the enemy were and how close they were to our site. The objective was to send as many V1s to London as was possible before we had to abandon the launch site and set up another out of reach of the advancing enemy.

In Germany we nicknamed the V1 the *Kirschkern* (cherry stone) or *Maikafer* (maybug). The official Luftwaffe service designation was Fi 103, the Fi standing for Fieseler which was the aircraft company involved in the manufacture of the V1. It was an odd-looking device, rather like a cigar shape with an engine mounted on top and stub wings fitted either side of the fuselage. It looked like a weird kind of aircraft, yet it wasn't strictly an aircraft as it carried no pilot. The engine which powered the weapon through the air was an Argus As 109-014 pulsejet engine which was a simple yet efficient design with a very distinctive engine tone when started up. The range was approximately 160 miles, and it flew at the top speed of 400mph, usually at a height of 2,000 to 3,000 feet altitude. The V1 was guided to the target area by a gyrocompass-based autopilot mechanism, which was a very clever technical innovation for its time. I certainly didn't see the destruction that I in part was responsible for. We were remote from seeing the carnage that these weapons caused the population of southern England. The Luftwaffe high command was convinced that a saturation bombardment of the English capital would create mass civilian unrest and force the English government into a negotiated surrender. The high command underestimated the resolve of the English people as we now understand.

It was only after the war that I saw what the weapons we were launching at England were capable of and the death and destruction they and the newer V2 army weapon caused. Yes, when I returned home, I didn't really think about it too much, but later I felt immense guilt about it. It was nothing

> I was proud of; it was just remote killing. We never saw the bodies of the victims, their grieving families or their destroyed homes. I couldn't have refused to report for duty; they would have arrested me had I done so, I don't know. All I can say is that today I look on it all and feel ashamed of myself and I don't really like to talk about it very often.

The population of London and southern England on the receiving end of the V1 blitz nicknamed the V1s 'doodlebugs' or 'buzz bombs'. The first of these German cruise missile weapons struck Swanscombe in Kent on 13 June 1944. Some 6,725 V1s were launched against England. Of these, 2,340 hit the densely populated capital. A total of 5,475 people were killed and 16,000 injured by these weapons.

There were many tragedies involving V1 flying bombs but perhaps the worst of all was that which befell Weald House which stood on Crockham Hill in Sussex during the early hours of Friday, 30 June 1944. At the time Weald House was being used as a refuge for babies and young children who had been evacuated from London. By all accounts they should have been safe there in the idyllic setting of the Sussex countryside. Despite the Allied landings in Normandy some twenty-four days earlier, V1 launch sites were still active in the Pas de Calais area. In the early hours of 30 June, a crew assembled and prepared one of their weapons for launch against London. Within minutes the pulsejet engine roared into life and the weapon was catapulted along its launch ramp; the crew watched as the trail of flame from the V1's engine rapidly disappeared into the dark sky. In a matter of minutes, the V1 would have made its flight across the English Channel, its pulsejet engine would have automatically shut off, falling to earth with its one-ton high explosive warhead. Its victims would neither see nor hear it coming.

On the English coast men of the Royal Observer Corps heard the characteristic growl of the V1's engine as it approached. The weapon's course, altitude and speed were plotted and the information was urgently relayed to the anti-aircraft gunners of the Royal Artillery stationed in the countryside near the English coast. The anti-aircraft gunners manned their 40mm Bofors guns, a weapon with rapid-fire capability found to be ideal for shooting down these robotic intruders. The gunners heard the V1 as it approached, the dull yellow glow of the flame from its engine soon visible in the night sky. There was a crescendo as multiple 40mm guns began to blaze away at the intruder passing overhead at 400mph. The sky was soon filled with the lethal two-pound high-explosive shells, red hot splinters of steel filling the area around the V1. One of the 40mm rounds exploded and found its mark, puncturing the thin sheet-steel skin of the missile. The V1's flight became erratic, and it began to oscillate, trailing a long sheet of flame behind it which eerily lit up the sky around it. Yet, the V1 had not exploded as the gunners had hoped; instead, it was now out of control and steadily plummeting earthwards.

Weald House at Crockham Hill was quiet and in darkness. The thirty children and babies were all in bed asleep, along with the eleven female staff members. At 3.37am there was a huge explosion which was heard for some considerable distance. The explosion caused nearby homes to tremble, forcing the occupants to go outside to investigate the cause of the disturbance. One of the locals, a woman named Barbara Foster, was one of those startled by the explosion and she recalled what happened:

> It was an enormous bang that shook the house like an earthquake. When you're fast asleep and that happens, you immediately wake in a state of terror, wondering what the hell is going on. I grabbed my dressing gown and slippers and quickly ran downstairs and out of the front door. By this time, I was joined by other residents coming out of their homes, wondering what was going on. There was a kind of yellowy-red glow in the direction of Weald House; the sky above was glowing like the embers of a fire. I remember one of the old people saying, 'Oh my God, it's hit the house; there are children in that house.' She began to cry. One of the other neighbours had a telephone and called the police but the police were already aware of what happened and the emergency services were rushing to the scene. We could hear the fire engines in the distance. I went back to bed, but I couldn't sleep; we knew something terrible had happened, but we did not learn of the scale of it until the next day.

It was a terrible tragedy that the V1 which the anti-aircraft gunners had damaged had fallen from the sky, struck a large tree next to Weald House, bounced off the tree and landed directly on the house where it exploded, killing twenty-two children and eight of the staff. Peter Findley was one of the children who survived as he had measles and was in isolation away from the other children in a nearby house at the time.

An auxiliary fireman named Bob Ferris who had attended the scene at first light was too traumatized by what he saw to talk about the incident for many years after the war. In an interview with me he spoke about the incident for the first time:

> As a fireman I had seen many horrors during the war. I expected to see terrible things as it was part of my job. Yet, what I saw at Weald House on the Saturday, 31 June were the worst things I have ever seen in my life. It was clear there were going to be no survivors and the task in hand was to remove the rubble to retrieve the bodies of the victims. It was just horrible as we were pulling what looked like little ragdolls out of the rubble; the bodies of the dead children looked just like ragdolls and they were removed and covered over. I recall parents arriving from London to identify the bodies of their children; do you know, that was the hardest part of it all for me. I saw many grown men cry that day. The parents, mostly young mothers as the husbands or most of them were away fighting, were totally broken, grief-stricken people. I remember one of the young women screaming frantically, 'Why, why my baby, I want my baby, I want my baby.' She was so distraught they had to take her away from the scene. I'd never suffered from nightmares in my life up until that point, but I did, and I still do to this day after seeing the things I saw that day. Some of the bodies were in bits, you know, an arm here or a leg there, or just bits of a torso with bits of clothing attached. I spent most of the day assisting in the recovery of the dead at Weald House. When I came home, I sat at my kitchen table and I cried my eyes out; yes, I sat there and wept. My wife, bless her, she understood what I had witnessed as she had heard all about it and she did what she could to offer some comfort, but it was horrible. I prayed I would never see anything like that again. It has stayed with me every day from that moment. I still see the bodies, the faces of those dead children; they never had a chance against that bomb.

> What did I think of the Germans afterwards? I hated them and far from defeating us, it hardened our resolve to destroy them, to take what they threw at us and carry on until they were destroyed. Those flying bombs were acts of war crimes in my view, but I guess there were innocent Germans being killed every day in the Allied bombings; war goes both ways, doesn't it. You have to think of it logically; it's war and we have to learn that war brings only death, misery and destruction more often to the innocent than anyone else.

Cyril Banks, nicknamed 'Cyril the Squirrel' by his school chums, lived a short distance from Weald House and remembers the blast that devasted the community that night in June 1944. In an interview with him at his home in Westerham, Kent, he recalled:

> It was a lovely quiet place to live until that V1 shattered the myth of being safe out in the countryside. I remember the explosion in the early hours that night; hell of bang and we guessed the Germans had dropped a mine or bomb or something, but there were no warnings of an air raid so knew it was something out of the normal, maybe even a gas explosion or something. We soon discovered it was one of the V1 doodlebugs, as we called them. I was only an 11-year-old kid at the time but me and some school friends went up to Weald House to have a look for ourselves; this was around a month after the incident, if I remember right. We weren't being morbid or anything; we were just curious. We made our way through a wood which surrounded the house, and through a clearing in the trees we could see the partially demolished building; it was eerily quiet there. We were aware that the local bobby [policeman] was frequently visiting the site and keeping an eye out on it, so we had to make sure he didn't catch us or we would have had a right thick ear off him; he was a stern old boy, he was. We just skirted around the site really near the clearing, scratching around like chickens and it was then I spotted a green-painted piece of metal with what looked like a shrapnel hole in it. I picked it up and examined it and it was silver metal

> one side and green-painted the other. I knew then that it was a fragment of the V1, a piece probably discarded or missed by the recovery teams. Ironically, it also had a hole in it which must have been made by a piece of shrapnel from the British anti-aircraft guns that had fired on it as it passed over. My mates were pretty envious of me for finding that; these things were prized souvenirs that could be traded in the school playground for sweets and comics. I don't know, to me at the time it was just another piece of shrapnel, its significance only dawning on me as I got older and had children of my own. It was kept in the garden shed in a tin for years as my dad put in there when I moved out. It only turned up again when both my parents passed away and I had to clear the house and shed.

At the close of the interview, we shook hands. As I walked out the front door, Cyril said, 'Hold on a minute – here, take this with you.' He handed me a padded envelope and I peered inside, curious as to what it might be. I could see it was the fragment of the V1 he had found at Weald House. It was an unusual parting gift, but Cyril explained that if he 'kicked the bucket', his wife would only put it in the bin. He told me to take it and tell the story of the Weald House bombing as so few knew about it, especially young people today. Since then, I have taken it along to many of the talks I have given over the years. It is a sombre reminder that war doesn't discriminate.

As to the question of the morality of weapons such as the V1, unlike modern guided or cruise missile weapons, the V1 could not be guided with precision to hit a specific target. It was in every sense an indiscriminate weapon of terror.

What of the brilliant minds who devised the V1, did they rest easily in their beds knowing of the death and destruction they in turn were party to? Men of science and intellect such as Paul Schmidt, Gorg Hans Madelung and Robert Lusser have a long history of often creating things they later lived to regret.

The last V1 flying bomb launched against England was on 29 March 1945. It was destroyed by anti-aircraft fire off Orfordness, Suffolk.

# Chapter 23

# The Collapse

The steady demise of the Luftwaffe can be blamed on many factors: political and tactical interference from Adolf Hitler and Hermann Göring, a failure to understand the resources required to fight a protracted campaign in the air, particularly in manpower, repair facilities and, of course, war production. Despite the Luftwaffe facing increasingly overwhelming odds in the skies above the Reich, it was at times able to pull off what could be considered the impossible and mount large-scale attacks on Allied forces in Europe. The problem was with each such large-scale, last-stand attack more pilots were lost; it was pilots with adequate experience not aircraft that the Luftwaffe desperately needed over the last few months of the war.

Monica Kieler Vanessa Dorsche, whom I had the pleasure of interviewing several times over the course of many years from 1997, was one of the unsung heroes of the Luftwaffe, and in many ways a maverick in much the same vein as Marseille and Galland. Monica had been fascinated with aviation well before the outbreak of the war. Her father had flown in the German air force of the First World War and in her own words, 'flying was in my blood'. She became a pilot when it was far from fashionable for women to attempt to enter this predominantly male domain in the post-First World War aviation boom. In the interwar years Monica flew twin- and single-engine mail delivery aircraft, learned to master fast and agile stunt aircraft and spent much time in Africa where she took wealthy photographers up on wildlife-spotting flights. When war looked certain to break out in Europe again, her father begged her to return home which she duly did.

During the course of the war, she persistently asked the authorities to let her fly military aircraft as a ferry pilot to help free up manpower, and each time she was refused despite her impressive flying resumé and logbook charting more flying hours than most Luftwaffe pilots. It was during those last desperate months that Monica was finally granted her wish, much to her parents' consternation. Monica recalled one particularly memorable incident:

> I had been assigned the task of taking a factory-fresh, brand-new Focke-Wulf Fw 190A-8 out to a local airfield being used by one of the fighter groups. I was not alone as there were twelve other aircraft in the flight of several brand-new aeroplanes plus our escort. The dangers of running into an Allied fighter patrol at that stage, in February 1945, were very real and we were given specific instructions on what to do if we were ambushed. This did not concern me at all as I knew manoeuvres that even some of the escorting fighter pilots did not know of and I knew I could look after myself. We left the departure facility, formed up and headed for the delivery airfield which was only a very short hop of around forty or so miles. After just ten minutes I noticed problems with my aircraft; it would not be the first time I experienced this problem, yet it was pretty scary. The big BMW engine began to make unfamiliar noises and the temperature gauge began to rise alarmingly and I could smell a little smoke in the cockpit. I asked the pilot flying at my port wing if he could see any smoke coming from my engine over the radio. He said he could see nothing. It was at that point that the flight leader, Helmut Frisch, told me to climb to get some clearance from the other aircraft and he followed me up. By this time smoke had begun streaming from the engine cowlings. I noticed the gauges were in the red and I made the decision to exit the aircraft. Frisch cleared me to bale out, so I initiated a shallow climb to approximately 15,000 feet before sliding the hood back and rolling the Focke-Wulf over onto its back where I immediately fell out of the cockpit into the cold air. Within seconds my parachute deployed and there I was hanging in my parachute admiring the German countryside. I watched as the Focke-Wulf turned over and almost levelled itself out before hitting the ground and breaking up.
>
> I landed not far away in a potato field and before my feet had even touched the ground, I could see a group of men from a nearby anti-aircraft gun emplacement running over to

me. I hit the ground, bending my knees and rolling to one side as taught so as to limit the chances of breaking my legs. I collected up my parachute and the young men from the gun emplacement asked me if I was okay. As I removed my helmet and goggles, they gasped in amazement on seeing the face not of a man but a woman. There was an argument later among them to see who would be taking me to dinner that evening. They looked after me well and I was given five-star treatment.

The next morning, I was taken out to where my aircraft had crashed. The recovery team wanted everything that could be found to try and determine what had happened. It was later discovered that the engine had been sabotaged: there was material inside it that should not have been there. Of course, this was down to the use of slave labour, but I felt uneasy at what was going to happen to that production line which had assembled the engine. I knew full well they might face execution or be sent to one of the camps. I did try to tell the investigating branch that it was fine, that I wasn't hurt and there were plenty more A-8s waiting to be delivered but they were having none of it. Their view was, 'We will not tolerate sabotage from anyone and when we find out who was responsible, they are going to be very fucking sorry.' That is what they said then they left, and I went home to my parents for a few days as I felt a bit ill.

After a brief few days' rest, I returned to my duties of ferrying aircraft to local fighter units. I was later forced to abandon another Focke-Wulf due to an engine fire – sabotage again – so by that time I was well accustomed to getting out of an aircraft about to burst into flames. It happened a lot and wasn't just me, but the men of the flight still used to tease me: just before I was about to deliver another new aircraft, they would say, 'Hey, Monica, say hello to God for us when you get there,' insinuating that one day my luck surely must run out. They weren't being nasty; it was typical of the dark humour we fliers shared.

Adolf Galland, never a man to suppress his opinions, had already fallen foul of both Hitler and Göring as a participant in the early-1945 'Fighter Pilots' Revolt'. The incident was a minor insurrection engineered by some of the high-ranking Luftwaffe pilots who were rightly dismayed at the state of affairs brought about by years of interference and inept leadership. Following this relatively minor rebellion, some officers were relieved of their positions or assigned to punishment duties. Such foolish retribution at that stage displays perfectly the vengeful mentality of individuals such as Göring who as a former fighter pilot himself should have known better. Not the kind of man to be deterred by the likes of 'Fatty Göring', Galland formed Jagdverband (hunting formation) 44 (JV 44), a unit which brought together some of the Luftwaffe's finest aces, or *Experten* as they were known, into a single unit operating the deadly Messerschmitt Me 262 jet fighter. Galland's idea, far from being blocked by his disgruntled superiors, was welcomed, as many secretly hoped that Galland would be killed in action, removing what was a proverbial thorn in their side. The top five fighter pilots of JV 44 were credited with a combined total of over 1,000 enemy aircraft destroyed. Tasked with the defence of the skies of southern Germany and Austria, the unit comprised the following fighter aces:

- Gerhard Barkhorn 301 victories
- Heinz Bär 220 victories
- Walter Krupinski 197 victories
- Johannes Macky Steinhoff 176 victories
- Günther Lutzow 110 victories
- Adolf Galland 104 victories
- Willhelm Herget 72 victories
- Alfred Heckmann 71 victories
- Herbert Kaiser 68 victories
- Hans Ekkehard Bob 60 victories
- Klaus Neumann 37 victories

Due to the Me 262 being vulnerable to air attack in the initial stages of take-off and landings, a unit protection squadron, or *Wurger-Staffel*, of Luftwaffe fighters was created to provide air cover for the jets as they taxied, took off and then powered up their engines. Commanded by Leutnant Heinz Sachsenberg, the unit was equipped with excellent Focke-Wulf Fw 190D9s and D11s, the 'Dora', the 'long-nosed' version of the famous fighter. The Fw 190s were painted bright red on their undersides with contrasting white stripes to ensure they were not mistaken for Allied aircraft by their own Flak batteries. The Fw 190s would take off ahead of the Me 262s and circle the airfield until all the jets were in the air and able to utilize the full power of their two engines. During its brief existence JV 44 performed with great success, amassing a kill ratio in their Me 262s of four to one. However, the unit struggled to maintain a sufficient flight of operational Me 262s: only six were available at any one time and the unit was constantly forced to relocate to other airfields due to the advances being made by enemy ground forces.

The first sortie flown by JV 44 took place in late March 1945 when a Soviet Ilyushin Il-2 Shturmovik was claimed. By the end of the war JV 44 had claimed a total of forty-seven Allied aircraft during April/May 1945. The top-scoring pilot was Oberstleutnant Heinz Bär with sixteen victories in the Me 262, followed by Hauptmann Georg-Peter Eder with fifteen. Galland claimed seven enemy aircraft before he was wounded and taken out of flying duties for what remained of the war.

US troops arrived at the Salburg airfield being used by JV 44; shortly before the unit surrendered, the remaining Me 262 jet fighters were destroyed by grenades in the engine intakes. At other Luftwaffe airfields across the Reich, Allied troops were amazed to find brand-new aircraft all ready for use but with empty fuel tanks and even fewer pilots capable of flying them. The surviving Luftwaffe pilots who had been milling around awaiting the arrival of American and British troops appeared relaxed, knowing their war was now at an end and that, at some point, they could all go back to their families to begin picking up the pieces of what remained of their lives.

However, many did not live to see the end of the war. The Luftwaffe Tagjagd (day fighter arm) lost some 12,000 pilots killed or missing in action, with a further 6,000 wounded. The *Zerstörer* (destroyer) crews suffered approximately 2,800 airmen either killed or missing in action, plus another 900 wounded. The Nachtjagd (night fighter arm) also suffered high losses with a figure of around 3,800 airmen killed or missing in action, with 1,400 wounded.

When the Luftwaffe was first revealed to the world back in March 1935, one could be excused for thinking it was an air force capable of conquering all in its path. Yet, by May 1945, it was an air force that had been destroyed as much by the complex bureaucracy espoused by its own inept leadership and the very individuals who had created it, as it had been unequivocally annihilated by the combined material resources of the Allies. With strong, intelligent and organized leadership, with better resources, training and manpower, things might have been very different indeed.

# Appendix

# Luftwaffe Facts, Ranks & Slang

## Ranks

| | |
|---|---|
| Flieger | Aircraftman 2nd Class |
| Obergefreiter | Leading Aircraftman |
| Gefreiter | Aircraftman 1st Class |
| Fahnenjunker-Gefreiter | Flight Cadet Lance Corporal |
| Hauptgefreiter | Corporal |
| Unteroffizier | Sergeant (Junior Sergeant) |
| Fahnrich | Flight Ensign |
| Unterfeldwebel | Sergeant |
| Feldwebel | Flight Sergeant |
| Oberfeldwebel | Warrant Officer |
| Stabsfeldwebel | Warrant Officer |
| Oberfahnrich | Flight Ensign |
| Leutnant | Pilot Officer |
| Oberleutnant | Flying Officer |
| Hauptmann | Flight Lieutenant |
| Major | Squadron Leader |
| Oberstleutnant | Wing Commander |
| Oberst | Group Captain |
| Generalmajor | Group Captain |
| Generalleutnant | Air Vice-Marshal |
| General der Flieger | Air Marshal |
| Generaloberst | Air Chief Marshal. |
| Generalfeldmarshalf | Marshal of the Air Force |

## Insignia Colours

*Waffenfarben* or colours of the arms denoted different branches of the service and were shown in two ways: as underlay on collar patches and officers shoulder straps, and as piping on NCO (non-commissioned officer) and OR (other ranks) straps and peaked dress caps:

- White — Air Marshals and General Göring Regiment (which also used red piping)
- Deep yellow — Flying Branch
- Bright red — Flak Artillery
- Carmine red — General Staff
- Rose — Engineer Corps
- Brown — Signals
- Dark blue — Medical Branc.
- Light green — Aircraft Flying Control
- Dark green — Administrative
- Black — Air Ministry

## German Aircraft Production All Types by Year

- 1939 — 1,928
- 1940 — 7,829
- 1941 — 9,422
- 1942 — 12,822
- 1943 — 20,599
- 1944 — 35,076

## Total German Aircraft Losses 1939–45

The figure for the total of German aircraft destroyed and damaged in the Second World War is estimated at 76,875 aircraft of all types. Of this quoted figure, 40,000 were recorded as total losses, the remainder significantly damaged beyond use.

## Some Commonly Used Luftwaffe Slang

Emil: a Messerschmitt Bf 109E, also referred to as the Flying Brick, Canoe, Box, Bathtub and Molle, this last being a large-sized glass found in German restaurants

*Esel aus Messing* (brass donkey): an all-metal aircraft

*Mobelwagen* (removal van): heavy bomber

*Pupchen* (Dolly): usually a small aircraft and/or term of endearment for a female.

*Müll* (junk): an unserviceable aircraft

*Holen und Tragen* (fetch and carry): Ju 52 transport aircraft

Blond arse: a homosexual

*Frontbrummel* (lit. front hum): a flight over enemy lines, a spree or joyride

*Hase* (hare): young airman

Flak: anti-aircraft fire

*Metzgervogel* (butcher bird): nickname for the Focke-Wulf Fw 190

*Heiss absteigen*: to dismount 'hot'/to be shot down in flames

*Falscher Propheten* (false prophets): the Reich weather forecasters

*Eier* (eggs): bombs

*Gluhwurmchen* (glowworms): searchlights

*Blitzmadchen* (lit. lightning girl): female Luftwaffe auxiliary

*Kuhe* (cow) a Heinkel He 111

# Acknowledgements

I would like to thank the following for their contributions which has made this particular account possible:

Gerhard Funck, the family of Hans Dietrich 'Bubi' Knoetsch, Karl Voght, Adolf Galland, Claude Hunnemeyer, Frau Ingrid Riedel, Monica Vanessa Kieler Dorsche, José Marguerass, Ernst Willi Gabel, Viktor M. Sinaisky, Johannes Trautloft, Christoph Oegen, Michael Ott, Gottfried Urquhart, Ernst Heinrich Husse, Heinz Gunsche, Günther Rall, Heinz Knoke, Anthony Scholl, Horst von Riesen, Ludwig Werner, Rolf Ickert, Fritz Herbert Scholle, Mark Simmons, Judy Finch, Helmut von Schieff, Werner Hans Messner, Walter Rath, Walter Schlecht, Erich Boerschelle, Rudolph Weiss, Albert Tuga, Beryl Weller, Phillip Hale, Keith Warren, Captain Erich Brown, Eugene Slimmer and Gerhard Wilshe.

Ministry of Defence, London; Volksbund Deutsche Kriegsgraberfursorge e.V, (German War Graves Commission) Kassel, Germany; Bob Collis (aviation historian); Colonel H. Kortge, Gemeinschaft der Jagdflieger e.V (German Fighter Pilots' Association), Koln, Germany; Andy Wight-Boycott, RAF (Retd); Air Historical Branch, RAF Bentley Priory; Angela Wootton, Department of Printed Books, Imperial War Museum, London; Herr Raimund Grundler of The Rathaus, Stuttgart, Germany; the German Information Centre, London; Herr Seemann of the Verwaltungsgemeinschaft Seegebeit Mansfelder Land, Roblingen am See, Germany; Royal Air Force Personnel Management Agency (RAF/PMA); Herr Euteneuer of the Deutscher Luftwaffenring e.V, Bonn, Germany; Berthold Kruger of the Kameradschaft ehem KG.2 (Kampfgeschwader 2 Association), Soest, Germany; Frau Lehnert the

Deutsche Dienstelle, Berlin; the Royal Air Force Museum, Hendon, London; Herr vonruden-Ferner the Stadt Archiv, Essen, Germany; the Public Record Office, Kew, Richmond, Surrey; Frau Jansen, the Bundesarchiv, Freiburg, Germany; Edmund L. Blandford (author); Peter Halliday (aviation historian); *The Armourer* magazine (Duncan Evans) and T. R. Boyce for all translation requirements.

# Bibliography

A.I.L (K) Air Intelligence Report No. 34/1943.

A.I.L (K) Air Intelligence Report No. 918/1940.

Brown, David, Christopher Shores & Kenneth Macksey-Guinness, *The Guinness History of Air Warfare*, Superlatives Ltd., Enfield, Middlesex, 1976.

Foreman, John, *The Battle of Britain: The Forgotten Months – November and December 1940*, Air Research Publications, Walton-on-Thames, 1988.

Gunston, Bill & Anthony Wood, *Hitler's Luftwaffe: A pictorial history and technical encyclopedia of Hitler's air power in World War II*, Salamander Books Ltd., Ladysmith BC, 1977.

*Handbook of Enemy Ammunition* (Pamphlet Five).

Latimer Needhamm C. H., *Aircraft Design Volume II*, Chapman & Hall Ltd., London, 1939.

Luftarchiv.de- Das Archiv der Deutschen Luftwaffe (The Archives of the German Air Force)- online photograph and data resource created and managed by Bert Hartmann, Germany.

Price, Alfred, *Spitfire at War*, Ian Allen Publishing, Shepperton, 1974.

Price, Alfred, *The Last Year of the Luftwaffe: May 1944 to May 1945*, Arms & Armour Press, London, 1991.

Prien, Jochen, Peter Rodeike & Gerhard Stemmer, *Messerschmitt Bf 109, Im Einsatz Bei Der III. Und IV./Jagdgeschwader 27 1938–1945*, Author publication, Eutin, 1996

Shores, Christopher, *Ground Attack Aircraft of World War II*, TBS T.H.E. Book Service Ltd., London, 1977.

The British Museum Library newspaper archive, Colindale, London.

Windrow, Martin C., *The Messerschmitt Bf 109*, Profile Publications, Leatherhead, Surrey, 1972.

# About the Author

Tim Heath was born into a military family. His interest in military history began at the tender age of 7. His initial research focused primarily on the aircraft and weaponry of the Luftwaffe in the Second World War. He later wrote extensively for the UK's leading military history magazine, *The Armourer*. In the process he has assisted a number of UK and Europe-based military history authors with their published works. During the course of his research, he worked closely with the German War Graves Commission at Kassel, Germany, meeting with war veterans and their families. For the past thirty-five years he has specialized in German social and military history, with particular emphasis on the roles of German females in the Third Reich and beyond. His first title for Pen and Sword Books, *Hitler's Girls: Doves Amongst Eagles*, was published in 2017, followed by *In Hitler's Shadow: Post-War Germany and the Girls of the BDM*, *Hitler's Germany: The Birth of Extremism*, *Women of the Third Reich: From Camp Guards to Combatants*, *Hitler's Housewives: German Women on the Home Front*, *Hitler's Lost State: The Fall of Prussia and the Willhelm Gustloff Tragedy*, *Anschluss and After: Resistance Heroines in Nazi- and Russian-occupied Austria*. He lives with his partner Paula in the old Worcestershire market town of Evesham.